A. F. Mummery

My Climbs in the Alps and Caucasus

A. F. Mummery
My Climbs in the Alps and Caucasus
ISBN/EAN: 9783743426344
Manufactured in Europe, USA, Canada, Australia, Japa
Cover: Foto ©Andreas Hilbeck / pixelio.de

A. F. Mummery

My Climbs in the Alps and Caucasus

THE WEISSHORN PIERCING THROUGH THE GREYNESS.

My Climbs in the Alps and Caucasus
By A. F. Mummery

ILLUSTRATED

LONDON T. FISHER UNWIN
NEW YORK CHAS. SCRIBNER'S SONS
MDCCCXCV

PREFACE.

FATE decrees that the mountaineer should, sooner or later, fall a victim to the *furor scribendi*, and, since it is useless for a mere mortal to contend with the gods, I have yielded to their behests. A fitting reward has been allotted me; though the delight of wandering among the great snow fields, of climbing the jagged ridges, and of plunging down through the primeval forest of some Caucasian valley, cannot be rivalled by the rarest fabric built of memory, yet the piecing together of old incidents, the interweaving of the laughter and the fears, the desperate struggles and the wild triumph of old-won victories, has tinged many a winter evening with the gorgeous colouring of Alpine sunsets and has knitted more firmly the bonds of well-tried friendships; to some extent, even, it has brought me nearer to that reckless, lucky, tireless youth, when the grass slopes, and the stones, and the other ills of life, had not found the art of troubling.

PREFACE.

I fear no contributions to science, or topography, or learning of any sort are to be found sandwiched in between the story of crags and séracs, of driving storm and perfect weather. To tell the truth, I have only the vaguest ideas about theodolites, and as for plane tables, their very name is an abomination. To those who think with me, who regard mountaineering as unmixed play, these pages are alone addressed. Should they, in some dim afterglow fashion, reflect the joy and frolic of sunshine holidays, their utmost mission will have been accomplished, and pride will mightily inflate their author.

My sincerest thanks are due to those friends who have so kindly placed drawings and photographs at my disposal; indeed, I feel that my debt to them is wholly beyond expression.

A. F. MUMMERY.

CONTENTS.

CHAPTER I.
THE MATTERHORN—ZMUTT RIDGE 1

CHAPTER II.
THE MATTERHORN—FURGGEN RIDGE . . . 24

CHAPTER III.
THE COL DU LION 45

CHAPTER IV.
DER TEUFELSGRAT 66

CHAPTER V.
THE AIGUILLE DES CHARMOZ . . . 96

CHAPTER VI.
THE GRÉPON 120

CONTENTS.

CHAPTER VII.
THE DENT DU REQUIN 161

CHAPTER VIII.
AIGUILLE DU PLAN 183

CHAPTER IX.
THE AIGUILLE VERTE—BY THE CHARPOUA GLACIER . 205

CHAPTER X.
THE AIGUILLE VERTE—BY THE MOINE RIDGE . 221

CHAPTER XI.
A LITTLE PASS—COL DES COURTES . . 239

CHAPTER XII.
DYCH TAU 258

CHAPTER XIII.
SOME CAUCASIAN PASSES . . . 285

CHAPTER XIV.
THE PLEASURES AND PENALTIES OF MOUNTAINEERING 324

LIST OF ILLUSTRATIONS.

ILLUSTRATIONS IN THE TEXT.

	PAGE
TOURISTS	2
From a drawing by Mr. Pennell.	
ZERMATT FASHIONS	3
From a drawing by Mr. Pennell.	
AN "OFF DAY" AT THE MONTE ROSA HOTEL	8
From a drawing by Mr. Pennell.	
CONSULTING THE GUIDES	10
From a drawing by Mr. Pennell.	
NEUBRÜCKE	26
From a drawing by Mr. Pennell.	
STALDEN	27
From a drawing by Mr. Pennell.	
NEAR ZERMATT	28
From a drawing by Mr. Pennell.	
THE HIGH STREET	46
From a drawing by Mr. Pennell.	
THE TRIFTBACH BRIDGE	48
From a drawing by Mr. Pennell.	
THE VILLAGE OF ZERMATT	67
From a drawing by Mr. Pennell.	
THE RIFFEL PATH	95
From a drawing by Mr. Pennell.	
THE "CRACK"	156
From a photograph by Miss Bristow.	
GOATS	186
From a sketch by Miss Bristow.	
THE BLAITIÈRE AND PLAN	188
From a photograph by Mr. Holmes.	

ILLUSTRATIONS.

	PAGE
IN THE VAL D'AOSTE	229
From a sketch by Miss E. Petherick.	
COURMAYEUR	240
From a sketch by Miss Bristow.	
GOING TO CHURCH	242
From a sketch by Miss Bristow.	
A STREET IN COURMAYEUR	256
From a sketch by Miss E. Petherick.	
DYCH TAU FROM THE SOUTH	270
From a photograph by Signor Sella.	
JANGA FROM THE BEZINGI GLACIER	286
From a photograph by Mr. Woolley.	
A SUANETIAN VILLAGE	302
From a photograph by Mr. Woolley.	

PLATES.

THE WEISSHORN PIERCING THROUGH THE GREYNESS	*Frontispiece*
A lithograph plate from a drawing by Mr. Pennell.	
MATTERHORN	to face page 17
A photogravure from a photograph by Signor Sella.	
CHARMOZ	,, ,, ,, 96
A photogravure from a drawing by Miss Bristow.	
THE GRÉPON	,, ,, ,, 128
A photogravure from a photograph by Mr. Holmes.	
THE LOWER PEAK OF THE GRÉPON	,, ,, ,, 135
A photogravure from a photograph by Mr. Holmes.	
A CRAG ON THE GRÉPON	,, ,, ,, 150
From a photograph by Mr. Holmes.	
MONT BLANC AND THE DENT DU REQUIN	,, ,, ,, 160
A photogravure from a photograph by Mr. Holmes.	
MONT BLANC AND THE AIGUILLE DU PLAN	,, ,, ,, 183
A photogravure from a photograph by Mr. Holmes.	
THE VERTE	,, ,, ,, 232
A photogravure from a photograph by Mr. Holmes.	
DYCH TAU	,, ,, ,, 261
A photogravure from a photograph by Signor Sella.	
GUIDES ON A CLOUDY DAY AT THE RIFFEL	,, ,, ,, 324
A lithograph plate from a drawing by Mr. Pennell.	

CHAPTER I.

THE MATTERHORN—ZMUTT RIDGE.

At the age of fifteen the crags of the Via Mala and the snows of the Théodule roused a passion within me that has grown with years, and has to no small extent moulded my life and thought. It has led me into regions of such fairy beauty that the fabled wonders of Zanadu seem commonplace beside them; it has brought me friends who may be relied on in fair weather and in foul; and it has stored my mind with memories that are treasures, corruptible neither by moth nor rust, sickness nor old age. My boyish delight in the great white peaks towering above the gloom of pines is still awakened when the lumbering diligence rolls through the gorge of the Diosaz or when the Matterhorn rises from out the foliage of the Val Tournanche. I remember, as if it were yesterday, my first sight of the great mountain. It was shining in all the calm majesty of a September moon, and, in the stillness of an autumn night, it seemed the very embodiment of mystery and a fitting dwelling-place for the spirits with which old legends people its stone swept slopes. From that moment I have been one of the great peak's most reverent worshippers, and whenever the mighty rock appears above the distant hori-

TOURISTS.

zon, I hail its advent with devoutest joy. Even the vulgarisation of Zermatt, the cheap trippers and their trumpery fashions, cannot wholly drive me from the lower slopes, and I still love to gaze at it from amongst the pines of the Riffelberg, or to watch its huge mass soaring above the flowery meadows of the Staffel Alp.

In those distant days (1871), however, it was still shrouded with a halo of but half banished inaccessibility, and, as I looked at it through the tangle of the pines or from the breezy alps, I scarcely dared to hope that one day I might be numbered among the glorious few who had scaled its frozen cliffs. Three years later, however, the ascent had become fashionable, the deluge had

ZERMATT FASHIONS.

begun, and with its earlier waves I was swept on to the long desired summit.

I am aware that from that moment my interest in the peak should have ceased, that the well-conducted climber never repeats an ascent; that his object is to reach the summit, and, that object once attained, his work is over and he should rest in ignoble ease. The true faith on this subject is crystallised and resplendent in a remark made to me last year by a bandbox inmate of the Monte Rosa Hotel: "I had to go to Grindelwald to ascend the Eiger; it was a beastly nuisance, but I wanted to *finish off* the Oberland: shall never go there again"!

For myself, I am fain to confess a deplorable weakness in my character. No sooner have I ascended a peak than it becomes a friend, and delightful as it may be to seek "fresh woods and pastures new," in my heart of hearts I long for the slopes of which I know every wrinkle, and on which each crag awakens memories of mirth and laughter and of the friends of long ago. As a consequence of this terrible weakness, I have been no less than seven times on the top of the Matterhorn. I have sat on the summit with my wife when a lighted match would not flicker in the windless air, and I have been chased from its shattered crest and down the Italian ridge by the mad fury of thunder, lightning, and whirling snow. Yet each memory has its own peculiar charm, and the wild music of the hurricane is hardly a less delight than the glories of a perfect day. The idea which cleaves unto the orthodox mountaineer that a single ascent, on one day, in one year, enables that same mountaineer to know and realise how that peak looks on all other days, in all other years, suggests that he is still wallowing in the lowest bogs of Philistinism. It is true the crags and pinnacles are the same, but their charm and beauty lies in the ever changing light and shade, in the mists which wreath around them, in the huge cornices and pendent icicles, in all the varying circumstance of weather, season, and hour. Moreover, it is not merely that the actual vision impressed on the retina reflects every mood and change of summer storm and sunshine; but the observer himself is hardly less inconstant. On one day he is dominated by the tingling horror of the precipice, the gaunt bareness of the stupendous cliffs, or the deadly rush of the rocks when some huge block breaks from its moorings and hurtles through the air—a fit emblem of resistless wrath. On yet another day he notices none of these things; lulled by the delicate tints of opal and azure, he revels in the vaporous softness of the Italian valleys, in the graceful sweep of the wind-drifted snow, or even in the tiny flowers wedged in the joints of the granite. While the mountain may sometimes impress its mood on the spectator, as often the spectator only sees that which harmonises with his own. A man may doubtless be so constructed that

> "A primrose by the river's brim
> A yellow primrose is to him"

and in no conceivable circumstance or time could it ever be aught else; but others more happily constituted, who can rejoice in the beauty of the external world, are scarcely likely to feel the "taint of staleness," no matter how thoroughly they may know the substantial basis of rock and ice on which the sun and cloud, mist, air, and sky are ever weaving the glory of the view.

It was, then, with an interest in the great mountain only intensified by my first ascent, that I crossed the Tiefenmatten Joch in 1879. Whilst descending the glacier, I gazed long and earnestly at the great Zmutt ridge towering above the long slopes of rock and stone swept couloirs of the western face. I was by no means the first who had so gazed; amongst others, Mr. Whymper, with his guides Michel Croz and Christian Almer, had studied it carefully from the crags of the Dent Blanche. The conclusions they came to may be gathered from the following paragraph: "My old enemy—the Matterhorn—seen across the basin of the Z'Muttgletscher, looked totally unassailable. 'Do you think,' the men asked, 'that you, or any one else, will ever get up *that* mountain?' And when, undismayed by their ridicule, I stoutly answered, 'Yes, but not upon that side,' they burst into derisive chuckles. I must confess that my hopes sank; for nothing can look, or be, more completely inaccessible than the Matterhorn on its northern and north-west sides."[*] It did not appear, however, that this judgment was wholly warranted. The snow ridge and the jagged rocks by which it is continued for some distance further, offered an

[*] "Scrambles amongst the Alps," p. 278.

obtrusively easy route to a height of about 13,000 feet, and on the final ridge, from about 14,000 feet to the summit, the climber had little to fear. Serious difficulty was limited to the short section of the route by which these two highways would have to be connected. From observations on this and previous occasions, it was evident that where the Zmutt ridge first steepens, till it verges on the perpendicular, it would be necessary to bear to the left into a deeply cut couloir, which falls in appalling precipices to the Matterhorn glacier. The upper part of this couloir, where alone we should have to deal with it, did not, however, look altogether hopeless, and, provided it could be ascended, the ridge would be regained above the first inaccessible step. A short distance further, where it again becomes perpendicular, or rather actually overhangs, it was apparently possible to swerve to the right on to the long slopes of the western face, and, after a considerable ascent, to regain the Zmutt ridge above all serious difficulty. Having decided upon this somewhat ambitious programme, I went down to Zermatt to find a suitable guide to carry it out.

In front of the Monte Rosa Hotel I met an old companion, Alois Burgener, who gave me the joyful news that his brother Alexander might possibly be able to join me for a few days. The broad-shouldered Alexander, his face half hidden in beard, was then interviewed, he bluntly expressed

AN "OFF DAY" AT THE MONTE ROSA HOTEL.

his opinion that to go on such an expedition with a Herr of whom he knew nothing would be a "verfluchte Dummheit." I was much taken by this bold expression of opinion, which appeared to me not merely indicative of a wise distrust of an untried climber, but also of a determination to drive home the attack, when once begun, to the utmost limits of possibility. My previous experience had been chiefly, if not exclusively, with men who were eager to start on any attempt, no matter how desperate, and who were far too polite to inquire whether their employer knew anything about the art of climbing. At an early stage in the proceedings, however, these men had invariably developed a most touching, but none the less most inconvenient, affection for their wives and families, and were compelled by these most commendable feelings to discontinue the ascent. The confident carriage of Alexander, and the honest outspokenness of his language, seemed to show that he was not of this sort, and to presage well for our future acquaintance. I gladly accepted his suggestions, and agreed that we should make a few preliminary expeditions together.

We accordingly crossed to the Laquin Thal by the Mischabel and Laquin passes, forcing our way back over the Fletschhorn by a new and remarkably difficult route. We then ascended the Portienhorn, and on the fifth day returned to Zermatt by the Ried pass and St. Niklaus. Our campaign having been thus successfully inaugurated, we were ready to turn our attention to the Zmutt ridge. We felt, however, that we had fairly earned a day's rest, so we spent the last of August lying among the haymakers of the lower slopes. Towards evening we heard that Mr. Penhall, with Ferd. Imseng and L. Zurbrucken, had started that very

CONSULTING THE GUIDES.

day to sleep on the mountain and assault the Zmutt ridge the next morning. We had little doubt about their success. The weather looked perfect, the mountain was in exceptionally good condition and the party was of most unusual skill and strength. We determined in consequence to vary our plans and cross the Col Durand. This would enable us to watch their progress and obtain useful information for the future, and we hoped that possibly the east ridge or north-east face of the Dent Blanche would afford us consolation for the loss of the Zmutt ridge.

The next morning, on our way to the Staffel Alp we found that so fierce a wind was raging on the higher peaks that it seemed hardly possible any serious ascent could be effected. Our thoughts and aspirations consequently veered back to the Zmutt ridge, and when we met Penhall's party returning, and heard that they had definitely abandoned the ridge route, we determined to spend the day at the Stockje and see whether the wind and clouds really meant mischief. On our arrival there the men soon came to the conclusion that the weather was hopeless. I was, however, much too young and too eager to dream of returning, and, being wholly ignorant of all meteorological lore, I was able to prophesy fair things with such an appearance of well-founded knowledge that Burgener was half convinced. A second difficulty then arose. Our provisions were calculated on the basis of a ten hours' walk, and were obviously insufficient for a two days' campaign. Gentinetta's feelings, stimulated doubtless by the contemplation of these limited supplies, at length overcame his usual taciturnity and, unabashed by " the dignity that doth hedge" a Herr, he expressed *his* opinion of my prophecies. He backed this up by stating his conviction that at no period since the creation of the world, nor for that matter anterior to it, had such wind and such clouds resulted in aught but the most desperate and lasting bad weather. We felt that exercise would be good for his spirits, and that in any case his company would be depressing, so he was sent back to Zermatt for extra supplies and the best man he could find to help carry them. We pointed out the place where we should camp, and undertook to intercept him on his way back should the weather appear to us too evil for sleeping out.

Ever darkening clouds rolled over the Col Tournanche, and the roar of the wind through the crags of the Matterhorn became distinctly audible, telling of the furious hurricane that was raging round its mighty ridges. Burgener's confidence began to waver, and he again suggested retiring to the Capuan luxuries of the Monte Rosa Hotel. I felt more than a tremor of doubt myself, but the die was cast, so I trusted to luck, kept a cheerful countenance and declared that, come what might, we should have fair play from the weather. Burgener was impressed. The constant blotting out of the distant ridges, the ever gathering mass of cloud round the Matterhorn and more than a suspicion of dampness in the fierce squalls of wind that smote us at short intervals, were signs so distinct and unmistakable that he thought even a Herr must recognise them. My persistence, therefore, suggested occult knowledge. I was, perhaps, a Mahatma (or its Saas Thal equivalent), and he settled himself in a sheltered corner and, charmed by the caresses of my Lady Nicotine, told me weird tales of the ghosts and goblins which still haunt the great circle of cliffs towering above the Val Anzasca. As the day wore on, the burden of a cheerful countenance became too much for me, so I retired to a quiet nook and, wrapped in numerous rugs, sought to drown my anxieties in sleep. Late in the afternoon Burgener awoke me with a great thump and bid me look at the weather. My first impression was that he had come to upbraid me as an impostor, and hold up my prophecies to scorn and derision. His jubilant air and a look of thinness about the lingering clouds, however, negatived these painful thoughts, and I found that the thump was intended to convey devout appreciation of my astounding wisdom! I shook myself free from the damp rugs, and a gleam of sunshine breaking through the mists, we welcomed the returning orb of day with ear-splitting yells and a "break down" as vigorous as hobnailed boots would permit. Our conduct would doubtless have suggested to competent critics that we were pious followers of Zoroaster (or escaped lunatics?). These ebullitions of joy having exhausted themselves and us, we packed the knapsacks and, appropriating the store of rugs belonging to the hut, made for the rendezvous appointed with Gentinetta.

At the extreme north-western corner of the great buttress or shelf on which rests the Matterhorn glacier, is a stony plateau from which the ice has long since retreated. We hoped to discover a sheltered hollow amongst the *débris* with which it is strewn, and thitherward we slowly wended our way. On our arrival we found a total absence of convenient hollows, and we were fain to content ourselves with such protection as the side of a big rock affords. Above us frowned the great ice cliffs of the glacier, cutting off nearly all view of the mountain. To their right, and out of reach of any fragments that might fall from them, was a long ridge of rock leading to the foot of the snow arête. Having lit our fire and set the pot to boil, we sat down at the edge of the cliff overlooking the Zmutt glacier, and soon discovered Gentinetta and another man making their way rapidly through the crevasses. Meanwhile the sun had set, and with the gathering darkness the last lingering clouds dispersed as by magic. About eight o'clock the men arrived, and we found that our new recruit was Johann Petrus. We were both delighted, for no bolder climber or more resolute man has ever delighted the heart of an eager Herr.

Gentinetta's commissariat arrangements had taken a very fluid form. Our dinner consisted chiefly of the remains of our original provisions and an heterogeneous mixture of red wine and marsala, bottled beer and cognac. During the continuance of this festivity, Burgener and Gentinetta vied with each other in extolling the weather wisdom of their Herr. Petrus was called upon to bear witness to its utterly uncompromising appearance in the morning, and, not content with his testimony, the absent Imseng was added to my triumph: for had he not also given it up as hopeless? "Yet their Herr had never faltered in his confidence"—little did they guess my feelings during the afternoon — "and had consistently borne true witness in the face of an adverse host." Subsequent experience has been quite thrown away on Burgener; he still regards me as of transcendent merit in this branch of the climber's craft. When, as usually happens, facts do not agree with my forecast, he, like the celebrated French scientist, is inclined to exclaim: "Tant pis pour les faits."

The night proved intensely cold. The clouds had prevented any sunshine reaching the plateau, and the small pools of water and patches of snow, even when we first reached it, were still hard frozen from the previous night's frost. These icy rocks below and a keen north wind above seemed to freeze us to the very marrow, and we shivered with the pain of cold under our scanty rugs. We were all glad when it was time to be moving, and at the first hint of dawn (4.15 a.m.) we began to scramble up the rocks and along the ridge leading towards the snow arête. At 5.20 a.m. we reached its foot, and on a sheltered ledge found the *débris* of Penhall's camp. Here we halted for breakfast and deposited the blankets, which, thinking it just possible we might have to spend another night on the mountain, we had brought with us to this point. After half an hour's halt we put on the rope and began to ascend the snow ridge. Reaching the rocky teeth, which, when seen from Zermatt, stand out conspicuously against the sky, we scrambled over the rickety piles of frost-riven rock. Beyond the third tooth we were pulled up by a deep cleft. Burgener and Petrus soon scrambled down the face of the rocks to our right and succeeded in getting into it. Further direct progress was, however, impossible, as the ridge rose perpendicularly above them, and a great rib supporting it bulged out in front and precluded all chance of traversing. Of itself this would not have stopped either of the men, as a narrow gully between this rib and the fangs of the tooth on which Gentinetta and I were sitting, offered an obvious means of descending below the obstruction; further in front and to the left, however, rose a slope with the unpleasant look that tells of a basis of rotten rock, glazed with ice and masked with powdery snow. Higher up it steepened till it seemed almost perpendicular. Up this slope we knew we must go or abandon the ascent, and, startled by its appearance, the men recoiled to the rocks where I was still posted.

For another three-quarters of an hour we examined it without being able to see a satis-

Matterhorn.
from the Dent d'Hérens

factory way across, and unpleasant doubts were being freely expressed when a distant jodel attracted our attention. Far away down the mountain we spied three dots, whom we at once and rightly guessed to be Penhall and his guides. We wasted the next half-hour in alternately watching their progress and studying our slope. At length they disappeared behind a projecting buttress, and this excuse for delay having disappeared, it was decided that we should pass the cleft in front and examine the slope more nearly. We descended into the gap. Burgener and Petrus then scrambled down the gully and soon found a way on to the face. On reaching this point* a few minutes later I found Burgener and Petrus already working upwards, and in a few minutes we were again on the arête. After following it a short distance, we reached the point at which it was necessary to take to the evil slope, and the discussion was once more renewed. Burgener was distinctly averse to attempting it, but as there was no other way, Petrus went forward to explore.

* This point is seen, in the illustration opposite, just beyond the rocky teeth which terminate the snow ridge. The route then turns to the left into the couloir, but again reaches the ridge beyond the first precipitous step. Higher up, near where this ridge merges in the great western face—to the left of three small snow patches—the route turns to the right, and the broken western face is followed till it becomes possible to traverse back on to the final Zmutt ridge, which is then followed to the summit.

I have not the slightest doubt that Burgener's objection to this slope was exclusively due to the fact that we had never previously been together on this sort of work. It was obviously practicable, but it was equally obvious that the slip of one meant the destruction of all who were roped to him. Subsequent experience enables me to sympathise with his feelings. The knowledge that you can do nothing to arrest a slip, combined with a lively fear that one may occur, creates as unpleasant a situation as it is easy to imagine. The fear of slipping oneself is almost a delight when compared with the trap-like feeling induced by the rope with an "unknown quantity" at the end of it.

Our halts at this point and on the third tooth had exceeded two hours, and we had no more time to lose. Petrus seemed to be getting on all right, so Burgener made ready for the traverse. Though by no means a big man in the valley, on an ice glazed slope he seems to visibly dilate, and looks like a veritable giant when wielding his resistless axe. For some reason, probably to get a decent excuse for unroping Gentinetta and saving him from the risk of the "unknown quantity,"* Burgener told us to pay him out till he should

---

* On more than one occasion I have found Burgener attempting to save others from risks which he himself was running, by various more or less transparent devices. To those who know him it is needless to add that he never allows others to run risks from which he himself is exempt.

be "ganz fest." We paid out a hundred feet of rope, and as there was no immediate prospect of his being "ganz fest," and as in the event of a slip it was tolerably certain that it would make no difference whether he were or no, I cautiously followed his track; Gentinetta bringing up the rear, free from the dangerous entanglement of the rope. Having traversed in all about a hundred and fifty feet we were able to turn up the slope, and soon reached firm rock, which, though very steep, offered good hold and plenty of it. Burgener dashed up at a furious pace. Suddenly a splinter of rock caught his coat, and an agonised yell told us that his pipe, his faithful companion in many a hard-fought climb, and the gift of his most trusted Herr, had been jerked out of his pocket and had plunged down to the Matterhorn glacier.

Soon afterwards we regained the ridge, and, without halting, followed it to the point where it not merely becomes perpendicular, but actually overhangs.* We had now to traverse to our right on to the great western face of the mountain. Burgener anxiously scanned the huge cliff and then gripped my hand and exclaimed, "The pipe is avenged, we are on the summit," which I took to mean that we should be there sometime.

* That this is no exaggeration may be distinctly seen either from the Mettelhorn or from the slopes above and to the west of Breuil. From these two opposite points this part of the arête is well seen.

The men began the construction of a stone man, whilst I utilised the halt in a diligent search for a diminutive chicken which Burgener averred was concealed in the knapsack. We then prepared one of our numerous bottles for the due reception of our names, and it was subsequently carefully built into the cairn. These duties having been performed, and Burgener having borrowed Gentinetta's pipe—which, by the way, he did not return till we got back to Zermatt—we began the ascent of the western face. We traversed a short distance and then turned straight up over slabby, icy and somewhat loose rocks. They were not, however, difficult, and we made rapid progress. Probably we should have done better still further to the right, but Burgener was very properly averse to this course, as he thought it might bring us too directly above the other party. Even where we were, he insisted on the utmost care to avoid upsetting stones. I subsequently learnt from Penhall that his party was too far to the right to be affected by anything we sent down, and the one or two fragments we did dislodge never came within sight or hearing.

After some steady climbing, we reached a point from which it appeared possible to work back on to the Zmutt ridge, but Burgener was not quite certain, and on hearing that Carrel had traversed by a ledge higher up, he preferred to take that course. We soon gained this ledge—the well-

known "corridor" of the early Breuil ascents—
and found no difficulty in following it to the
fault that bars access to the ridge. Petrus was
promptly swung over to see if the last man could
get down unaided. This being pronounced impossible, our second rope was got out. A good
deal of time was spent before it could be fixed,
the only available knob of rock being too round
to admit of its being easily attached. Meanwhile,
I had time to look along the ledge which winds
like a pathway, round all the irregularities of the
mountain, to the southern ridge. It was quite
free from ice and snow, and in its then condition
could have been traversed with ease. I also
came upon a deeply rusted hook driven into
the rock, a relic, I suppose, of Mr. Grove's ascent
in 1867. Having slid down the rope, we found
the remainder of the ledge was very different.
Instead of offering firm foothold on the rock,
it was loaded with incoherent snow, and the few
knobs which protruded through this were glazed
with ice, and, for the most part, rotten. It was,
however, of no great extent, and we were soon
able to plunge through the snow on to the ridge
(12.50 p.m.). Petrus, who had been more or less
erratic in his movements all day, had disappeared.
We followed his traces, occasionally on the arête,
but more often on the steep slope to the left,
and in three-quarters of an hour found him on
the summit (1.45 p.m.).

The day was perfectly calm and the view cloudless. Time fled swiftly, and when Burgener came up to me with the rope at 2.30 p.m. I could hardly believe we had been three-quarters of an hour on the summit.

Then we descended the chain-clad north-eastern arête to the elbow, where we waited a few minutes to watch Penhall's party, which had just come in sight on the Zmutt ridge. With a parting jodel to our friends we plunged down the slopes to the cabane. Great care, however, was required to avoid the broken glass and sardine boxes which had accumulated in large quantities. After a short halt we ran down to the Furggen glacier, and at 5.30 p.m. were unbuckling our gaiters on the moraine under the Hörnli. An hour and a half later we tramped down the high street of Zermatt, and were soon enjoying the rewards of the faithful.

NOTE.—So far as I can learn, the ascent had till 1894 been only once repeated. On the 27th of August of that year, however, S. A. R. il Duca degli Abruzzi, with Dr. Norman Collie and myself, left a gîte, rather below my previous quarters. Under the lead of young Pollinger, who was the only professional member of the party, we kept to the right of my old route, and, reaching the Tiefenmatten glacier, skirted it where it abuts against the cliffs of the Matterhorn. Then turning straight up, we climbed to the snow ridge just where it merges into the rocky teeth.

We found the mountain almost completely free from snow and ice, and were able to climb without serious difficulty on the face to the left of the ridge—in the gully falling away to the Matterhorn glacier—which, when I was there previously, had been excessively dangerous. Similar good luck followed us when we emerged on the western face, and we found places, which in 1879 had been very formidable, comparatively easy and simple. By 9.10 a.m. we gained the upper Zmutt ridge. This, owing to the absence of snow, was quite easy, and a little before 10 a.m. we reached the summit. The fear of approaching bad weather had, however, driven us ever forward at our best pace, and it is not likely the ascent will often be made as rapidly.

Four days later, three parties were on this face of the mountain together. Miss Bristow, with young Pollinger and Zurbriggen (ascended by the Hörnli route and *descended* by the Zmutt ridge—the first descent effected on this side of the mountain); Dr. Güssfeldt with Rey; and Mr. Farrar with D. Maquignaz (both ascended by the Zmutt ridge; Dr. Güssfeldt descending by the Hörnli route and Mr. Farrar returning by the Zmutt).

CHAPTER II.

THE MATTERHORN—FURGGEN RIDGE.

A YEAR later, at Couttet's Hotel, I was dreaming peacefully of my *bien aimée* the Aiguille des Charmoz—whom we had successfully wooed the previous day—when Burgener broke in upon my slumbers and ejected me, ruthlessly, from the soft comfort of my bed.

Protests were vain. The huge ridge of the Furggen Matterhorn had long tempted his desires, and what are such things as sleep, rest, or blissful ease, when weighed in the balance with the wild joy of gripping grey-brown ledges, and hacking and beating the long gullies of black ice into submission? All the ingrained fighting instinct was aroused in him. He wished to hurl himself once more at the cliffs and ridges, matching his skill against their dumb, passionless resistance, and forcing them now, as ever, to yield to his reckless onslaught. Time, however, pressed, and if this attempt was to be made, without prejudicing other long-cherished hopes, it was necessary to reach Stalden that very night.

We hurried along to Argentière, and then the driver, thinking he had fairly got us in his power, coolly told us that it was quite impossible to catch the mid-day train at Martigny; at all events, neither his horses nor any one else's could do it. We were not, however, to be beaten. Seizing our axes and knapsacks, we left the voiture disconsolate on the road, and trudged manfully up the path towards the Col de Balme. The driver, who saw the piled-up wealth of the Martigny tariff dwindling into a mere ten francs, protested with all the vigour of a Chamoniard.

We were buoyed up, during the ascent, by the hope that a voiture would be procurable at the Forclaz inn. But when we arrived there, we found that luck had abandoned us, and we must face the grim terrors of the road down to Martigny. Half choked by dust, and more than half baked by the blazing sun, we reached the railway station with just twenty minutes to spare. Burgener quickly recognised the necessities of the situation—borrowing a franc, he dashed into the town, and, before we could realise the nature of his quest, he returned with a great stoneware jar full of foaming beer. Jolly John Barleycorn quickly appeased our miseries, and by the time the lumbering train had arrived happiness was once more enshrined in the party.

We reached Stalden about 4 p.m., and halted for the night. By so doing, Burgener and Venetz were enabled to make those ecclesiastical arrangements which the peculiar enormities of the Furggen ridge seemed to render desirable. Such elaborate and careful preparations appeared to me a trifle uncanny, and subsequent events showed very clearly the evil effects which this

NEUBRÜCKE.

sort of indulgence in religious festivities has upon the nerves. However, both Burgener and Venetz appeared to be in excellent spirits when they returned, and we whiled away the summer evening with stories of chamois hunting and the great deeds wrought amongst the winter snow.

The next day we strolled up to St. Niklaus, and drove merrily on to Zermatt, starting about half-past ten the same evening for our ridge. Near the last châlets, the guides, allured by the pleasing appearance of a small hollow, curled themselves up and went fast to sleep. I soon found that the grass was damp, not to say wet, and the wind bitterly cold. The contemplation of

STALDEN.

these discomforts gradually exhausted my patience, and, as there were no signs of waking, I gently stirred the sleepers with an ice-axe. The knapsacks were picked up, and we went slowly on our way. From this point our pace became steadily worse, until, at last, Burgener confessed to being very unwell. In consequence, I took his load.

NEAR ZERMATT.

and we struggled onwards till we came to a great stone, close to the Schwarzer See. It was quite obvious by this time that the ascent must be abandoned, and, after an hour's halt, we tramped wearily back to Zermatt, where we arrived too early for breakfast and too late for bed.

After a bathe in the Triftbach, I returned to a sad and solitary meal in the Monte Rosa Hotel, and, from a secluded corner, heard my chances of success discussed on all sides; the more eager folk even neglecting their breakfasts in favour of the painful attitudes requisite to watch the Furggen ridge through the big telescope.

A well-known climber has expressed a doubt whether the Christian virtue of good temper is binding on a man before 9.30 a.m. I sincerely trust it may not be, or Venetz and I most certainly have a "mauvais quart d'heure" before us. Burgener, with much wisdom, went to bed, and was thus free from the wrangles with which Venetz and I sought to pass the dragging hours. As the day wore on, things began to take a more hopeful turn. Burgener was reported better, and, towards evening, even in favour of a renewed attempt. Two other parties were leaving for the Hörnli route at 11 p.m., so, to avoid the bustle and discomfort of an innumerable host, we determined not to start before midnight.

Owing to the usual delays, we did not actually get off till 12.45 p.m., and, once more, tramped up the slopes to our last night's halting place. Whilst the men were consuming a sort of preparatory breakfast, I watched the curious movements of a light, far below on the Gorner glacier. The light, obviously, proceeded from a lantern, but its movements were most extraordinary and undecided. At one moment it would make good progress up the glacier, then it would halt, wobble up and down, in and out, dodge behind intervening rocks or ice, again reappear, and finally re-descend to the original point of departure. These proceedings were then repeated, and there seemed to be no possible aim or object in its vagaries. However, my mind was chiefly occupied with the Furggen ridge, and, so soon as we again got under weigh, I thought no more of its strange behaviour. The men were evidently determined to make up for our slow progress on the preceding night by the rapidity of their movements on this, and it was with no small delight that I hailed our arrival on the level stretch of boggy ground, under the Schwarzer See.

A few minutes later we were surrounded by the weird, unearthly flicker of innumerable will-o'-the-wisps. At every step they floated away on either hand, yet, seemingly, no sooner had we passed, than they crept up stealthily behind, dogging our footsteps with a cruel vindictiveness from which there appeared no hope of escape or flight.

The men were horror-struck. Burgener gripped

my arm and hoarsely whispered—"Sehen Sie, Herr, die todten Leute!"

We were marked out for the vengeance of the immortal gods. The fiends who haunt the crags of the Matterhorn were already gloating over their prey! Such was the purport of the agonised whispers of the men. I am fain to confess, the crawling, bluish flames, the utter silence, and the contagion of my companions' superstitious fear, thrilled me with instinctive horror. I perceived, however, that if we were not to return to Zermatt baffled and beaten a second time, the delights of a spiritualistic *séance* must be abandoned in favour of a matter-of-fact explanation. My efforts in this direction led Burgener and Venetz to the somewhat erroneous belief that every square yard of England, Scotland, and Wales is illuminated, nightly, by similar, but far more brilliant and nerve-shattering, displays. Despite the unfortunate way in which my German would give out just as I was making a really effective point, the men were evidently inclined to think that these "Geister" were, perhaps, impostors; but, alas! this was not all.

"Ach lieber Herr, did you not see the wandering light on the Gorner glacier? There is no boggy ground there. That *was* a Geist."

In vain I protested that it was a lantern. "A lantern! What could any one want there? It was on the road to nowhere; besides, it did not move forwards like a lantern, but kept wandering to and fro, twinkling and dodging, precisely as a disembodied spirit, with no particular business on hand, might be expected to do."

The position was serious enough in all conscience. It is a well ascertained fact (attested by all the ecclesiastical authorities of the Saas, Zermatt, and Anzasca valleys) that any one seeing a "Geist" is certain to be killed within twenty-four hours! I pointed out to Burgener that this being so, there could be no advantage in turning back; for, either they were ghosts, in which case we must be killed, or they were not ghosts, in which case we might as well go on. The men admitted the dilemma, but suggested that even so, climbing up a peak for the purpose of being chucked off it by mischievous "Geister" is not pure and unalloyed joy. I readily assented to this proposition, but pointed out the inconvenience and discomfort, both mental and bodily, of being haled from the Monte Rosa Hotel, perhaps from the very *table d'hôte* itself, by the foul fiend and his myrmidons. I asked him to consider the scorn and contempt with which the Zermatt priesthood, ever jealous of their Saas Thal brethren, would witness his flight, as, clutched by the huge talons, the black wings bore him to the under world. Burgener, who, like Luther and the early Christian fathers, had had personal acquaintance with his Satanic Majesty, agreed that this would be altogether too grievous, and, taking everything into consideration, that the balance of advantage lay with an advance. Being the most sceptical of the party, I was allotted the post of leader.

Suddenly, in the distance, appeared two lights. "The other parties!" I exclaimed, thinking the men's fears would be somewhat allayed by company. But Burgener and Venetz had "Geister" on the brain, and vowed that these also were undoubted specimens of that genus. I urged them to force the pace and find out. "What!" cried they, "do you know so little of Geister as to attempt such a thing as that?" Burgener, after much persuasion, consented to jodel, a proceeding attended with very grave danger—"Geister" don't like being jodelled at—and only to be effected in doubtful and tremulous sort. To our delight, however, back came a cheery yell, that the men recognised as belonging to Peter Taugwalder.

The sceptics in the party being much strengthened by this most opportune support, we pushed onwards more cheerily. When, lo! a great luminous figure with outstretched arm sprang across our path, and, as instantly, melted into the blackness of night. I will freely admit that the inveterate sceptic was startled at this apparition, and stood motionless with horror and superstitious fear. The men, however, were actuated by other feelings. They knew that only a few yards off were the consecrated walls of the Schwarzer

See chapel, and, dashing past me, they rushed, wild with panic fear, towards this tiny oasis of safety.

A second time the apparition stood before us, but now we could see that our mysterious foe was naught else than the door-post of the sacred edifice itself. A candle left in the chapel by Taugwalder throwing a fitful light on the timbered porch, as the unlatched door swung to and fro in the light breeze.

The men entered for devotional purposes, whilst I proceeded slowly on my way. Reaching the Furggen glacier, I sat down on a stone and waited. Half an hour past, and I began to wonder whether a fresh troop of ghosts had driven them incontinently back to Zermatt. Happily, just as the first grey light of dawn began to show in the east, my shouts were answered, and, once more united, we tramped rapidly up the glacier. As the sun rose, its earliest beams fell on long wisps of snow torn from the crest of the Matterhorn, and though of fairy-like beauty, suggestive of more wind than we quite cared for.

We had by now reached the base of the steep glacier that clings to the eastern face of the Matterhorn, and as our ghostly adventures had most unduly delayed us, we determined to try a short cut and ascend transversely over the distorted ice to a rock couloir that obviously gave access to the broken cliff immediately under the Furggen ridge. The adoption of this line of ascent illustrates very clearly the errors to which even the best ice men are occasionally subject. I have no hesitation in saying, that Burgener is second to no one living, in the skill with which he can steer his party through an ice fall, and the instinctive art of taking the best route. But on this occasion he was hopelessly astray. An easy route to the foot of our couloir can be found, either by keeping close under the north-eastern ridge till the upper level of the glacier is reached, and thence traversing across slightly inclined snow; or the climber may push over the flat glacier to the foot of the Furggen-grat, and find an equally easy way to the upper snows, close to its base.

We, however, took neither of these courses, and were soon involved in ice work of the most sensational kind. At one point it appeared as if we should be forced to retreat. The upper lip of a huge crevasse towered forty feet or more above us, and it was only by the most brilliant skill, that Burgener and Venetz succeeded in forcing their way up in a small transverse crevasse that, luckily, intersected it. Above this obstruction we halted a few minutes, to examine our line of attack.

From the Breuil Joch to the great snow slopes of the eastern face, a steep cliff guards all approach to the upper part of the mountain, and the rock couloir, referred to above, seemed to be the only point at which we could break through these defences. The main objections to it were the obvious frequency of stone avalanches, and the impossibility of conveniently gaining its base, save by the ascent of the deep groove cut by these same stones in the ice slope below. However, we all agreed that well-behaved stones in the nineteenth century were scarcely likely to be on the move at 5 a.m., so we turned a couple of Bergschrunds, scrambled into the avalanche groove, and dashed up at a furious pace; an occasional rattle overhead stimulating our movements to the utmost. The rock couloir proved to be ice-glazed, and not free from difficulty; moreover, we could only ascend exactly in the line of fire. It was, therefore, with feelings of great delight that we perceived a flaw in the cliff on our left, and were able to find a way through to the easy slopes of the face.

Here we halted to take breath, for our desperate exertions had been more than even the most active amongst us quite appreciated. A little stream, which the sun had just woke from its icy sleep, then suggested breakfast, and we unpacked the knapsacks and settled ourselves for half an hour's rest. Far below, a party bound for the Furggen Joch spied us on our lofty seats, and roused the echoes of the mountain with their jodels.

Bearing to our left we soon reached the ridge, and ascended without difficulty of any sort, till at 9 a.m. we reached the great tower, seen from Zermatt on the left sky line just beneath the final peak. Standing in the gap between this tower and the mass of the mountain, we looked down a couloir of most appalling steepness. Far beneath us, amongst its lower crags and ridges, mists were curling and seething, seeming in their restless activity to be the half-awakened "Geister" hungering for their victims. So strange and mysterious did that deep chasm seem, that I half expected to see the writhing vapour take form and substance, and sweep to their doom those rash mortals who had surprised the dead amid their nightly revels.

Far above, the great ridges armed with fantastic icicles, at one moment would stand out hard and sharp against a blue-black sky, and the next be lost in a blurred cloud of driving snow, the roar of each furious gust being followed by the ominous clatter of broken icicles, and the crash of great stones torn from the summit rocks.

The final peak looked very formidable, and, in such weather, could not have been assailed with any reasonable approach to safety. We resolved, in consequence, to traverse on to the ordinary Hörnli route. Scrambling up to a second tower, just above that already mentioned (also visible from Zermatt), we halted for a few minutes and made ready for a rapid traverse. So far, we had not been in the line of fire, but we were now compelled to break cover, and run the gauntlet of the hail of broken ice and stones that the gale was stripping from the topmost crags. The process of avoiding these missiles was rendered exceptionally difficult, by the way in which the furious wind would deflect them from their course, and bring those which seemed to be falling well in front of the party, right into its very midst. After more than one extremely narrow escape, we reached a point somewhat sheltered by a projecting crag above. Burgener turned straight up the slope towards it, and, at racing speed, led us to a secure ledge at its foot.

Immediately in front, the long, pitiless slabs, ceaselessly swept by whizzing, shrieking fragments of all sorts and sizes, suggested to Burgener—who has a most proper and prudent objection to every form of waste—that it would be well to drink our Bouvier, and consume our other provisions, before any less fitting fate should overtake them. The knapsack was accordingly unpacked, and, in the grave and serious mood befitting the solemnity of the occasion, we proceeded to demolish those good things with which the thoughtful Seiler had stored our bags. Under these various benign influences our spirits rose rapidly, and Burgener's face resumed its wonted look of confidence; he once more shook his beard with defiance at the falling stones, and called " Der Teufel " to witness that we had been in quite as bad places before. Looking back on that distant lunch, I have little doubt that Burgener fully realised that a rollicking, self-confident party can dodge falling stones and dance across steep slabs, in a manner, and at a pace, which is impossible to anxious and disheartened men. His object was fully attained; by the time we had tied on our hats with sundry handkerchiefs, seen to the lacing of our boots, and otherwise pulled ourselves together, we felt quite satisfied that the stones and ice would exhibit their usual skill in missing the faithful climber.

We were soon springing across the slabs like a herd of frightened chamois. At one or two places, where the whole party was simultaneously on extremely insecure footing, we were forced to moderate the pace a little; but even then our leader would brook no hesitation, whether we liked it or whether we did not, his "Schnell nur schnell" hurried us ever forwards. An occasional rap on the head by a splinter of ice, or the hurtle of a great stone, as it spun playfully between the various members of the party, most thoroughly accentuated Burgener's admonitions.

It is needless to say, a very few minutes of this sort of progress took us out of range, and we were able to rest in safety. A short distance further was the well-known "shoulder." Scattered up and down it, were the two parties ascending by the ordinary route. To reach them, however, was not easy. Bare rock, destitute of hold and extremely steep, intervened. Burgener made an effort to creep across, but one of the guides on the "shoulder" scrambled towards us, and after inspecting the cliff shouted that it was "ganz unmöglich." Our leader retreated on hearing this, and we tried to traverse on a line some thirty feet below. This proved wholly impracticable, and the guides on the ridge kindly recommended us to go back by the way we had come. The advice was doubtless well meant, but it roused our ire, and we turned once again to Burgener's original line of effort. After considerable difficulty we succeeded in working our way across and refuting our timorous advisers. We reached the "shoulder" just at the point where the ridge abuts against the final summit.

The other parties, having seen our success was assured, were already ascending, so we tucked ourselves under a great rock, and expressed heartfelt regrets for the Bouvier that was no more, and the good things that we had devoured. Subsequently we scrambled to the top, rattled back to the "shoulder," and should have been in Zermatt by 5 p.m. had I not made an unlucky remark concerning Geister and Todten Leute. These good (or bad?) people had been forgotten amidst the excitement of the climb, but my unlucky remark awakened Burgener to the imminence of the catastrophe that must necessarily overtake us. For some reason which he could not make very clear, he considered it certain that the Geister would either push us off the mountain or drop something hard and heavy on our heads before we reached the point where the new hut now stands. It was in vain I pointed out to him that the various supernatural powers would be able to effect our destruction as easily in Zermatt as on the mountain. Burgener, whilst admitting the theoretic excellence of my doctrine, evidently did not accord it any actual acceptance. His position on this subject appeared to be as illogical as his views on Sunday mountaineering. On this latter great question, he holds that difficult expeditions are an obvious and distinct " tempting of Providence." Easy expeditions, on the other hand, he considers may be undertaken, for, says he, on such and such mountains you can hang on no matter what happens, and he proceeds to back up this opinion with arguments of a painfully materialistic type. In the present instance he clearly thought that the natural advantages of the ground would give us a good chance of defeating the lurking enemy. We descended with the utmost elaboration of care, only one moved at a time, and constant entreaties were even then required before rope enough was paid out to enable anybody to move. These elaborate precautions were backed up by a great profusion of pious (and sometimes the reverse) ejaculations, and we each vowed a candle of peculiar splendour and size to a saint of Burgener's acquaintance, subject, of course, to the provision that the said saint enabled us to baffle the malignant Geister. When we had duly arrived on the Furggen glacier, Venetz suggested a doubt as to whether the saint had really earned the candles. He showed us a small necklet he was wearing, which contained the tooth or thumb-nail, or other decaying *débris*, of an exceptionally holy saint, and which, he averred, was, as cricketers would say, " quite able to lick all the Zermatt Geister off its own bat." However, Burgener assured me that, in bargains of this sort, it is always the better plan to pay, "especially," he added, " when a few francs are alone at issue." So we subsequently duly discharged our debts. We got back to Zermatt just in time for *table d'hôte*, after a day of the most varied interest and excitement.

The next day we walked, railed, and drove back to Chamonix. Our minds were chiefly occupied with the various apparitions we had encountered. Burgener, after a protracted talk with the priest at Stalden, had come to the conclusion that the candles and Venetz's amulet would have been wholly ineffective against Todten Leute, and that, consequently, the apparitions we had seen could not have been real, *bonâ fide* specimens. My explanation of the will-o'-the-wisps was accepted, and they were dismissed as mere natural phenomena. But it was less easy to dispose of the light on the Gorner glacier. Burgener and Venetz thought that probably a big lump of gold had seen fit to "wachsen" on or near the glacier, and they supported this theory by much ingenious argument. Was there not gold in the Macugnaga valley? And if there was gold on one side of Monte Rosa, why not on the other? Now it is evident that the only way in which gold could get there would be by a " wachsening " (if that is the right derivative) process, and if this happened at Macugnaga, why not in Zermatt? It was further obvious that during the growing stage, gold would be likely to shine with just such a light as we had seen. I was prepared to accept all these propositions, but I could not agree that gold in its infantile stages would be likely to take such idiotic and senseless walks on the glacier. On the other hand, I pointed out that the place was well suited to be the home of a dragon, and the movements we had seen appeared exactly appropriate to what is known of that reptile's habits. The men, however, were deplorably sceptical on this point, and even with the well authenticated instances related by Scheuchzer to back me, they would not admit the existence of this most interesting animal.

On our arrival at Chamonix, a friend joined our councils and threw fresh and startling light on the problem. A girls' school, with mistresses and all the paraphernalia of learning and wisdom, had been staying in Zermatt. Wishing to acquire close and intimate acquaintance with a glacier, they had walked up to the Gorner and scattered themselves about the ice. One of the girls, with the instincts of a born mountaineer, fearing to be late for the *table d'hôte*, had tracked back by herself. Accordingly, when her companions were once more assembled and ranged under the stern eye of the "genius tutelary," her absence excited alarm, and the whole school once more distributed itself over the glacier, seeking for some traces of the lost demoiselle. The sun meanwhile set, and both teachers and taught found themselves unable to escape from their entanglements. Monsieur Seiler ultimately became alarmed, and sent a guide with a lantern to look for them; and this guide spent the rest of the night in rescuing the disconsolate maidens from the various holes and chasms into which they had fallen.

Thus Burgener's hopes of fortune, and mine of discovering a real nineteenth century dragon, were rudely shattered. Still, as Burgener said, Geister or no Geister, we had had a splendid day, and stored up memories that would last us through many a winter evening. He added "it was a pity we were in such a hurry about those candles."

CHAPTER III.

THE COL DU LION.

ONE glorious day at the end of June, 1880, in fact a week or two previous to the events just described, Burgener and I had finished the more important part of our day's work (crossing the Col Tournanche), and were whiling away the time basking on a warm rock just above the level expanse of the Tiefenmatten glacier. The pipe of peace was wreathing tiny clouds and threads of smoke amongst the overhanging rocks, whilst before us towered the grandest wall the Alps can boast, the huge western face of the Matterhorn. Gradually my attention was riveted by the Col du Lion, and it was brought home to my mind, that no more difficult, circuitous, and inconvenient method of getting from Zermatt to Breuil could possibly be devised than by using this same Col as a pass. I communicated this brilliant and, as I fondly imagined, original idea to Burgener, but he did not immediately respond with the enthusiasm I had anticipated. On the contrary, he told me

that many Herren and many guides had been possessed of the same desire, but on closer examination had invariably abandoned it. However, as we discussed a bottle of Bouvier, first one bit and then another of the couloir was pronounced practicable, and by the time Burgener had indulged in a final and prolonged pull at the brandy flask, to obviate any ill effects that well-shaken Bouvier might cause in the human system, he decided that, "Es geht gewiss," provided, firstly, that we could get into the couloir at the bottom, and secondly, that we could get out of it at the top.

It is true that there was a most repulsive section of the couloir about two-thirds of the way up, where some precipitous rocks broke through the broad ribbon of snow, leaving two narrow gullies of black shining ice up which the climber would have to force his way. There was the further very serious objection that if we were turned back near the Col, it would be very dangerous to retrace our steps, as the couloir was obviously and obtrusively raked by falling stones, as soon as the sun reached the great rock faces of the Matterhorn and Tête du Lion, and released the frost, which alone held the *débris* in position. This latter objection was, however, promptly dismissed, being in reality nothing but an additional reason for not turning back. Once in the couloir, we must, no matter what difficulties might be met, force our way to the top. We ultimately deter-

THE TRIPTBACH BRIDGE.

mined to go down to Zermatt, and make the necessary preparations for delivering an assault the next day.

On our arrival there, however, Burgener heard that one of two recent additions to his family had died, so our expedition had to be temporarily postponed. Meanwhile I gathered much unfavourable information concerning the couloir.

Mr. Whymper, looking at it from the Col above, describes it in these words:

" On one side a sheer wall overhung the Tiefenmatten glacier. . . . Throw a bottle down to the Tiefenmatten—no sound returns for more than a dozen seconds.

". . . . How fearful
And dizzy 'tis to cast one's eyes so low!"

Whilst, in "Hours of Exercise," I came upon the following: " On the other side " of the Col du Lion " a scarped and seamed face drops sheer on the north, to what we know is the Zmutt glacier. Some hopes I had entertained of making a pass by this gap from Breuil to Zermatt vanish immediately." Happily my confidence in Burgener was equal to even these shocks, and I felt sure that if he were once fairly started on the expedition, he would bring it to a happy issue.

On Monday, the 5th of July, Burgener duly arrived, but he was tired with his hot walk, or possibly from the effects of the funeral festivities, which appeared to have been carried on with great vigour and persistence. We decided, therefore, to start from Zermatt at 10 p.m., instead of sleeping at the Stockje and taking the expedition from thence. After *table d'hôte* I thought a short nap would be advantageous, so, telling the hotel porter to call me at half-past nine, I went to sleep. When I was awakened by the dazzling blaze of a dip candle, I felt that it was after time, and a reference to my watch disclosed the painful fact that it was eleven o'clock! I swallowed the cup of tea brought me by the porter, and hurried down to the hall, where I found Burgener in that frame of mind which is suitable to a sleepy man who has been sitting in a straight-backed chair for an hour and a half. He at once gave it as his opinion that we were too late, and that I might as well return to my much loved bed. However, when I had expressed my contrition and explained that my late appearance was due to an error on the porter's part, he consented to overlook my delinquencies.

The knapsack was promptly adjusted and we were ready to set off, when each asked the other for the rope. Burgener averred that I must have it, while I was equally certain that it had been left in his possession. We sought diligently through the lower regions of the hotel, but it was nowhere to be found; indeed, if Burgener was to be trusted, our search should have been directed to certain other "lower regions." At length in desperation we sallied out and sought to beg, borrow, or buy a rope from one or other of the Zermatt guides. Though we succeeded in bringing various night-capped and indignant heads to various windows, no rope could we obtain; indeed, it was scarcely likely that a Zermatt guide would come to the aid of a Saas Thal trespasser. We returned disconsolately to the hotel, and the porter, horrified at the strength of our language and our furious mien, produced a rope which, he told us, some confiding monsieur had left in his charge for the night. Our consciences were fully equal to the occasion, no single qualm or quiver affected their serenity: we seized the rope and started.

By this time it was nearly one o'clock, and we walked up the valley as fast as we could. The night was very dark, and, as we tramped along the moraine-covered glacier, it was a matter of some difficulty to see the crevasses. Every now and then, a larger crack in the ice would necessitate the lighting of a lucifer match, and on the rare occasions when the wind did not blow it out, we crossed the obstruction triumphantly. At other times, when the waste of lucifer matches was becoming excessive, we exercised the Christian virtue of faith and jumped, trusting that we should land on something. Getting through the moraine on to the clear ice, we were able to see a little better, and made relatively good progress till we reached the small glacier coming from the direction of the snow ridge of the Matterhorn. At its base were one or two formidable crevasses, so my companion halted, urging as a reason that we should have such excellent opportunities of coming to grief later in the day, that it was quite needless to take advantage of those immediately at hand.

We found a convenient stone, and, taking off our loads, proceeded to breakfast. We chatted over old scrambles till the faint light in the east had intensified into a fiery glow, lighting up the mountains with a strange unearthly radiance, made doubly brilliant by contrast with the sombre night which still lingered in the deep valley below. Once more we began to ascend, when suddenly, with one consent, we leaned on our axes and gazed mutely at the "aged pinnacle" before us. The rising sun had just touched its summit, and the snowy Zmutt ridge was blazing with crimson light. We watched the red sun creeping ever down the slopes till, at length, it reached the broad glacier below, then Burgener struck his axe into the snow and we breasted the slope: the day had begun.

Keeping well to our right, we reached a sort of col, which leads from this small glacier on to the broad basin of the Tiefenmatten glacier. The latter was rather below us, but, by traversing along the snow slopes heaped up against the Matterhorn, we were able to avoid losing much height, and gradually the glacier rose to our level. Keeping close to the tremendous cliffs on our left, we reached the Bergschrund, and were able to examine the first of the problems we had to solve. It was obvious that the upper lip was quite impregnable to direct assault. Even had it been possible, two great masses of rock broke through the slope about three hundred feet above, over which the ice bulged in great dirty green bosses that formed an obviously impregnable wall. To the right of these two masses of rock, but separated by a narrow slope and slightly above them, was a third mass, also surmounted by a bulging roof of ice. It appeared quite evident, that the only way to get into the couloir, was by the slope between the second and third bulge. Luckily a great sérac had kindly bridged the Bergschrund, not, indeed, exactly below this bulge, but still not unduly far to the right of it.

We put on the rope, and, Burgener having coached me over the bridge, I began cutting up the slope, bearing well to the left. The angle steadily increased, and, before reaching the base of the mass of rock for which we were aiming, Burgener took the lead. The traverse under this was very formidable. The right leg, which was next the slope, could no longer be passed between the left leg and the ice, a very unpleasant change of feet being thereby necessitated at each step. Happily this did not last very long, and we gained the ice slope between the second and third masses of protruding rock. Turning sharply, though still bearing a little to the left, we crept slowly up the bare, shiny slope, till the broad expanse of the couloir above the rocks and their overhanging roofs of ice, was reached. To our left, under the shadow of the gaunt cliffs of the Matterhorn, great patches and streaks of snow still adhered to the ice. The snow was not of great thickness, nowhere exceeding four or five inches, but it was slightly frozen to the slope below, and we mounted rapidly on shallow notches chipped in this loose veneer. In places the snow had slipped away, and we had to cut across the intervening patches of ice, but, as we advanced, the snow became more continuous, and our spirits rose rapidly. It was, however, obvious that the aid of this thin covering of snow was only to be had at the cost of deliberately abandoning all possibility of retreat. So soon as the sun should touch this slope and the frost be relaxed, any attempt to meddle with it could only result in a swirling slide, a long bounce at the point where the rocks protrude, and a final drop into the Bergschrund. This consideration urged us forwards, and kept the steps at the smallest size compatible with standing on them. From time to time we paused a moment to gaze upwards at the sun-tipped ridge, towering at a tremendous height above us, and across which delicate films and streamers of mist were curling. Could we ever reach it? The grim cliffs of the Matterhorn and Tête du Lion

shut us in to the couloir, and, far above, black
overhanging rocks broke through the snow and
seemed to bar further passage. It looked scarcely
possible to get up, and there was more than a
touch of anxiety in Burgener's "Wir mussen,
Herr Mommerie, sonst sind wir beide caput."

Meanwhile my companion's knuckles were
beginning to suffer severely from that occasional
contact with the slope, which is unavoidable
when cutting up steep snow. As he had
evidently plenty of work before him, it was considered desirable that less valuable fingers should
be sacrificed at this stage of the proceedings. I,
accordingly, took the lead. Now and again the
snow thinned out and heavy blows were required
to cut into the ice, but ever, as we advanced,
the labour became less, and at length a single
chip with the axe, backed up with a few good
blows from a hobnailed boot, sufficed to make a
reliable step. We advanced, rapidly and easily,
to the foot of the rocks to which reference has
previously been made, and which constitute one
of the most serious difficulties of the pass. These
rocks, as we had noted on our preliminary survey
of the mountain, were flanked on either hand
by narrow ice-glazed gullies. That on our right
looked the easier, but, unluckily, the sun was
already blazing on the Tête du Lion, and its
rays were loosening the frosty bonds that alone
held the icicles and stones in their places, with

the result that a ceaseless hail of fragments was whizzing and humming down it. We were forced, therefore, to take the gully on the Matterhorn side, which, so far, was quite free from the mountain musketry. Burgener took the lead again, and soon found that he had no ordinary work before him. The ice was bare and as hard as well-frozen ice can be; it was, moreover, excessively steep. So evil did it look above, that he halted and gazed anxiously at the rocks of the Matterhorn to see if we could escape in that direction. It was, however, obvious that we should encounter prolonged difficulty on them; besides which, it would leave the problem of the couloir unsolved. Once more he turned sullenly to the wall of ice, and foot by foot hewed out a way. The projecting rocks on our right, ever tilting the slope outwards, forced us to the left into a sort of semicircular recess in the cliff. Suddenly the step-cutting ceases. " Der Teufel " is apostrophised in soul-curdling terms, and half the saints in the Romish calendar are charged, in the strongest language known to the German tongue, with the criminal neglect of their most obvious duties.

Burgener's axe had broken!

Midway in an ice couloir two thousand feet high, a single axe alone stood between us and utter helplessness. I untied and carefully lashed my axe to the rope and sent it up to Burgener.

The rope then declined to come back anywhere within my reach, and I had the pleasure of ascending the next eighty feet without its moral support, and, which was worse, without an axe. Rejoining Burgener, the broken weapon was made over to me. We were now on a level with the top of the projecting rocks, and could see that, supported by their topmost crag, a long ribbon of snow led upwards. Once on this snow it seemed as if our progress would be comparatively easy, though, as Burgener showed, by the simple expedient of chucking a knob of ice across, it was of that evil, powdery sort that the guides call "pulverischen." Since, moreover, it was lying at the very steepest angle consistent with remaining at rest, it was evident that greater reliance would have to be placed in Providence than is usually considered desirable in these degenerate days. The difficulty, however, was to reach it. I have already explained that the projecting rocks had forced us to the left into a sort of blind, semicircular hollow. A few feet above, the ice, up which we had been cutting, thinned out against overhanging rock; while to cross to the snow involved the passage of an almost perpendicular wall, thickly glazed with ice. This traverse of fifteen feet or more looked scarcely possible. For once in his life Burgener suggested retreat, and we should have both returned incontinently down the couloir, running the gauntlet of falling stones, and facing even the horrors of that hideous ice slope, with its thin surface of snow already relaxed by the warm rays of the mid-day sun, had it not been for the absolute belief I reposed in certain previous utterances of my brave companion, to the effect that retreat was impossible, and to attempt it certain destruction. Confident in this belief, I thought the best thing to do was to keep up the spirits of the party, to scout the idea of turning back, and to shout "vorwärts," strengthened by such allusions to the supernatural powers, as my limited knowledge of Saas Thal patois would render effective. The aid of other spirits, called from the "vasty deep" of my pocket, was also invoked, and then the attack was begun.

The ice was too thin to allow steps of such depth to be cut as would enable us to change our feet in them. Burgener therefore adopted the expedient of cutting a continuous ledge along which, by the aid of handholds cut in the ice above, one could just manage to shuffle. This involved an extraordinary amount of labour. One hand had always to be clinging to the hold above, whilst the other wielded the axe. Before the traverse was half completed Burgener had to retreat, both to rest and to rub some warmth and feeling into his left hand, chilled by constantly clinging to the ice. After a short halt he returned to the attack, but another five minutes again forced him to recoil, and, with a melancholy air, he showed me his right wrist, badly swollen with the strain of one-handed step cutting. Happily the shelf was nearly completed, and, advancing once more, he was able to reach the snow ribbon with his axe. It afforded, however, no support, being loose and incoherent to its very core; so the weary cutting had to go on till he could set his foot on the treacherously piled mass. Very cautiously he tried to tread it down, and then slowly swung his weight on to it. Needless to say, I watched eagerly the behaviour of the snow. If it slithered away bodily, as it seemed much inclined to do, nothing could prevent our making a short and rapid descent to the Bergschrund.

Happily, though a good deal streamed down in incipient avalanches, the core stood firm, and a hoarse shout of triumph relieved the pent-up feelings of the party. Burgener immediately began to force his way up the knife-edge which formed the upper surface of the ribbon, one leg on one side and one on the other. Our whole length of rope being paid out I shuffled along the shelf, past the corner, and up to my companion. Before us was a long open ice slope, through which occasional rocks projected. The slight support so afforded had sufficed to hold long ribbons of dust-like snow in position above them, and we perceived with joy that the final wall, surmounted by a broken cornice, was the only serious obstruction now before us. The cliffs on the Matterhorn side here recede considerably, greatly adding to the width of the couloir, and giving a sense of freedom and daylight that is lacking lower down. Our chief delight, however, was the snow, of the worst and most powdery description it is true, but still snow. I am aware that all authorities agree in preferring ice to incoherent snow, but when the ice slope is measured by hundreds of feet, and when the northern couloir of the "Lion," swept by the afternoon avalanches, is below, I will frankly confess that any snow, however bad, is a delight, and its treacherous aid most thankfully accepted.

We made our way upwards on ribbon after ribbon, cutting across the intervening stretches of ice, and in this way mounted rapidly till we reached a continuous slope of snow that led us to the foot of a low rocky wall, surmounted by a projecting, square-cut cornice from which the flimsier portions had broken away. The face of this final cliff consists of loose, disintegrated rock. It appeared, indeed, to be only held together by the snow and ice with which it was plastered. However, it had to be ascended, so we once more rubbed a little life and warmth into chilled fingers, and then Burgener set to work. Inch by inch and yard by yard, I paid out the rope till he reached the base of the cornice. It was soon evident that a direct assault would not be successful, so he made his way to the right, to a point where the outer fringes and icicles had torn a mass of the more solid cornice away with them in their fall. Once in this gap, he soon gets one hand on to the hard-frozen Col, the other waves his hat, and with a triumphant though breathless jodel, he draws himself over the edge of the grimmest wall it has ever been my luck to scale. Owing to the traverse Burgener had made, the rope did not afford that sense of security and comfort which is so pleasing to the amateur, and it was with no little delight that, on reaching the gap in the cornice, I saw a red hand appear, and a moment later was hauled bodily on to the pass.

I threw off the knapsack, and we set to work to thaw our fingers, or rather those portions of them that still remained. The process proved excessively painful, one or two of them having got badly frozen on the last rocks. Then Burgener's wrist, still suffering from the work on the great shelf traverse, had to be bound up in all the handkerchiefs we could muster. These various operations were, each and all, much delayed by the derisive jodels which it was necessary to hurl at intervals down the couloir. We next made ourselves comfortable, at the very edge of the great cliff, quaffing our wine, and warming ourselves in the glints of hot sunshine, which burst through wind-torn rents in the surging mists. Now and again Burgener would slap me on the back and bid me lean over to note one or other of the more startling obstructions we had had to surmount. After an hour's halt, we turned our attention Breuilwards. The couloir on that side was filled with impenetrable mist, but the few feet we could see did not look very formidable. Burgener suggested a standing glissade, and the next minute we had quitted the sun and blue sky, and were spinning through fog, surrounded by a seething avalanche of snow. From time to time we jumped sideways out of the gathering torrent, fearing lest its growing mass might involve us in danger. Suddenly through the fog I caught sight of the Bergschrund, and with a warning shout to Burgener, who was eighty feet above me, the brakes were applied, regardless of skin and knuckles, and we pulled up on the very brink of the chasm. Traversing to the left we found a bridge, and, as it was much too rotten to crawl over, we trusted to luck and a sitting glissade. We then dodged a few crevasses and glissaded a few slopes, and, turning sharply to the right, got off the glacier. We were now almost below the clouds, and a sun-warmed rock suggested to devout worshippers of the goddess Nicotine the observance of certain solemn rites. Half an hour soon passed, and then the rope was squeezed into the knapsack and we ran, helter-skelter, down to Breuil, where we arrived in one hour and a quarter of actual going, or one hour and three-quarters including halts, from the Col.

My second guide, Venetz, had been sent across the Théodule, partly because the knapsack was too heavy for the Col du Lion, but mainly because Burgener thought that two were a better party than three on ground of that sort. We had strictly enjoined him not to give way to his prevailing weakness, a love of sleep, but to watch for our arrival in the Col. So soon as he saw us we had bidden him to pursue and slay sundry of the bony fowls which, in those remote days, constituted the only form of nutriment attainable at the head of Val Tournanche. We arrived, therefore, with the fond anticipation of a hot lunch. But on reaching the inn we found the silence of death reigning. We battered at the door with our axes, or more correctly with my axe, and such parts of Burgener's as still survived; we even attempted to force the window-shutters off their hinges. But all was of no avail; the Val Tournanche carpenters had done their work too well, and I was just on the point of tracking down the valley when Burgener emerged from the cow-shed, dragging a sleepy native from its pestilential interior. So soon as this native, by dint of much shaking on Burgener's part, and much rubbing of eyes, coughing, and other sleep-destroying processes on his own, had fairly recovered consciousness, he directed us to one particular window, and, regardless of paint and woodwork, we battered on the shutters with such fury that Venetz's slumbers were abruptly terminated. He soon unlocked the door and expressed the utmost surprise at our arrival. He excused his failure to wring the necks of the fowls on the ground that he fully expected that the mountain would have broken ours. He had also considered it a wise precaution, with the fatigues of a "search party" before his eyes, to put in a good sleep as a preliminary!

The lady of the house was, it appeared, some distance away, so we despatched Venetz in quest, and soon saw the pair of them in full chase down the valley with the afore-mentioned bony fowls well in front. Later in the day we tramped down to Val Tournanche, and ended the day in feasting and comparative luxury.

NOTE.—The subsequent history of the pass is soon told. The next year Dr. Güssfeldt, with Alex. Burgener as sole guide, crossed it in the opposite direction (Breuil to Zermatt). By the simple expedient of driving a stake into the snow above, and looping two hundred feet of rope round it, the difficulties near the Col were easily evaded. Owing to the exceptionally fine weather of 1881, the snow on the upper part of the couloir was in much better condition, and no very serious difficulty appears to have been encountered till the party were half-way down. The same cause which had rendered the upper half easier, greatly increased the difficulty of the lower. The fine weather had stripped the snow from the ice and left nothing but a bleak, stone-swept slope. Luckily they were able to take refuge on a small shelf of rock, where they were protected to some extent from the hail of shot and shell discharged by the mountain, and, after a terrible night, reached the Tiefenmatten glacier safely the next morning.

One other passage, and one only, has been effected. On this occasion, Herr Kuffner, with Alex. Burgener and Kalbermatten, crossed the pass from Zermatt to Breuil, but of this passage I have heard no details. Possibly the experience gained by Burgener enabled him to avoid some of the difficulties we encountered. I do not, however, think that in any conditions it is likely to be easy.

CHAPTER IV.

DER TEUFELSGRAT.

BY MRS. A. F. MUMMERY.

The slopes of the Breithorn and the snows of the Weiss Thor are usually supposed to mark the limit of ascents suitable to the weaker sex—indeed, strong prejudices are apt to be aroused the moment a woman attempts any more formidable sort of mountaineering. It appears to me, however, that her powers are, in actual fact, better suited to the really difficult climbs than to the monotonous snow grinds usually considered more fitting.

Really difficult ascents are of necessity made at a much slower pace, halts are fairly frequent, and, with few exceptions, the alternations of heat and cold are less extreme. Snow grinds, on the contrary, usually involve continuous and severe exertion—halts on a wide snow field are practically impossible—and the danger of frost-bite in the early morning is succeeded by the certainty of sun-burning at mid-day. The masculine mind,

THE VILLAGE OF ZERMATT.

however, is, with rare exceptions, imbued with the idea that a woman is not a fit comrade for steep ice or precipitous rock, and, in consequence, holds it as an article of faith that her climbing should be done by Mark Twain's method, and that she should be satisfied with watching through a telescope some weedy and invertebrate masher being hauled up a steep peak by a couple of burly guides, or by listening to this same masher when, on his return, he lisps out with a sickening drawl the many perils he has encountered.

Alexander Burgener, however, holds many strange opinions; he believes in ghosts, he believes also that women can climb. None the less it was with some surprise that I heard him say, "You must go up the Teufelsgrat." Now the Teufelsgrat, as its name implies, is a ridge of exceptional enormity, and one, moreover, that a few days previously, while we were ascending the Matterhorn, he had pointed out to me as the very embodiment of inaccessibility. I was proud of the compliment, and we solemnly shook hands, Burgener saying the while that the nominal proprietor of the ridge and all his angels should not turn us back, once we were fairly started.

For the benefit of those who may not be well acquainted with the Alpine possessions of his Satanic Majesty, it may be pointed out that the Teufelsgrat is the south-western ridge of the Täschhorn. A short distance north of the Täsch-

THE TÄSCHHORN.

Alp this ridge ends in the little peak called the Strahlbett. Our plan was to sleep at the Täsch-Alp and, crossing the Weingarten glacier, to climb up to a very obvious col immediately on the Täschhorn side of that small peak. From thence to the summit we hoped to be able to follow the ridge.

Accordingly, on July 15, 1887, we started from Zermatt to sleep in the highest châlet—in those days the Täsch Inn was still an unimagined luxury. A merry afternoon was spent on the Alp. Some friends, thinking it a good opportunity to see a sunrise, had joined our party, and, being much interested in our expedition, partook of our high spirits. We greatly astonished the various beasts of the neighbourhood by encroaching on their domain. During the afternoon an irate bull made various endeavours to slay us, and at length succeeded in driving the whole party, guides and travellers, on to the roof of the châlet. Finally, when we began to find our perch inconveniently small, a general sortie was ordered, and with wild yells and much flourishing of axes and hats, the brute was put to rout and sent bellowing down the Alp.

When the last tint of sunset had faded off the Weisshorn, we lit our candles and converted the châlet into a ball-room. It was only twelve feet square, and made perilous by low and unexpected beams. None the less, we had a brilliant dance, diversified with songs from the guides and porters. Andenmatten, our second guide, was even provided with a strange and wonderful musical instrument, from which much exhausting blowing would extract reedy dance music and other nondescript melodies. The evening's entertainment having been wound up by the usual discussion about the weather, we betook ourselves to our rugs and tried to sleep. But the boards were hard and the rugs were rough and we were all very restless, and our tempers were getting irritable, when, towards eleven o'clock, the door received a mighty bang, followed by a terrific roar. We all leapt up and seized on ice-axes and telescopes, sticks and hobnailed boots, as weapons wherewith to slay, or at any rate put to flight, the monster who had dared to attack our stronghold. The door was then thrown open and with loud shouts we sallied forth, and once more saw our old enemy the bull. Realising the vigour and fury of his assailants, he again fled, waking the echoes with his indignant snorts and grumbles.

We seized on this incident as a favourable excuse, and abandoned all further idea of sleep. Soon our preparations for the start were begun, and at 1.30 a.m. everything was ready. The two lanterns, skilfully constructed by knocking the bottoms out of empty champagne bottles, were duly lit and, saying good-bye to our friends, we plunged through the long wet grass. The track was soon hopelessly lost, so we worked our way towards the torrent and followed its left bank to the moraine.

I do not wish to make any heart ache by recalling the feelings that followed an unwholesome and indigestible supper at 8 p.m., a sleepless night, and a still less digestible breakfast at 1 a.m.; truth, however, compels me to admit that when these feelings were further accentuated by a loose and very inferior moraine lit by the flickering light of a farthing dip in a Bouvier bottle, I agreed most fully in the short and comprehensive denunciation of things in general which various masculine lips now and again expressed. As we tripped and stumbled up the endless stones we became aware that the day was breaking, and by the time we reached the snout of the Weingarten glacier, Monte Rosa was blazing in brightest sunlight. We halted a few minutes in order that Burgener might consider which of two rock couloirs immediately in front of us would offer the best route. I will confess this problem did not arouse my enthusiasm, and, turning my back to the cliffs, I watched the stately advance of the great red sun, as it drove the last lingering darkness from the lower snow fields.

Burgener's survey was soon completed, the men once more swung the knapsacks on to their shoulders, and we strode across the moraine and loose stones towards the couloir nearest the

Täschhorn. The rocks proved very easy, and we made rapid progress till, at 4.45 a.m., we reached a convenient spot for breakfast. Just in front the cliff became much steeper and was intersected by more or less continuous bands of precipitous rock.

Burgener rejoiced in the approach of our first struggle, and could hardly restrain his exuberant spirits. He employed his time, when his mouth didn't happen to be more seriously occupied, by using his best English to try and shatter my nerves. He gave me various and most graphic pictures of the awful precipices which were to greet my inexperienced eyes, always ending each sentence with, "It is more beautifuls as the Matterhorn," that being the only peak we had previously ascended together.

Having exhausted the regulation time for feeding, the rope was got out and a business-like air settled on Burgener's countenance. He, of course, took the lead, I followed, then came Andenmatten, and my husband last. The rocks were fairly good for a little while, but as we got higher they became steeper and very rotten. Our leader took the greatest care not to upset any of the stones, and kept hurling frightful warnings at me to be equally careful. "You kill your man, you not like that!" I did not "kill my man," but, nevertheless, it was here that our first accident occurred.

We had reached a sort of platform cut off from

the upper slopes by a precipitous wall of rock. At one point, however, where the end of an overlapping slab had weathered and decayed, it seemed just possible to surmount the barrier. Burgener was soon at work upon it, but the splinters of rock were so loose that no reliable grip could be found, and progress had to be made with foot and hand-hold equally uncertain. Still he steadily advanced, and, at length, could just reach his hands over the top of the rock and clutch at a great stone which seemed firm. Firm it was to a certain extent. Firm enough not to roll over on our heads, but, alas! not firm enough to prevent a slight movement on to Burgener's hand. A stifled groan, a trickle of blood down the rocks, followed by a long and impressive sentence in patois, was all the intelligence vouchsafed us till, with a last effort, Burgener clambered on to the top of the wall. We quickly followed, and, finding a convenient ledge, proceeded to make our diagnosis. A somewhat mangled, swollen, and bleeding thumb offered an interesting problem to a student of the St. John's Ambulance Association. The bleeding was soon checked, and the offending thumb bound up in a variety of pocket-handkerchiefs, Burgener murmuring the while in most pathetic tones, " I no more strong in that hand."

We suggested an immediate retreat, but after a glance at the pinnacled ridge, now well within view, a half bottle of Bouvier (we had forgotten to bring any cognac) and a bite off the limb of a tough poulet, there issued from the invalid's lips sneering remarks at the idea of returning. "Vorwärts," he cried, and vorwärts we went, amidst a strange mixture of joyful jodels at the towering gendarmes which seemed to challenge us to wrestle from afar, and dejected looks and mournful voice repeating, "I no more strong in that hand."

About 5.30 a.m. we reached the ridge, here covered with snow. Andenmatten took the lead, and, as the snow was in excellent condition, we were able to make good pace. This was soon succeeded by queer, slabby, stratified rocks, piled at a steep angle, like rows of huge slates, one on the other. Their sharp edges, however, offered good hold for hands and feet. After a short time these broken rocks were interspersed with an occasional bold, precipitous turret, forcing our leader to show his metal. This first gendarme was, nevertheless, successfully passed, and the second stood before us—a large, piled-up mass of brownish yellow, rotten rock, blocking entirely from our view the rest of the arête.

After a short consultation between the guides the best route was singled out, and Andenmatten once more advanced to the attack. The base of the tower went well, and little by little the difficulties seemed to be yielding. Our leader's face beamed with pride and pleasure, as he stormed crag after crag, but, alas! he forgot the well-worn proverb, "Pride goeth before destruction, and a haughty spirit before a fall."

Solomon was once more to be justified, and the joyful Andenmatten was to be the victim. A last small, rocky tooth impeding his progress, and not being able to find sufficient hold, he summoned Burgener to his aid. The suggestion that he should take off the knapsack was treated as an insult, and a minute later, aided by a friendly shove, he had not merely got good hold on the top of the tooth, but was actually resting his arms on it. The tooth was to all intents and purposes climbed, when, to our horror, we saw his arms sliding off, and with a last convulsive effort to find grip for his fingers, he toppled outwards and plunged head downwards over the cliff. Long before the command "hold" could be given we saw him, heels uppermost, arms outspread, knapsack hanging by one strap, and hat rolling into space, on a sloping ice-glazed rock some fifteen feet below us. Burgener, with admirable readiness, had caught hold of the rope as Andenmatten was in the very act of falling, and his iron grip, luckily for us, had stood the strain. I was still clinging to a projecting crag, whilst our last man had thrown himself half over the opposite side of the ridge, and was ready for all emergencies. The fall being checked, all hands seized the rope, but no immediate results ensued. My husband then climbed down, and found that Andenmatten's coat had hitched on a rock. This being loosened, a few strong tugs hauled the victim on to the ridge. The deathly silence was broken only by the sobs of the nerve-shattered bundle which lay at our feet, and it was difficult to realise that this was the same active, sturdy, high-spirited man who had piped for us to dance—who had kept us merry by jodels, making the echoes resound amongst the rocks, and whose cheerfulness had made even the stony moraine and endless screes lose something of their horror. Still the silence remained unbroken save for the injured one's sobs—when, suddenly, a solemn voice remarked, " How providential both bottles of Bouvier are not broken." And, looking round, I found my husband had employed the awe-stricken moments in overhauling the contents of the knapsack. One of these same bottles was promptly opened, and a glass of the foaming fluid poured down the throat of the gasping guide.

After again displaying my great surgical skill, mainly by banging the injured one in the ribs, bending his limbs, and generally treating him in a reckless and unmerciful manner, I declared him more frightened than hurt. " Vorwärts," shouted Burgener; " Vorwärts, wir wollen nicht zurück," and once more he took the lead. I followed, then my husband and last of all Andenmatten, his face deathly pale, his limbs trembling, and his head

THE TÄSCHHORN.

enveloped in a voluminous red handkerchief. At every small rock that came in our way he uttered either bitter curses on the past or prayers for his future; matters, we assured him, of trivial import so long as he placed his feet firmly. A short distance further we were forced off the arête on to the Weingarten face. Every ledge and shelf was here so piled with loose, rolling *débris*, that it was impossible to move without upsetting great slabs and stones. They slid from under our feet, collecting perfect avalanches, as they bounded from ledge to ledge, before taking the last tremendous plunge to the glacier. Coming to the end of these shelves and ledges, we were pulled up by "Blatten" and forced to ascend to the ridge once more. By this time the mournful appeals of the crestfallen Andenmatten enlisted our sympathies, and we halted a few minutes to once more examine his back and apply a certain well-known remedy to his lips. At the same time a gentle hint was given that it was quite useless to develop pains of any sort, either in the back or elsewhere, until a more favourable spot should present itself for their treatment.

We then again set to work. A pyramid in front being impracticable, we were forced over on to the Kien glacier face, along a steep ice slope of most uninviting aspect. Here and there a slab of rock protruded through the ice, suggesting slight hold for the hands, but almost invariably proving to be loose and coming away at the slightest touch. The amount of step-cutting involved was extremely irksome to Burgener. His hand was by this time bleeding afresh, and a groan of pain escaped his lips as each stroke of the axe sent the brittle chips sliding and slithering down the glassy slope. In spite of the wounded hand, the step-cutting had to continue for half an hour or more —half an hour that appeared to me absolutely interminable, as I listened to the groans from in front and to the intermittent sobs and complaints from behind. Andenmatten appeared, indeed, to be in such a deplorable condition that he might faint at any moment; a contingency which suggested that, after all, the Teufelsgrat might have the best of the game.

Further progress on the ice slope was now barred by an impassable buttress of smooth, black rock, the fangs of a huge tooth which towered high above the ridge. Burgener was forced in consequence to work back to the right, and make his way to the ridge up the chimney or rock couloir by which the tooth was flanked. There was, of course, the obvious objection that this chimney would bring us to the arête on the wrong side of the great tooth, but, as our leader remarked, "Es giebt keinen anderen Weg!" Some rather difficult climbing brought him into the gully. When he had found secure footing, I scrambled up and was stowed away into a small ice-filled cleft. He then kindly took my axe and perched it for me in the gully, and, with an authoritative "You stay there" to me, he proceeded on his way. Stones and chips of ice soon whizzed past, followed, a few minutes later, by a great flake which swept down, upsetting my axe, and in a moment my cherished weapon had disappeared into space.

At length the rope became taut, and in obedience to the order "come on," I climbed up the ice-glazed, snow-masked rocks to a big step cut into deeper ice near the top of the gully. Above, snow and easy rock led us to the ridge. But as we had feared, the great tower in front was impassable, and it was evident that another traverse would have to be made. On coming quite close, however, we were overjoyed to find an extraordinary cleft in the rock. The cleft was just wide enough to enable one to squeeze through, and led along the ridge, apparently turning the obstruction.

I feel sure my companions shared the thrill of delight which this awoke within me, by the inspiriting jodel which Burgener shot into the air, the merry chuckle from my husband, and the absence of sound of any sort from Andenmatten. To explore this dismal and uncanny tunnel was the next business. For this purpose one of the party unroped and dived into the semi-darkness. His grunts and groans as he squeezed himself through the narrow passage, and a final volley of those unreportable words in which the troubled masculine mind invariably seeks relief, acquainted us with the fact that the hole was a delusion, and that the mountain had been merely playing us a practical joke.

The only alternative was to get round the obstruction on the right. Burgener at once led us along a narrow ledge, which was more or less covered with the *débris* fallen from above. It was necessary to be extremely careful, as the cliff on our left was cased with a veneer of rotten stones, and it seemed as if the disturbance of any single one of them might bring the whole rickety mass down on our heads. On the right was a dizzy precipice of fifteen hundred feet or more, with the crevassed Weingarten glacier below. After a while we reached an arm of rock which blocked the ledge; climbing over, or rather round this, we found a secure nook where we sat down whilst Burgener unroped and went ahead to explore. He was soon hidden from our view by the crags, and, for a time, all the news we had of him was the ceaseless rattle of the stones he upset. At last we saw him reappear, but there was no life in his movements; his face was serious, and in response to our queries he said: "Herr Mommerie, it is quite impossible." During our enforced idleness we had had time to thoroughly study the wall of rock cutting us off from the ridge. A very sanguine member of the party had even declared that,

"If old Burgener can't get up that slope, it is a pity."

Putting on the rope once more, the great man of the party advanced to the assault. With great care he got his hands well fixed in a crevice, but above and on either side, as far as he could reach, everything he touched came away, covering me with showers of crumbling shale. I jammed my head against the cliff, but this gave scanty shelter from the sharp-edged, slate-like chips that came flying by, and by the time the order "Come on" was sounded, my fingers and arms were a good deal the worse for wear, and my eyes were full of anything and everything small enough to get into them. But the worst was now to come; how was I to get up without at least slaying those behind me, or, which seemed much more likely, upsetting the whole unstable veneer that covered the face of the cliff? Whenever one stone gave way, those above it came sweeping down in a perfect avalanche, so exciting Burgener's fears that he kept shrieking, "You kill your man if you not more careful are." My own impression was that I should not merely "kill my man," but that the whole party and most of the mountain would be hurled to the glacier beneath. It was, therefore, with a most joyful heart that I at length found myself seated securely on a rock overlooking the snow slope on the left of the arête, and could watch in comfort the miseries of my companions below.

So soon as we had thoroughly realised that no serious injury had been done either to us or the mountain, Burgener carefully examined our route. In a few moments forth came the joyful words, "Herr Mommerie, das geht."

Once more we advanced, this time "Herr Mommerie" leading. The arête proved fairly easy, though there were short steps of precipitous rock where a shoulder from Burgener or a hoist on his axe were needed. At one place a more formidable step was encountered, and the knapsacks, coats, Andenmatten and myself were left below, while the cragsmen of the party grappled with the difficulty. Shouts at length announced their success, and with a great swish down came the rope for the various baggage. As soon as this had been hauled up, the rope came down again for me, and, with unmixed delight, I prepared to follow. My half-hour's halt had been anything but pleasant, as a bitterly cold wind had sprung up, and the sun was obscured by driving mist. A third time the rope was thrown down, and after much hauling and advice Andenmatten joined our company. We then kept along the ridge till a larger "step," precipitous and impassable, barred the way. Our leaders again consulted, and, after a short halt, led us on to the Kien glacier face, where a convenient snow slope seemed to afford an easy, though not very expeditious, method of turning the obstruction.

THE TÄSCHHORN.

The snow being in good condition we got over the ground quickly, but as we advanced the axe occasionally reached the underlying ice, and at last the snow dwindled down to an inch or less in thickness, and every step had to be hacked out of hard black ice. The cautious Alexander, thinking that it was no longer a place in which an amateur should lead, unroped, and cutting a few steps below me, went to the front, and swung mighty blows against the relentless slope. It was desirable to go as fast as possible, for the rock above us was constantly sending its superfluous icicles and stones across our track, and we feared at every moment that larger missiles might follow, and sweep us with them in their mad flight of bounds and leaps to the gigantic blue crevasses far, far below. But the ice was hard, and Burgener was hampered by his wounded hand. Slowly we seemed to crawl along, and ever, when we reached rock, found nothing but smooth slabs, slippery with a glazing of ice. Wearily we plodded on. Fingers and feet had long since lost all sensation, and the only hope that buoyed our sinking spirits was the belief that, on passing a rib of rock not far in front, our difficulties would be at an end and the ascent practically accomplished. In due time we reached this rib, and beyond it the snow was certainly thicker, and, as far as we could see, there was nothing ahead that need cause us uneasiness. Judging by the time we had already spent on the mountain and the many difficulties we had surmounted, I concluded that the summit must be nearly won. The lead was again made over to my husband, and Burgener having resumed his old place on the rope, the traverse continued.

"Oh! vain hope and frivolous conclusion!" The crucial test was yet to come. Snow, rocks and ice had astonished us in the past by their forbidding nature; now, in addition to these, we were handicapped by the lateness of the hour (1.30 p.m.), a driving mist, and, worst of all, by fatigue, cold and hunger.

The snow once more began to thin out, leaving nothing but a huge sheet of ice. To cut across would have taken days. There was clearly nothing for it but once more to regain the ridge. Burgener was of opinion that we were past the more serious towers and pinnacles, and that, if we could only reach the crest, a sure and not too lengthy road to the summit would be ours. He therefore directed our leader to make straight up the slope towards some great slabs of rock that projected through the ice. These, however, soon became too precipitous and smooth, and we were reduced, as our last chance, to cutting up a hideous ice-gully that flanked the rocks. In places snow covered the ice, and, the gully being bent and narrow, it afforded more or less precarious footing. Burgener's injunctions were constant, "Keep where the snow is thickest."

But the snow soon dwindled down till it nowhere exceeded an inch or so; still, as long as the beat of the axe could hew out a step, we advanced steadily. At length, however, the cheery chip of the axe ceased, and in response to Burgener's query came the reply, "Es giebt gar kein Eis." To the right and to the left the smooth slabs of the rock-gully were but thinly glazed, and above this again was a thin coating of loose snow. The wall of rock on the right suggested, however, some possibility of continuing the ascent, and to this our leader made his way and climbed a short distance, when it became so ice-glazed and precipitous that he was brought to a stand. It was even doubtful whether he could descend, and it was evident that his position was critical in the extreme. Luckily, he had for the moment fairly reliable footing.

Burgener's strong points now showed themselves; without a moment's hesitation or delay he untied, and, holding the rope as a banister, rapidly ascended by its aid. Arrived at the point where my husband had traversed, to the right, he quitted the rope and made his way rather to the left, and succeeded in finding ice deep enough for very shallow steps. Aided here and there by a projecting stone, he worked up till the slope of the gully eased slightly, and considerable quantities of snow had accumulated. This snow was of the worst possible quality, and poured away like flour at every step; still, bad as it was it rendered progress possible, and, working upwards with indomitable courage, we saw him at last reach reliable footing. Our feelings found vent in loud shouts and jodels, but all the same it was grim work standing in a small step three-quarters of an hour, with splinters of ice and a stream of snow from above chilling fingers and toes till it seemed impossible to endure it longer. Indeed, nothing but the sure and certain knowledge that the only alternative was to move and slip, could have kept me inactive so long. Welcome were the occasional cheery assurances from above, "Hold on a bit longer and we shall get up all right." But Burgener, being unroped, could give no direct help to my husband, and it was some time before the latter could effect the traverse back into the gully and up the treacherous steps to the snow above. When the safety of the party was once more in Burgener's hands, I ascended, finding that my husband had already cut his way to the ridge. Then the order to untie reached me, and the rope was sent down for Andenmatten.

With a hasty glance at the never-to-be-forgotten gully, we bent our somewhat weary steps onward, scrambling, climbing and crawling over the various crags, pinnacles and flying buttresses which constitute the arête. Compared to our recent experiences it seemed easy, and progress was rapid. Suddenly, however, our leader came to a halt, and though Burgener urged him to proceed, he utterly refused, and after a few moments summoned Alexander to the front. I could not see his usually expressive face, but the words, "Herr Gott, unmöglich!" reached my ears, and I hurried forward to see what new peril threatened us.

To understand the position of affairs it is necessary to describe the very curious rock formation in some detail. The ridge where we stood projected in a huge rock cornice, far over the precipice. Immediately beyond, this cornice had broken away. In consequence, the ridge by which we had been ascending appeared to end abruptly, and there was no question of going forwards—immeasurable space yawned in front. Twenty feet or more to our left the true ridge, there denuded of its rock cornice, mounted rapidly in a series of precipitous steps, but from our point of view we looked, not at the ridge, but at the bare precipitous face below it. Even could we have reached that face, no climber could hope to cling to it; but we could not even reach it; between us and it was the most awful chasm it has ever been my lot to see. This formation of ridge is, so far as the experience of any member of the party extended, unique. It gave, indeed, the impression that there were two ridges, separated from each other by an impassable gulf.

No wonder, then, that black horror seized us. Return was not to be thought of, and advance seemed impossible. There we four stood, absolutely powerless, our teeth chattering with the bitter cold, and the damp, cruel mist ever driving across, threatening to add obscurity to our other bewilderment.

Happily, after a few minutes we began to recover from the mental shock caused by this most dramatic break in the ridge, and proceeded to reduce its tremendous appearance to the dull and narrow limits of actual fact. So soon as we had realised that we were on a cornice overhanging the precipice, it became obvious that we must climb down the cornice to the real ridge, and from that point seek to attack the difficulties in front. This descent was not very easy, the slabby rocks shelving steeply towards the Kien glacier, and all the interstices and cracks being filled with ice. However, some slight hold was obtainable on the extreme edge, and after the ice had been dug from various irregularities and fractures my husband arrived at a point immediately above a deep cleft, which cut off the corniced section of the ridge from its uncorniced continuation. Beyond this point the comfortable assurance of the rope was gone. Any one dependent on it would necessarily swing free in mid-air, and it may well be doubted whether "all the king's horses and all the king's men" would suffice to replace that aerial dangler on the ridge. Happily, minute search revealed a small notch in the rock, and though it was evident that a rope drawn from time to time through it would be certain to slip out, it appeared likely that a fixed rope would be held in position so long as only a perfectly steady pull was applied to it. In dubious tones, therefore, came the words, "Fix the rope and I'll try." To which Burgener replied, "Herr Je, es muss gehen sonst sind wir alle caput." The rope being securely lashed to a crag on the top of the cornice, the other end was passed down, and our leader squeezed it into the tiny notch. First carefully pulling it taut to prevent any "run" when his weight should come on it, we saw him swing over and disappear. An instant later we heard the welcome news, "It's all right, there is good hold all the way down."

At length he came in sight, stretching over the yawning gulf, and we saw him grip the rock beyond and climb warily along the side of a great block of uncertain stability, poised like a logan stone on the arête. An ugly ten feet or more followed, and then we heard the joyful, "Kommen sie nur, Alexander." The sheet anchor of the party having got over, I had to follow, and great was my elation to find that I could accomplish without help a mauvais pas that had for a minute or two seemed impassable to the stronger and more daring members of the party.

Looking back, the crag we had just left was weird in the extreme; though at the top it was twenty feet or more in breadth, it narrowed down at the bottom of the cleft to less than two feet, and the whole mass looked as if a good blow from an ice-axe would send it bodily on to the Weingarten glacier. Indeed, as the mist whirled and eddied through the cleft, it seemed to totter as in the very act of falling. But it was already 4 p.m., and we were far from the wished for snow; so, whilst Andenmatten was being coached across, my husband unroped and went to work, crawling up a steep "step" in the arête. The rope was then thrown up to him, and Alexander, scrambling up by its aid, was ready to help the rest of the party. This procedure was then repeated. Still crag followed crag, here loose rocks that rolled away at a touch, there precipitous buttresses, access to which could only be gained by using Burgener's broad shoulders as a ladder. All at once, however, difficulties seemed to cease, our leader again put on the rope, and we rattled along the arête till it broadened out into a great snow ridge.

"Der Teufelsgrat ist gemacht!" shouted Burgener, and we began to race along the snow, which rose in front and to our right into a steep crest. Up these slopes we could see the footprints left

by a party which, under the leadership of Franz
Burgener, had made the ordinary ascent on the
previous day. "Half an hour more and it is done,
and the Teufelsgrat is ours," added the excited
Alexander as we hurried along, feeling that success
was within our grasp. The footprints grew per-
ceptibly larger, and on we ran till we actually
placed our feet in the tracks. Here all unnecessary
luggage was deposited, and Burgener, seeing I was
very cold, arrayed me in his coat and gloves. We
hastened up the snow, finding no difficulty other
than its extreme softness. A scramble over some
sharp slate-like rocks followed, then a little more
snow, and at 5.30 p.m. we stood on the summit.
But for one moment only. At once Burgener
began with serious face to say, "I not like a
thunderstorm on this ridge." There was no doubt
about it, the clouds were wrapping round us, and
the distant grumble rolled in our ears. "Go on,
go on quicker, Herr Mommerie!" and then with a
push he hustled me along the arête. "You must go
on, I could a cow hold here," were the encouraging
words I heard as I went helter-skelter over anything which happened to be in the way. Soon the
snow slopes were reached, and our property once
more picked up. We ran our hardest through the
blinding storm, almost deafened by the reverberating peals of thunder; but what mattered it?
True it was late; true we were cold, hungry, and
tired; true we were sinking into the snow above

our knees, and the "trace" had disappeared beneath the rapidly falling snow; but "the Teufelsgrat was ours," and we cared little for these minor evils, and we laughed the tempest to scorn with jodels and triumphant shouts. A short traverse to the left and we crossed the Bergschrund; a weary drag over gentle snow slopes, a little care in winding through some open crevasses, and our dangers were ended. At 8 p.m. we reached the snout of the Kien glacier, and once more stepped on to moraine. We descended stony slopes for another hour, and then I remembered that our last meal had taken place at 10 a.m. It being obvious that we could not get to Randa that night, I suggested a halt, and the idea was received with applause. In a few minutes we were sitting on various stones munching our evening meal, the only drawback being that we were distinctly cold. My hands and feet were numb, and what remained of our clothing (we had left a good deal of it on the Teufelsgrat) was soaking wet, and, worst of all, my boots, viewed by the flickering light of a candle, seemed hardly likely to hold out till we got to Randa.

Our hunger being somewhat appeased, I noticed symptoms of sleepiness amongst the guides. In consequence, I reminded Burgener of his promise to take us, in any case, down to the trees, so that we might rejoice in a fire. We started off once more, carefully roped. The slope being steep and intersected by low cliffs, and the night being so inky black that we could see nothing, it was really necessary to take this precaution. We proceeded down the hill much as a pack of cards might be expected to do. Burgener sprawling on his back and upsetting me, and I passing the shock back to the others. This mode of advance kept up till 11 p.m., when our guides suddenly pulled up, and inquired, in an awestruck whisper, whether we could see a tiny light on the right? With great glee I said, "Yes, it must be a chalet." The suggestion was treated with silent contempt. "What can it be then?" In funereal tones Burgener said, "I do not know;" but Andenmatten timidly whispered, "Geister!" From that moment I could see there was no fire for us; that we should be lucky if we could sneak under the cover of a rock to shelter us from the storm that threatened once more to burst over our heads.

A few steps further and a huge black object faced us. On examination we found it to be a suitable place for spending the next few hours. In five minutes the guides were snoring peacefully; but we, after wringing the water out of our dripping clothes, were reduced to dancing various war dances in the vain hope of keeping warm. When these exercises became unduly fatiguing, we watched the lightning play round the peaks and ridges, and finally stirred up the guides with an ice-axe and urged them to continue the descent.

They did not at all approve this course of action, as they considered their quarters luxurious and most thoroughly calculated to induce refreshing sleep. The next two hours were spent in slowly slipping and tumbling down stony grass-grown slopes. We then turned to the right on to somewhat smoother ground. The men, however, refused to go further, alleging that there were fearful precipices in front, and that, in the blackness of the stormy night, it was quite impossible to do so with reasonable safety. The guides again went soundly to sleep, whilst we watched wearily for the first sign of morning. When a streak of light did at length illumine the darkness, we saw the dim outline of trees not far distant, and promptly went down to them. A fire was soon blazing, and we endeavoured to warm ourselves; but though we well nigh roasted our toes and fingers and scorched our faces, the rest of us seemed, perhaps by contrast, colder than before, and we shivered painfully before the crackling pine wood.

As soon as it was fairly light, we dragged our weary bodies through the forest and along and down the pastures, till at 5.30 a.m. we entered the little white inn at Randa. We woke the landlord, and he promptly provided us with a big fire. A hot breakfast followed, and when we had done due justice to his culinary efforts, we climbed into a shaky char-à-banc and drove back to Zermatt.

Burgener was in the highest spirits; his chief

source of delight appeared to be a belief that our non-return the previous night would have excited alarm, and that we should probably have the proud privilege of meeting a search party, properly equipped for the transport of our shattered remains. My husband, however, did not altogether sympathise with these feelings, and seemed to have a keen appreciation of the Trinkgeld, tariffs, and other pecuniary concomitants of such luxuries. Happily, we knew our friends were not very likely to think we should have come to any harm, and when two hours later we drove into Zermatt, we found they were still peacefully slumbering in their rooms.

THE RIFFEL PATH.

CHAPTER V.

THE AIGUILLE DES CHARMOZ.

AFTER the passage of the Col du Lion, already described, we drove to Courmayeur, intent on mighty deeds. Bad weather, however, made us prisoners, and for four consecutive days a strong south-west wind poured a ceaseless deluge of rain into the valley, washing haystacks and even an occasional châlet into the great muddy torrent below the village.

I was the only guest at the Hotel Royal, and its skilful *chef* devoted his whole time and thought to the ruin of my condition and form. During the rare intervals when I was not actually enjoying the good things provided for my delectation, he occupied himself with careful inquiries as to my likes and dislikes.

On the fifth day symptoms of improvement in the weather became visible, and during the afternoon Burgener, Venetz, and I walked up to the Mont Fréty Inn, with some vague idea of trying to make a new pass to Chamonix. Before day-

break, however, a terrific thunderstorm and furious squalls of wind and rain put an end to all thoughts of new ascents, and made even the Col du Géant seem a reckless and perilous adventure. But as the day wore on the clouds began to break, and by the time we reached the séracs, a brilliant sun was making the new snow stream from the rock faces and steeper slopes in avalanches of every sort and size.

At Chamonix I was once more in danger of falling an utter victim to the wiles of innkeepers and their cooks, but happily some friends recognised my perilous position and took me up to the Grands Mulets. No sooner had we got there than yet another storm assailed us, and kept us in the hut till it was too late to descend. When we awoke the next morning, we found ourselves halfway up to the Grand Plateau, Burgener and Venetz being evidently under the impression that we intended to spend the rest of the day in the tread-mill like occupation of ascending Mont Blanc. Revolutionary ideas quickly gained possession of the party, and culminated in the absolute refusal of its amateur members to go another step. Despite the indignation and scorn of the professionals, we tumbled and glissaded back to the Grands Mulets, picked up our few belongings and ran down to the Pierre Pointue and Chamonix.

The same afternoon we held a solemn council

and decided that this sort of thing must go on no longer, and in desperation we determined to start for the Charmoz. It was true that the continuous bad weather was likely to have materially damaged our chances of success, but as the mountain has a south-western exposure, and is not very high, we hoped nothing really serious would be amiss.

The next morning (or shall I say the same night?) we started, and, being provided by M. Couttet with an admirable lantern (this expedition took place in the pre-folding-lantern age), we made very fair progress for the first half-hour. We then began to ascend something which Burgener averred was a path, but which, insensible of, or possibly made bashful by, such gross flattery, hid itself coyly from view at every third step. After a long grind the grey light of morning began to overpower our lantern, so, finding a suitable stone, we carefully hid it and marked the spot with a sprig of pine. Sad to say, on our return, though we found many stones with many sprigs of pine on them, none had our lantern in the hole underneath, a circumstance much to be regretted, as, from an item which subsequently appeared in my bill, it seems to have been a lantern held in high esteem by Monsieur Couttet.

We soon got clear of the forest, and, reaching a stream under the lateral moraine of the Nantillon glacier, halted for breakfast. Here we discovered that three slices of meat, a tiny piece of cheese, ten inches of loaf, and a big bag of raisins were all the provisions the hotel porter had thought necessary. Luckily, Burgener had been left in charge of the commissariat, and, as I prefer raisins on the side of a mountain to any other food, I was able to look on the porter's conduct with philosophy, a state of mind by no means shared by my companions.

We very injudiciously turned the lower ice fall by keeping to the right and ascending a couloir between the cliffs of the Blaitière and the precipitous rocks over which the glacier falls. The couloir proved very easy, but a rock buttress on our left being still easier we took to it and rattled to the top at a great pace. Immediately over our heads towered an endless succession of séracs, huge sky-cleaving monsters, threatening us with instant destruction. The spot was not a desirable one for a halt, so we turned to the left to see how we were to get on to the glacier. At one point, and one only, was it possible to do so. A sérac lurching over the cliff, and apparently much inclined to add to the pile of broken ice-blocks some hundreds of feet below, was the only available bridge. We scrambled along it, crossed a crevasse on avalanche *débris*, and dashed up a short ice slope to the open glacier. Ten minutes sufficed to take us into comparative safety, and we traversed to the island of rock, by which the ice fall is usually turned.

Here we made a halt and proceeded to search the knapsack for possibly hidden stores of food. While Venetz and I were engaged in this duty, Burgener screwed himself and his telescope into a variety of extraordinary attitudes, and at length succeeded in making a satisfactory examination of our peak. An hour later we started again and tramped up to the base of the long couloir which leads to the depression between the Grépon and the Charmoz.

We crossed the Bergschrund at a quarter to nine, and at once turning to the left, out of the couloir, worked our way up some good rocks for three-quarters of an hour, only one or two slabs offering any sort of resistance to our progress. By this time we had reached the top of a secondary ridge, which here abuts against the final cliffs of the mountain. We sat down on an ice-coated rock and, producing our limited supplies of food, once more solemnly reviled the Chamonix porter. We then deposited the wine tin in a safe corner, and unanimously discarded coats and boots, which, with two out of three hats and the same proportion of ice-axes, were packed away in a secure cleft. The baggage, consisting of a spare rope, two wooden wedges, the food, a bottle of Bouvier, a tin of cognac, and an ice-axe, was made over to me.

The two men began to worm their way up the cliff, Venetz usually being shoved by Burgener and then helping the latter with the rope. Progress, however, was painfully slow, and when at last good standing ground was reached, the rope declined to come anywhere near me. Ultimately, I had to make a difficult traverse to fetch it, as it was quite impossible to carry the ice-axe and knapsack without its aid. This sort of work continued for three-quarters of an hour, and then a longer delay suggested that there was something seriously wrong. An eager query brought back the reply that the next bit was quite impracticable, but, added Burgener, "Es muss gehen." Anxious to see the obstacle which, though impracticable, was yet to be ascended, I swarmed up the edge of a great slab to a narrow shelf, then, working round an awkward corner, I entered a dark cold gully.

A mighty block, some forty feet high, had parted from the main mass of the mountain, leaving a rounded perpendicular couloir, which was now everywhere veneered with ice. A tiny stream trickled down the back of the gully, and about mid-height had frozen on to the rocks, forming a thick column of ice flanked on either hand by a fantastic fretwork of the same material. A green bulge, about fifteen feet above, prevented our seeing the back of the gully beyond that point. Nothing could appear more hopeless, there was not even decent foothold where we stood, everywhere the black glazing of ice filled up and masked the irregularities of the rock below.

Some ten minutes later both men appeared to my inexperienced eye in extremely critical positions. Venetz, almost without hold of any sort, was gradually nearing the aforementioned green bulge; an axe, skilfully applied by Burgener to that portion of the guide costume most usually decorated by patches of brilliant and varied hue, supplying the motive power, whilst Burgener himself was cleverly poised on invisible notches cut in the thin ice which glazed the rock. Before, however, Venetz could surmount the green bulge, it became necessary to shift the axe to his feet, and for a moment he was left clinging like a cat to the slippery wrinkles of the huge icicle. How he succeeded in maintaining his position is a mystery known only to himself, and the law of gravity. With the axe beneath his feet, he once more moved upwards, and with a desperate effort raised his head and shoulders above the bulge. "Wie geht's?" yelled Burgener. "Weder vorwärts noch zurück," gasped Venetz, and to a further query whether he could help Burgener up came the reply, "gewiss nicht." However, so soon as he had recovered his wind he renewed his efforts. Little by little his legs, working in spasmodic jerks, disappeared from sight, and at last a burst of patois, a hauling in of the rope, and Burgener advanced and disappeared. The whizz of icicles and other small fragments, and the hard breathing of the men showed they were advancing. Then Burgener shouted to me to squeeze well under cover for fear of stones, but as the crack to which I was holding only sufficed to shelter my nose, fingers, and one foot, I thought it wise to work back out of the gully on to the warm rocks, being, moreover, much persuaded to this line of conduct by my toes, which, unprotected by boots and with stockings long since cut to ribbons, were by no means unwilling to exchange frozen rock and ice for warmth and sunshine.

Presently a startled shout and a great stone leapt into space, followed by a hoarse jodel to announce the conquest of the gully. As I scrambled back the rope came down with a swish, and I tied up as well as I could with one hand, while the other hung on to an ice-glazed corner. Having accomplished this important operation I began the ascent. Everything went well for the first few feet, then the hold seemed to get insufficient, and a desperate effort to remedy this ended in my swinging free, unable to attach myself to either rock or ice. A bearded face, with a broad grin, looks over the top of the gully, and cheerily asks, " Why don't you come on ? "

Then a few vigorous hauls, and I am above the green bulge, and enter a narrow cleft. Its smooth and precipitous walls were everywhere glazed with ice, and their parallel surfaces offered no grip or hold of any sort. It was just possible to jam one's back against one wall and one's knees against the other, but progress under these conditions was not to be thought of. After a few minutes had been allowed to convince a possibly sceptical Herr that the knapsack and the ice-axe were not the only impedimenta in the party, the persuasive influence of the rope brought me to more broken ground, and a scramble landed me in the sunshine.

The men were ruefully gazing at their torn and bleeding elbows, for it appears they had only succeeded in attaching themselves to the gully by clasping their hands in front of them, and then drawing them in towards their chests, thus wedging their elbows against the opposing walls. They were both very thoroughly " blown," so we halted and circulated a certain flask. Then I lay down on the warm rocks and wondered how long my internal organs would take to get back into those more normal positions from which the pressure of the rope had dislodged them.

A quarter of an hour later we were once more *en route*. Above, a long series of broken cliffs, seamed by a fairly continuous line of vertical cracks, assured our progress as far as the ridge. How I crawled up great slabs hanging on to impossible corners—how at critical moments the knapsack hooked on to sharp splinters of rock, or the ice-axe jammed into cracks, whilst the holes in my toes got deeper and bigger, and the groove round my waist more closely approximated to the modern ideal of female beauty—is fixed, indelibly, on my mind; but these are things too painful for words, and I will therefore limit myself to saying that on some rocks, in due accordance with the latest mountaineering fashion, I expostulated with Burgener on the absurdity of using a rope, at the same time taking very good care to see that the knot was equal to all emergencies. On other rocks I just managed to ascend by adopting new and original attitudes, which, despite certain adverse criticisms, I still believe would have won renown for any artist who could have seized their grace and elegance, and would, moreover, have afforded a very distinct departure from all conventional models. On yet other rocks a method of progress was adopted which has since, I regret to say, given rise to fierce disputes between the amateur and professional members of the party; it being alleged on the one hand that there is no difficulty in ascending such rocks if the climber be not hampered by a knapsack and ice-axe; and on the other, that a waist measurement of eighteen inches ought, for some mysterious reason, to be taken into account, and detracts from the climbing merit of its possessor. Without, however, entering into controversial matter of so painful a character, I may briefly say that at a quarter-past eleven we scrambled on to the ridge and feasted our eyes with a near view of the summit.

The more sanguine members of the party at once concluded that a projection on the left, of easy access, was the highest point; but certain gloomy dissentients averred that an ugly tooth on the right, of a most uncompromising character, was the true peak. Laughter was the portion of these unbelievers, and the easy crag was scaled amid a wild burst of enthusiasm, only, however, to find that here, as elsewhere, the broad and easy path is not for the faithful.

Returning to the gap where we had attained the ridge, we made our way to the foot of the real summit. Venetz was promptly lifted up to Burgener's shoulders and propelled onwards by the axe; but the first attack failed, and he recoiled swiftly on to Burgener. The despised Herr was then used to extend the ladder, and by this means Venetz was able to reach indifferent hold, and ultimately to gain the summit. At 11.45 a.m. we all crowded on to the top, the men rejoicing greatly at the reckless waste of gunpowder with which Monsieur Couttet welcomed our arrival. Burgener, as a fitting recognition of this attention, planted our one ice-axe on the highest point, whilst the rank and file of the expedition diligently sought stones wherewith to build it into an upright and secure position. To this a handkerchief of brilliant pattern and inferior repair, the product into which the Zermatt wash had resolved two of more ordinary dimensions and colour, was securely lashed.

Whilst these details were being satisfactorily completed, the heavy luggage of the party was quietly sunning himself in a comfortable nook, and absorbing that mixture of sunlight, atmosphere, glittering lake, and jagged ridge, which make up a summit view. Long hours of exertion urged to the utmost limit of the muscles, and the wild excitement of half-won but yet doubtful victory, are changed in an instant to a feeling of ease and security, so perfect that only the climber who has stretched himself in some sun-warmed, wind-sheltered nook, can realise the utter oblivion which lulls every suspicion of pain or care, and he learns that, however happiness may shun pursuit, it may nevertheless be sometimes surprised basking on the weird granite crags. To puzzle one's brains at such moments by seeking to recognise distant peaks, or to correct one's topographical knowledge, or by scientific pursuits of any sort, appears to be sacrilege of the most vicious sort. To me it seems the truer worship to stretch with half-shut eyes in the sun, and let the scenery

> " Like some sweet beguiling melody,
>   So sweet we know not we are listening to it "

wrap us in soft delight, till with lotus-eaters we had almost cried—

" Let us swear an oath . . .
. . . to live and lie reclined
On the hills like gods together, careless of mankind."

But Burgener did not altogether share this view, and at 12.30 p.m. he insisted on our sliding down a doubled rope to the ridge below the summit. All went merrily till we reached the ice couloir. Here Burgener tried to fix one of our wooden wedges; but do what he would, it persisted in evading its duties, wobbling first to one side and then to another, so that the rope slipped over the top. We all had a try, driving it into cracks that struck our fancy, and even endeavouring to prop it up with ingenious arrangements of small stones. Some one then mooted the point whether wedges were not a sort of bending the knee to Baal, and might not be the first step on those paths of ruin where the art of mountaineering becomes lost in that of the steeplejack. Whereupon we unanimously declared that the Charmoz should be desecrated by no fixed wedges, and finding an insecure knob of rock we doubled our rope round it, and Venetz slid down. I followed, and to prevent as far as possible the chance of the rope slipping off the knob, we twisted it round and round, and held the ends fast as Burgener descended.

By 2.20 we rejoined our boots, and ideas of *table d'hôte* began to replace those of a more poetic type. We rattled down the rocks, and raced across the glacier in a way that, we subsequently learnt, created much astonishment in the minds of sundry friends at the opposite end of M. Couttet's telescope. The further we got the faster we went, for the séracs that looked unpleasant in the morning now lurched over our heads in a way that made Burgener's " schnell, nur schnell," almost lift one off one's feet. After the usual habit of séracs they lurched and staggered, but did not fall, and we got down to the lower glacier much out of breath, but otherwise uninjured. Reaching the neighbourhood of our lantern we sought diligently but found it not, so we made for a châlet Burgener knew of.

We found the fair proprietress feeding pigs. She brought us milk, and, though of unexceptionable quality, the more fastidious members of the party would have liked it better had not some of the numerous denizens of her abode and person previously sought euthanasia in the flowing bowl.

Happily the zigzags did not take long to unwind, and at 5.30 p.m. we were warmly welcomed by Monsieur and Madame Couttet and much excellent champagne.

THE AIGUILLE DES CHARMOZ—WITHOUT GUIDES.

The ascent was not repeated for several years, but at length Monsieur Dunod and F. Simond found their way to the southern summit, and the following year they recovered the axe we had left on its northern peak. The mountain soon after became the most popular climb in the Montenvers district, and the traverse of the five peaks (as it is now called) is recognised as the best and merriest introduction to the Chamonix rock scrambles.

In 1892 I once again started for the mountain. This time we were without guides, for we had learnt the great truth that those who wish to really enjoy the pleasures of mountaineering, must roam the upper snows trusting exclusively to their own skill and knowledge. The necessity for this arises from many causes, and is to no small extent due to the marked change that has come over the professional mountaineer. The guide of the "Peaks, Passes and Glaciers" age was a friend and adviser; he led the party and entered fully into all the fun and jollity of the expedition; on the return to the little mountain inn, he was still, more or less, one of the party, and the evening pipe could only be enjoyed in his company. Happy amongst his own mountains and skilled in ferreting out all the slender resources of the village, he was an invaluable and most pleasant companion. But the advantage was not wholly on one side, thrown constantly in contact with his employers he acquired from them those minor rules of conduct and politeness which are essential if guide and traveller are to develop mutual friendship and respect. Of these early pioneers Melchior, Anderegg and a few others still remain; but, amongst the younger men, there are none with whom one could associate on the old terms and with the old intimacy. The swarming of the tourist has brought with it the wretched distinctions of class, and the modern guide inhabits the guide's room and sees his Monsieur only when actually on an expedition. Cut off from the intercourse of the old days, the guide tends more and more to belong to the lackey tribe, and the ambitious tourist looks upon him much as his less aspiring brother regards his mule.

The constant repetition of the same ascent has, moreover, tended to make the guide into a sort of contractor. For so many tens or hundreds of francs he will take you anywhere you like to name. The skill of the traveller counts for absolutely naught; the practised guide looks on him merely as luggage. Of course, if he be of abnormal weight and bulk, he must pay an additional number of francs, precisely as a man who rides sixteen stone has to pay a high price for a hunter; but, apart from the accident of weight, the individuality of the Herr is not considered.

The guide, having undertaken a contract, naturally wishes to get it satisfactorily completed at the earliest possible time. To this end, the way up the mountain is mapped out with great minuteness. The contractor knows to a second the time at which he should arrive at each rock and every ledge. The slightest variation from these standard times hurts his feelings and ruffles the serenity of his temper. There is, of course, no fun or merriment during the ascent. The travellers, pushed to the very utmost limit of their speed, are in no state to enjoy themselves; you might, indeed, as well ask a man trying to break the one mile cycling record to look at the view, or the members of an Oxford racing crew to see the point of a joke. The party is simply driven onward, checked only when the wind or legs of its Herr absolutely refuse to proceed a step further. During the short halt thus involved—usually designated breakfast, though no one ever eats anything—the amateurs gasp and pant and feel all, or more than all, the pangs of incipient mal de mer, whilst the guides gloomily commiserate themselves on the slowness of the Herrschaft. It is needless to say that the conditions essential to the pleasures of talk and contemplation enjoyed by the founders of the craft are wholly lacking. Woe to the town-bred Englishman, hurried along by a couple of Swiss peasants in the very perfection of wind and muscle.

The guideless climber is free from all these baneful and blighting influences. So long as there is time in hand, and very often when there is not, he prefers to lie on sheltered rocks and watch the ever changing shadows on the distant hills, or to peer down enormous depths on to the restless mists floating above the glacier. Toiling up snow slopes or screes at his top pace never commends itself to him—at such times every flat stone suggests a halt and every tiny stream deep draughts of water.

I once met a man who told me, at 11 a.m., that he had just been up the Charmoz. He seemed mightily proud of his performance, and undoubtedly had gone with extraordinary speed. "But why," I asked myself, "has he done it?" Can any one with eyes in his head, and an immortal soul in his body, care to leave the rugged beauty of the Charmoz ridge in order to race back to the troops of personally-conducted tourists who pervade and make unendurable the mid-day and afternoon at the Montenvers? And this is not exceptional; at Zermatt one may frequently meet men, early in the day, who have wantonly left the most beautiful and inmost recesses of the Alps, the Gabelhorn, Rothhorn, or other similar peak, to hurry back to the brass bands and nigger minstrels of that excursionist resort. The guideless climber does none of these things; rarely is he seen returning till the last lingering glow has died out of the western horizon. It is night, and night alone, that drives him back to the crowded haunts of the tourist. This love of living amongst the sunshine and upper snows is the true test of the enthusiast, and marks him off from the tribe of brag and bounce and from all the "doers of the Alps." It must not be assumed that the love of mountains is to be regarded as the first of human duties, or that a man's moral worth can be determined by the usual time of his arrival at a mountain inn; but merely that the mountaineer, the man who can sympathise with every change of light and shadow and who worships the true spirit of the upper world, is distinguished from unregenerate imitators and hypocrites by these characteristics.

My main objection to guide-led parties, however, is to be found in the absolute certainty with which the day's proceedings are carried out. Not merely can the guide "lie in bed and picture every step of the way up," but he can also, whilst so reposing, tell you to the fraction of a minute the exact time you will get to each point in the ascent, and the very moment at which he will return you, safe and sound, to the smiling landlord of your hotel. Now I agree with Landor, that "certainties are uninteresting and sating." When I start in the morning I do not want to know exactly what is going to be done, and exactly how it is all to be carried out. I like to feel that our best efforts may be needed, and that even then we may be baffled and beaten. There is, similarly, infinite delight in recalling all the varying chances of a long and hardly fought victory; but the memory of a weary certainty behind two untiring guides, is wholly colourless and soon fades into the indistinguishable past.

Few scrambles have yielded more pleasure to my companions and myself than the ascent of the Brenva Mont Blanc. Owing to a foolish mistake, in which, contrary to the advice of my friends, I persisted, we hurled ourselves at a huge wall of séracs and fought with a vigour and, "under the correction of bragging be it spoken," with a plucky determination, that afforded us then, and will, so long as memory lasts, ever afford us, unmixed delight and pleasure. Recoiling, baffled, we camped on an exposed ledge of rock, and, the next morning, for the third time traversing the far famed knife-edge of ice, we repeated our assault on the séracs, this time at a more vulnerable corner. Victory still hung in the balance, and it was only when Collie had constructed a rickety staircase, by jamming our three axes into the interstices of a perpendicular wall of frozen ice *débris*, that he scaled the obstacle and we strode in triumph on to the great rolling fields of snow below, but within certain reach of, the Calotte. Such moments are worth living for, but they are sought in vain, if a guide who can "lie in bed and picture every step of the way up" is of the party. Mountaineering, as Mr. Leslie Stephen has pointed out, is "a sport—as strictly as cricket, or rowing, or knurr and spell," and it necessarily follows that its enjoyment depends on the struggle for the victory. To start on an ordinary expedition with guides, is, from the sporting point of view, as interesting—or the reverse—as a "walk over" race.

There is, doubtless, another side to the question. The pious worshippers of the great god "Cook" regard the facilitation of the ascent as an unmixed good. The be-roped and be-cabined Matterhorn, the lie-in-bed-and-picture guide are welcomed by them as the earlier stages of that progress which will culminate in Funnicular railways and cog-wheels. To ascend the Matterhorn in a steam lift, and all the time remember that brave men have been killed by mere stress of difficulty on its gaunt, ice-bound cliffs, will be to the Cockney and his congeners unmixed delight. When they read of the early mountaineers, of their bivouacs, their nights spent in châlets, their frozen toes, and even of whole parties carried to destruction by a single slip, the halo of danger and suffering will seem to envelop them as they sit in their comfortable railway carriages, and they will feel themselves most doughty warriors.

Perchance even we of the older school should reconstruct our ideals. We are told that in a few centuries the English language will be a mixture of Cockney and bad American, why not also set about evolving a new creed of mountaineering? Abandon the old love of cold nights in the open, of curious meals with the hospitable curé, of hare-brained scrambles on little known glaciers and traverses of huge unclimbed ridges; and, instead, let us frequent the hotels and churches of Grindelwald and Zermatt, and, in the short intervals between the various functions appropriate to these two classes of building, run up the Jungfrau in a steam lift, or climb the Matterhorn on cog-wheels.

But the thought is too horrible. Let the snowstorm blow the reek of the oil-can from our nostrils, and the thundering avalanche and the roaring tempest drown the puny tinkle of cast-iron bells and the blare of cheap German bands. Let us even cherish a hope that the higher Alps will resist the navvy and the engineer for our time, and that we may still be left to worship peacefully at the great shrines of our fathers.

The delights of guideless climbing have, however, led me far from the crags and towers of the Charmoz; they have, I fear, even betrayed me into that greatest of indiscretions, a confession of faith. Prudence suggests, therefore, that I should quit this perilous ground and return to the solid granite of our peak. Till we reached the point where, on our first ascent, we had left our boots, it proved neither more nor less difficult than I had expected; from thence onward it was far easier. Possibly during that expedition the absence of our usual foot-gear impeded, rather than helped, our progress; possibly the extraordinary diminution of ice in the gully, rendering easy what had previously been most terribly difficult, lowered the impression conveyed by the mountain as a whole; or possibly, and the thought brings balm to the more aged members of the party, the passing years had not been able, so far, to work havoc in either muscle, wind or nerve. But these speculations are absurd; I forget that inspiration was enshrined in our party. Doubtless the presence of two ladies, who had honoured us with their company, endued us with a strength and agility that no mere guides, or even youthful activity, could hope to rival. Our progress to the first summit was, in consequence, a mere series of easily-won victories.

From that point, we strode along the ridge, scaling on the way the curious pinnacle, most irreverently known as Wick's stick, and finally squeezing through a very narrow letter-box * to

---

* A letter-box is the name given in the Montenvers district to split rocks. Such rocks are very frequently met with among the Chamonix Aiguilles, and are utilised either horizon-

the last summit. When we were ready to descend, we managed to find a more convenient way down the final tower, and reached the head of the great couloir that divides the Grépon from the Charmoz, without difficulty. We descended this with much trepidation, for the stones were loose, and we were a very large party. Happily no one was hit except Pasteur, and he, to all appearances, rather enjoyed it than otherwise.

Our descent of the ice slope to the breakfasting rocks was cheered by the sight of a great array of bottles, lemons, and a huge Dampfschiff, the whole being evidently manipulated with the most consummate skill, and awaiting the arrival of the first ladies who had braved the perils of the Charmoz traverse.

Far on in the evening, the lights of the Montenvers blessed our vision. Jodels and shouts were succeeded by rockets; and, as we descended the rhododendron-covered slopes, we saw the tallest member of the Alpine Club executing a brilliant *pas seul* on a rickety table, silhouetted against the dazzling glare of red lights and other pyrotechnic displays. A tumultuous welcome greeted our arrival, and protracted festivities concluded the evening.

tally as passages, or perpendicularly, by dint of much wriggling and wedging, as ladders.

CHAPTER VI.

THE GRÉPON.

AN INACCESSIBLE PEAK—THE MOST DIFFICULT CLIMB IN THE ALPS—AN EASY DAY FOR A LADY.

WHILST on the summit of Charmoz in 1880, the Grépon had struck me as rivalling the Géant itself in the wild grandeur of its cliffs. The ridge from that point looked wholly impassable; great towers, rising a hundred feet or more in single obelisks of unbroken granite, seeming to bar all possibility of progress. We had previously examined the cliffs of the Nantillon face with a telescope, and seen that they were nearly, if not quite, perpendicular, and of that peculiarly objectionable formation known to the German guides as "abgeschnitten." Feeling none the less certain that there must be a way somewhere, we were led by the process of exclusion to infer that it would be found on the Mer de Glace face. We decided, in consequence, to deliver our first assault from that side.

On the way up the Verte from the Charpoua glacier, Burgener and I had utilised our halts for the careful study of this eastern face. We discovered excellent gullies at the top, convenient snow couloirs below, and the eye of faith was able, with some effort, to discern pleasing cracks, ledges, and traverses which connected the one system with the other. Having thus worked out a most excellent route—assuming that the eye of faith was to be depended on—we determined to put it into execution. Accordingly, on the 1st of August, 1881, we assembled in the salon of the Montenvers Hotel at 1 a.m. Burgener, unluckily, proved to be very unwell, and had to be dosed with chartreuse and brandy before he could be got under weigh. Somewhat delayed by this, it was 2 a.m. before we started. We spent the rest of the night miserably floundering amongst endless stones and moraine-choked crevasses. Having turned the promontory of Trélaporte, we left the Mer de Glace and worked up to some grass ledges. These we followed, bearing always to the left, till we got on to the little Glacier de Trélaporte. From this glacier we had seen, on our previous inspection from the Verte, that three couloirs lead up into the mountain. Our affections had been fixed on the middle one, which had appeared from every point of view the most suitable to our enterprise.

On reaching its base, we found it open to the serious objection, that it was wholly and totally impossible to get into it. The Bergschrund was without a bridge, its upper lip was twenty or thirty feet above the lower, and more than a hundred feet above a mass of broken *débris* on which the chasm could alone be crossed. The rocks on either hand were smooth and quite unassailable, so we were compelled to abandon the couloir of our choice. We accordingly traversed to the left to see whether the next gully would be more favourable. We found that while the upper lip of the Bergschrund was equally hopeless, the ice in the gully had so shrunk from the rock that a sort of precipitous chimney was left, up which, Burgener thought, a way might be forced. Venetz was accordingly lowered into the Bergschrund, and, having got across on a bridge of ice *débris*, attacked the chimney. He had not climbed more than ten feet when he found himself pounded and unable to move up or down. The *débris* bridge did not run quite home to the foot of the chimney, but left a yawning chasm very conveniently placed for him to fall into, and his position appeared extremely critical. Burgener, seeing the necessity for instant action, laid hold of the spare rope, and without waiting to tie on, let me lower him into the Schrund. He promptly scrambled across the confused heap of rickety ice-blocks and was soon able to lend Venetz the requisite aid. The latter, after a short halt on Burgener's shoulder, succeeded in wedging his axe between the rock and ice, and, subsequently using it as a footing, was able to gain tolerable standing ground on a shelving rock. I then threw the end of the rope on which Venetz had been climbing across to Burgener, who, as soon as he had tied on, went up to the shelf. Meanwhile I had fixed one of our axes in the snow, and having fastened a short length of rope to it, slid down on to the bridge and crossed to the foot of the chimney, where the rope was already waiting for me. The rock was painfully cold, and it was with great satisfaction that I reached the top of the chimney and could join the men in the endeavour to rub a little life into our fingers.

Fairly easy rocks now enabled us to make rapid progress. A little stream which also used these rocks as a pathway, though in the opposite direction, submitted us to an occasional douche. After a time it struck us that even the pleasures of a shower-bath may be overdone, and we turned to our right and got on to the snow of the couloir. We followed this till its walls began to close in on either side in such grim sort, that we feared we should find no way out if we ascended it any further. Turning to our left we effected, after much difficulty, a lodgment on the cliff, and were able to ascend with tolerable ease for a few hundred feet. We were then confronted by an impassable slab that blocked, or rather terminated, the gully we had been climbing, and we were compelled to escape by traversing to our left along its lower overhanging edge. We were supported mainly by gripping the lower edge of this slab between our fingers and thumbs, whilst our legs sprawled about on the next slab below in a way which suggested that such useless appendages would have been better left at home. Having surmounted this difficulty, a few yards of pleasant scrambling brought us to the top of the great red tower that forms a fairly conspicuous object from the Mer de Glace.

It was obvious that though we had been going eight hours we had hardly begun the real climb, and we halted with one consent to see whether the attempt was worth further effort. The col between the Grépon and Charmoz appeared accessible, and it also looked as if a way might be forced to the gap between the summit and the tower which is now known as the Pic Balfour. Each of these points, however, was, we knew, more easily reached from the Nantillon Glacier. Our object had been to force an ascent straight up the face, and thus avoid the difficulties of the ridge. This we now saw was nearly, if not quite, out of the question. Burgener expressed his willingness to go on, but added that it would, of necessity, involve our sleeping on the rocks. The provisions were too scanty for this to be desirable, and after an hour's halt public opinion clearly favoured a descent.

We returned by the way we had ascended, only varying our route when we reached the Glacier de Trélaporte. Instead of going down the glacier and the slopes below to the moraine of the Mer de Glace, we kept to our left and used the great gap (Professor Tyndall's cleft station) as a pass, thus materially reducing the number of loose stones we had to traverse before reaching the Montenvers.

The idea that the Mer de Glace face was the true line of attack did not survive this expedition. We once more determined to turn our attention to the Nantillon side, and, as a beginning, to attempt to get along the ridge from the Charmoz-Grépon Col. It did not occur to us that the easiest way to the Nantillon Glacier would be to traverse the lower buttresses of the Little Charmoz from the Montenvers inn, the route which is now invariably taken, but, in our ignorance, we went down to Chamonix as a preliminary to the assault.

On August 3rd, accordingly, I was remorselessly ejected from my bed at 1.30 a.m., and informed that there was not a cloud or even a rag of mist for laziness and a love of slumber to modestly shelter beneath, so, reviling guides, mountains, and early starts, I got into my clothes and came down to the chill and comfortless salon. I then found that neither hot tea for the Monsieur nor breakfast for the guides was forthcoming. Doubtless the just retribution awarded by Providence (or M. Couttet) to those who bring Swiss guides to Chamonix.

We got on very slowly at first, our progress being much hindered by a bottle lantern. Happily, before the loss of time became really serious, Venetz took advantage of a smooth rock and some interlaced brambles, and went head-over-heels, no one exactly knew where, though, from some remarks he let fall, I gathered that it was one of the less desirable quarters of Hades. When he reappeared the lantern was no more, and we were able to make better progress, till, after a weary grind, we reached the Nantillon Glacier.

We did not much like the idea of repeating the traverse by which we had reached the upper slopes on our way to the Charmoz. We therefore halted and looked for a better method of turning the ice fall. A steep tongue of glacier between the cliffs of the Charmoz and the buttress of rock which projects from the Blaitière seemed to offer an easy and fairly safe line of ascent, and we unanimously decided in its favour.

Having settled this preliminary to our day's work we strolled up to the foot of the tongue. We kept straight up it, and found that it was just steep enough to require step cutting the whole way. The process was tedious, and, much to Burgener's chagrin, a party bound for the Blaitière were catching us up, hand over hand, on the easy rocks to our right.* Our leader exerted his utmost strength, and by herculean efforts managed to

---

* This is the proper route and is, I believe, now invariably taken by parties on their way to the upper slopes of the Nantillon Glacier.

reach the upper glacier simultaneously with the other party. We found them to be led by a well-known Oberland guide, who was not a little elated by his judicious lead. We kept together as far as the foot of the couloir running up to the Charmoz-Grépon Col. Here our ways diverged, so with mutual good-byes, and wishing each other all sorts of luck and success, we parted company, the Oberlander first giving Burgener much good advice and ending by strongly advising him to abandon the attempt, "for," said he, "I have tried it, and where I have failed no one else need hope to succeed." Burgener was greatly moved by this peroration, and I learnt from a torrent of unreportable patois that our fate was sealed, and even if we spent the rest of our lives on the mountain (or in falling off it) it would, in his opinion, be preferable to returning amid the jeers and taunts of this unbeliever.

Having found a rock which protected us from falling stones, we halted for a second breakfast. Turning once more to the ascent we found that the couloir, though not absolutely free from falling stones, is fairly easy, and it was not till about seventy feet below the col, when we had traversed to the right and assaulted a great slab, that we met with our first serious difficulty, and found it necessary to put on the rope. Both Venetz and I made sundry attempts, but, so soon as we got beyond the sure and certain support of Burgener's axe, progress upwards became impossible, and though we reached points within a few feet of broken and fairly easy rock, we were forced on each attempt to return. Whilst still doubtful whether a yet more determined attack might not conquer our enemy, Venetz wisely climbed back into the couloir and up to the col to see if any more convenient line could be discovered. He soon called on us to follow, and, leaving Burgener to pick up the rope and knapsack, I scrambled round and found Venetz perched some ten feet up a huge slab. This slab rests like a buttress against the great square rock, which shuts in the col on the Grépon side with a perpendicular wall. Its foot, accessible by a broad and convenient ledge, is about twenty feet below the col, whilst its top leads to the foot of a short gully, at the top of which is a curious hole in the ridge dubbed by Burgener the "Kanones Loch."* From this, once attained, we believed the summit was accessible.

So soon as Burgener had brought round the rope and knapsack, Venetz tied up and set to work. At one or two places progress was very difficult, the crack being in part too wide to afford any hold, and forcing the climber on to the face of the slab. I subsequently found that at the worst point my longer reach enabled me to get hold of a small protuberance with one finger, but how Venetz, whose reach is certainly a foot less

* I am not responsible for Saas Thal grammar.

The Grépon.
from the Charmoz

AN INACCESSIBLE PEAK.

than mine, managed to get up has never been satisfactorily explained. At the next stage the crack narrows, and a stone has conveniently jammed itself exactly where it is wanted; beyond, the right-hand side of the crack gets broken, and it is a matter of comparative ease to pull oneself on to the top. This top then forms a narrow, but perfectly easy and level, path to the gully leading up to the hole in the ridge. We found this hole or doorway guarded by a great splinter of rock, so loose that an unwary touch would probably have been resented with remorseless severity, and the impertinent traveller hurled on to the Nantillon Glacier. Squeezing through, we stepped on to a little plateau covered with the *débris* of frost-riven rock.

Burgener then proposed, amid the reverent and appreciative silence of the company, that libations should be duly poured from a bottle of Bouvier. This religious ceremony having been fittingly observed (the Western form, I take it, of the prayers offered by a pious Buddhist on reaching the crest of some Tibetan pass), we proceeded to attack a little cleft overhanging the Mer de Glace, and cleverly protected at the top by a projecting rock. Above this we found ourselves in a sort of granite crevasse, and as this, so far as we could discover, had no bottom, we had to hotch ourselves along with our knees against one side, and our backs against the other. Burgener at this

point exhibited most painful anxiety, and his
"Herr Gott! geben Sie Acht" had the very
ring of tears in its earnest entreaty. On my
emergence into daylight his anxiety was explained.
Was not the knapsack on my shoulders, and
were not sundry half-bottles of Bouvier in the
knapsack?

We now boldly struck out on to the Nantillon
face, where a huge slice of rock had been rent
some sixteen inches from the mass of the mountain,
leaving a sharp, knife-like edge, destructive of
fingers, trousers, and epidermis, but affording a
safe and certain grip. This led us on to a spacious
platform, whence a scramble of some twenty feet
brought us to the sharply-pointed northern
summit. Burgener self-denyingly volunteered to
go down and send me up a stone wherewith to
knock off the extreme point of the mountain, but
the pleasing delusion that I was to occupy the
convenient seat thus afforded was quickly dis-
pelled. Stones were hauled up by Venetz in considerable quantities, and the construction of a
stone man—or, having regard to its age and size,
I ought, perhaps, to say a stone baby—was undertaken. A large red handkerchief was then
produced, and the baby was decorously draped in
this becoming and festive attire. These duties
finished, we partly scrambled and partly slid back
on to the big platform, and proceeded to enjoy
ourselves, feeling that our work was over, our

summit won, and that we might revel in the warm sunshine and glorious view.

That night my dreams were troubled by visions of a great square tower—the great square tower that at the other end of the summit ridge had thrust its shoulders above the snows of the Col du Géant, and though the men had stoutly maintained that our peak was highest, I felt that the delights of an untroubled mind and a conscience void of offence must be for ever abandoned if up that tower I did not go. After breakfast, I sought for Burgener, but I found that he was invisible, an essential portion of his clothing being so terribly damaged that the protracted exertions of the local tailor were requisite to his public appearance. However, in response to my urgent entreaties, Venetz retired to bed, and Burgener emerged resplendent in the latter's garments.

It turned out that Burgener had to be in Martigny the next morning but one, so, to give him time on our return from the Grépon to drive over the Tête Noire, we resolved to go up to Blaitière-dessous that evening and make an early start. The tailor duly accomplished his labours and released Venetz, and about four o'clock, with the addition of a porter, we strolled up to the chalet.

We got under weigh at two o'clock the next morning, and, following the route just described, reached the base of the first summit. Passing to the right of this we dropped down a fifteen-feet step and crawled up a smooth rock to the edge of the great cleft which divides the summit ridge into two equal sections. After a careful examination, as there did not appear any other method of descent, we fixed our spare rope, having first tied two or three knots at suitable intervals. Venetz went down first, and after he had made a short inspection he called on us to follow. Burgener descended next, and I brought up the rear in company with the knapsack and an ice-axe. I found the first twenty feet very easy, then I began to think that the Alpine Club rope is too thin for this sort of work, and I noted a curious and inexplicable increase in my weight. To add to these various troubles the axe, which was held by a loop round my arm, caught in a crack and snapped the string. Luckily, by a convulsive jerk, I just managed to catch it in my left hand. This performance, however, greatly excited Burgener, who, unable to see what had happened, thought his Herr and not merely the ice-axe was contemplating a rapid descent on to the Mer de Glace. Having restored our spirits by a quiet consideration of the contents of a certain flask, we set off in pursuit of Venetz, who had carried away our only remaining rope. A convenient flake had split from the mountain on the Nantillon side and offered a fairly easy zigzag path to the top of the tower, which shuts in the great cleft on this side.

We here found one of the many excellences of

AN INACCESSIBLE PEAK.

the Grépon peculiarly well developed. On the Mer de Glace face, from ten to twenty feet below the ridge, a broad road suitable for carriages, bicycles, or other similar conveyances, led us straight along to an obvious chimney by which the last gap was easily attained, thus obviating the necessity of following the ridge and climbing up and down its various irregularities. It is true that this desirable promenade was only to be reached by rounding a somewhat awkward corner, which my companion professed to think difficult, and its continuity was interrupted at another point by a projecting shoulder, which pushed one's centre of gravity further over the Mer de Glace than was wholly pleasant; but, the passage of these minor obstacles excepted, we were able to walk arm in arm along a part of the mountain which we had expected to find as formidable as anything we had encountered. Reaching the last gap, we rejoined Venetz and proceeded to examine the final tower.

It was certainly one of the most forbidding rocks I have ever set eyes on. Unlike the rest of the peak, it was smooth to the touch, and its square-cut edges offered no hold or grip of any sort. True, the block was fractured from top to bottom, but the crack, four or five inches wide, had edges as smooth and true as a mason could have hewn them, and had not one of those irregular and convenient backs not infrequently possessed by such clefts. Even the dangerous helm of a semi-loose stone, wedged with doubtful security between the opposing walls, was lacking. Added to all this a great rock overhung the top, and would obviously require a powerful effort just when the climber was most exhausted.

Under these circumstances, Burgener and I set to work to throw a rope over the top, whilst Venetz reposed in a graceful attitude rejoicing in a quiet pipe. After many efforts, in the course of which both Burgener and I nearly succeeded in throwing ourselves over on to the Mer de Glace, but dismally failed in landing the rope, we became virtuous, and decided that the rock must be climbed by the fair methods of honourable war. To this end we poked up Venetz with the ice-axe (he was by now enjoying a peaceful nap), and we then generally pulled ourselves together and made ready for the crucial struggle.

Our rope-throwing operations had been carried on from the top of a sort of narrow wall, about two feet wide, and perhaps six feet above the gap. Burgener, posted on this wall, stood ready to help Venetz with the ice-axe so soon as he should get within his reach, whilst my unworthy self, planted in the gap, was able to assist him in the first part of his journey. So soon as Venetz got beyond my reach, Burgener leant across the gap, and, jamming the point of the axe against the face of the rock, made a series of footholds of doubtful security whereon Venetz could rest and gain strength for

*The lower peak of the Géant
from the highest point*

each successive effort. At length he got above all these adventitious aids and had to depend exclusively on his splendid skill. Inch by inch he forced his way, gasping for breath, and his hand wandering over the smooth rock in those vague searches for non-existent hold which it is positively painful to witness. Burgener and I watched him with intense anxiety, and it was with no slight feeling of relief that we saw the fingers of one hand reach the firm hold offered by the square-cut top. A few moments' rest, and he made his way over the projecting rock, whilst Burgener and I yelled ourselves hoarse.* When the rope came down for me, I made a brilliant attempt to ascend unaided. Success attended my first efforts, then came a moment of metaphorical suspense, promptly followed by the real thing; and, kicking like a spider, I was hauled on to the top, where I listened with unruffled composure to sundry sarcastic remarks concerning those who put their trust in tennis shoes and scorn the sweet persuasion of the rope.

The summit is of palatial dimensions and is provided with three stone chairs. The loftiest of these was at once appropriated by Burgener for the ice-axe, and the inferior members of the party

* M. Dunod heard at Chamonix that I took three ladders of ten feet each on this ascent ("Annuaire Club Alpin Français," 1886, p. 99); it is needless to say that this is a Chamonix myth. It, however, led him to encumber himself with three ladders of twelve feet each.

were bidden to bring stones to build it securely in position. This solemn rite being duly performed, we stretched ourselves at full length and mocked M. Couttet's popgun at Chamonix with a pop of far more exhilarating sort.

The aged narrative from which I have been quoting ends abruptly at this point.* Before, however, quitting the summit of one of the steepest rocks in the Alps, I may perhaps be permitted to ask certain critics whether the love of rock-climbing is so heinous and debasing a sin that its votaries are no longer worthy to be ranked as mountaineers, but are to be relegated to a despised and special class of " mere gymnasts."

It would appear at the outset wholly illogical to deny the term " mountaineer " to any man who is skilled in the art of making his way with facility in mountain countries. To say that a man who climbs because he is fond of mountaineering work is not a mountaineer, whilst a man who climbs because it is essential to some scientific pursuit in which he is interested, is a mountaineer, is contrary to the first principles of a logical definition, and I trust will never become general. It may be freely admitted that science has a higher social

---

* Portions of this chapter were written for the Alpine Club some years since, and though the following paragraphs are not perhaps very well adapted to a wider audience, old associations have made me unwilling to excise them.

value than sport, but that does not alter the fact that mountaineering is a sport, and by no possible method can be converted into geology, or botany, or topography. That the technique of our sport has made rapid progress is alleged against us as a sort of crime, but I venture to say, in reality, it is a matter, not for regret, but for congratulation. To emulate the skill of their guides was the ideal of the early climbers, and I trust it will still be the ideal that we set before ourselves. A terminology which suggests that as a man approaches this goal, as he increases in mountaineering skill he ceases to be a mountaineer, stands self-condemned, and must be remorselessly eliminated from the literature of our sport.

Probably most mountaineers would agree that the charm of mountain scenery is to be found in every step taken in the upper world. The strange interfolding of the snows, the gaunt, weird crags of the ridges, the vast, blue, icicle-fringed crevasse, or the great smooth slabs sloping downwards through apparently bottomless space, are each and all no less lovely than the boundless horizon of the summit view. The self-dubbed mountaineers, however, fail to grasp this essential fact. To them the right way up a peak is the easiest way, and all the other ways are wrong ways. Thus they would say, to take an instance from a well-known peak, if a man goes up the Matterhorn to enjoy the scenery, he will go by the Hörnli route;

if he goes by the Zmutt ridge, it is, they allege, merely the difficulties of the climb that attract him. Now, this reasoning would appear to be wholly fallacious. Among the visions of mountain loveliness that rise before my mind none are fairer than the stupendous cliffs and fantastic crags of the Zmutt ridge. To say that this route with its continuously glorious scenery is, from an æsthetic point of view, the wrong way, while the Hörnli route which, despite the noble distant prospect, is marred by the meanness of its screes and its paper-besprinkled slopes, is the right, involves a total insensibility to the true mountain feeling.

The suspicion, indeed, sometimes crosses my mind that the so-called mountaineer confounds the pleasure he derives from photography or from geological or other research, with the purely æsthetic enjoyment of noble scenery. Doubtless, the summit of a peak is peculiarly well adapted to these semi-scientific pursuits, and if the summit is the only thing desired, the easiest way up is obviously the right way; but from a purely æsthetic standpoint, the Col du Lion, the teeth of the Zmutt ridge, or Carrel's Corridor, whilst affording as exquisite a distant prospect, combine with it the dramatic force of a splendid foreground of jagged ridge, appalling precipice, and towering mist-veiled height.

The importance of foreground cannot, I think, be overrated, and it is obvious that the more difficult an ascent the bolder and more significant will usually be the immediate surroundings of the traveller. In other words, the æsthetic value of an ascent generally varies with its difficulty. This, necessarily, leads us to the conclusion that the most difficult way up the most difficult peaks is always the right thing to attempt, whilst the easy slopes of ugly screes may with propriety be left to the scientists, with M. Janssen at their head. To those who, like myself, take a non-utilitarian view of the mountains, the great ridge of the Grépon may be safely recommended, for nowhere can the climber find bolder towers, wilder clefts, or more terrific precipices; nowhere, a fairer vision of lake and mountain, mist-filled valleys, and riven ice.

A variety of attempts were made to repeat the ascent of the Grépon, but the mountain defied all attacks till the 2nd of September, 1885, when M. Dunod, after a month of persistent effort, succeeded in forcing the ascent by the southern ridge. Curiously enough, though he twice reached the Charmoz-Grépon Col, he failed on each occasion, not merely to hit off my crack, within six yards of which he must have passed four times, but also to strike the variation of this route which leads up some slabs on the Mer de Glace face. This latter was invented by some unknown party, whose existence is only deduced from numerous wooden wedges driven into a crack. These wedges were certainly not there when we ascended in 1881, but seven years later Mr. Morse, who, with Ulrich Almer, reached the first summit by this route, found them securely fixed and of great use. Unluckily, owing to lack of time (he was taking the Grépon on his way down from the Charmoz traverse!), it was impossible to complete the ascent, and he had perforce to remain content with the lower summit.

In 1892, therefore, the ascent had never been fully repeated by my route, and had only been twice effected by the southern ridge. In each of these latter ascents F. Simond had been leading guide. Early in August of that year, a party consisting of Messrs. Morse, Gibson, Pasteur, and Wilson, without guides effected the ascent by this same route, and left an ice-axe, with a fluttering scarf attached, as a challenge to the habitués of the Montenvers. A few days later, Hastings, Collie, Pasteur, and myself made up our minds to recover the derelict property. We intended to ascend from the Charmoz-Grépon Col and descend by the south ridge, and as the step known as C. P.* was reported to be absolutely inaccessible from the Grépon side—previous parties having always left a rope, on their way to the peak, hanging down the precipitous step so as to help them on their return—we

---

* An early explorer having ascended the southern ridge to this point, and not liking its appearance beyond, painted his initials on the rock, and it is now always known by them.

chartered two porters to go up to C. P. and fix the rope; we also provided such provision and refreshment for them to carry as would, we thought, add to our comfort and happiness.

At 2 a.m. on the 18th of August, Simond gave me the unpleasant intelligence that the very name of Grépon had so frightened the porters that they had surreptitiously left their beds and fled to Chamonix. The difficulty appeared very serious. 2 a.m. is usually an inconvenient hour to charter porters, and Simond was quite sure that C. P. was impassable from the Grépon side without a rope previously fixed. It appeared, then, likely, that if we reached the gap leading to it we should have to retrace our steps all the way along the ridge. After much talk, Simond offered to lend us the herd-boy attached to the establishment, and also to wake and interview a one-eyed guide, who was sleeping in the hotel, and who had been with M. Dunod on some of his unsuccessful attempts.

This guide, Gaspard Simond,* proved willing, and with the herd-boy as second man we started gaily for the valley of stones. Each amateur member of the party was quite sure that the route taken along the detestable slopes of the stone man ridge, was far inferior to the line that such amateur had

---

* A few days later this same guide lost his way on the Dôme du Gouter in a snowstorm, his employer, Mr. Nettleship, losing his life in consequence. The guides, thanks to the thickness of Chamonix clothes, survived the cold and escaped.

worked out and was prepared to lead us on; but I noticed that none the less we carefully kept to the herd-boy's lead, and for the first time we reached the moraine of the Nantillon Glacier without feeling the need of any seriously bad language. Concealing our lanterns beneath a stone, we struck up the glacier just as the soft lights of morning were silhouetting the rugged limestone ridges of Sixt.

At this point Gaspard indulged in some very depressing statements. He told us that he had recently been up the Charmoz, and with true prophetic insight had devoted his time whilst there to an examination of the particular slab up which our route lay. This slab, he had been able to see, was coated with "verglas," and most ingenious defences of snow, rock, and ice had been skilfully erected at the top; in short, it was simply courting defeat to go on with our attempt. It appeared to us, however, that these complicated defences were likely to be merely the products of our guide's imagination, and were, perhaps, in part referable to an objection to carrying a heavy knapsack up to C. P. We therefore proceeded; but on reaching the top of the rocks known as the "breakfasting station," Gaspard gave us further details; this very slab had, it appeared, fallen, crashing down to the glacier several years since, leaving a blank, unbroken wall that could by no manner of means be ascended. We were struck dumb by this accumulation of difficulties; not only was the slab impassable by reason of the accumulated ice, but it was not even there! A state of affairs recalling to our minds the celebrated legal pleas entered relatively to the cracked jar—"We never had it. It was cracked when we had it. We returned it whole!"

Pasteur, however, by an interesting deductive argument, reached an equally gloomy conclusion. "It was," said he, "extremely unlikely that I should have the luck to get up the Grépon at all this year; now, having been up once, it is absurd to suppose I shall get up a second time." He suggested we should tell the porters to halt at the foot of the couloir till we got to the col, and, if we found that we could not storm the Grépon ridge, we would shout to the guides and they could then deposit the baggage and return as fast as they liked. This suggestion was duly accepted by the party. Indeed, a telescopic examination of the peak had not enabled me to trace my old route—for the excellent reason, as I subsequently discovered, that it is not visible from this point of view. This, and the wide prevalence of a rumour that a great crag really had fallen from this part of the mountain, led me to fear that it might be all too true, and that the peak was closed for ever from this side. We started up the couloir, with chastened feelings and hopes little higher than the Charmoz traverse backwards. On reaching the neighbourhood of the col, I looked around for my old route to the "Kanones Loch," but I could not recognise it, and the col itself did not seem familiar to me. The furious wind whistling and howling through the crags did not help to awaken my memory, and it was only when I had climbed round a crag on the Charmoz side of the col that I recovered my bearings and recognised the cleft up which we had to go.

Possibly the knowledge that I was going to try to lead up to it made it look worse than it really was, but for the moment I was startled at its steepness. With the exception of two steps where the rock sets back slightly (to the extent, perhaps, of two feet in all), the whole is absolutely perpendicular. In this estimate I exclude a preliminary section of seven or eight feet, which bulges out and overhangs in a most painful manner. On the other hand, it was distinctly more broken than I had expected, and the longer we looked the better we liked it, till with fair hopes of success I climbed down to the foot of the crack, scrambled on to Hastings's shoulders, and tackled the toughest bit of rock climbing I have ever attempted. For the first twenty feet or so the climber is to some extent protected by the rope, which can be hitched round a great splinter close to the col; beyond that point the rope is simply worn as an ornament, though doubtless it supplies one's companions with pleasing sensations whenever a slip seems imminent. About half-way up is an excellent step on which one can take breath. When I say excellent, I only mean relatively to the rest of the crack, not that it is suitable for lunch, or even that one can balance on it without holding on; indeed, on the first occasion that I ascended, my meditations at this point were rudely interrupted by my foot slipping on the shelving rock, and I was launched into thin air. Wiser by this memory, I hung on with my fingers as well as the absence of anything to hang on to would permit, and then, having somewhat regained my wind, began the second half of the ascent. This section was, by the general consent of the party, voted the hardest. There is really very little hold for the hands, and nothing at all for the feet, the climber proceeding chiefly by a pious reliance on Providence, eked out at intervals by loose stones wedged with a doubtful, wobbling sort of semi-security into the crack. Above, the need for piety is replaced by excellent hand-hold on the right, though the gasping and exhausted climber still finds it difficult to propel his weight upwards. Ledges then become more numerous, and at length one's arms and head hang down the Grépon side of the slab, whilst one's legs are still struggling with the concluding difficulties of the other side. At this juncture wild cheers broke from the party below, and awoke in me the dread that the porters would regard them as the wished-for signal and fly incontinently to Chamonix.

In the intervals of gasping for breath I suggested these fears to my companions, and a silence, as of death, instantly showed their appreciation of the danger.

In order to prevent the remainder of the party scrambling up with undue facility and thus exposing the Grépon to scorn, I judiciously urged them not to waste time by sending up the axes and luggage on the rope, but to sling the axes on their arms and distribute the luggage amongst the rest of the party. I found this eminently successful, and a most material aid in impressing my companions with a due respect for the crag.

We then scrambled up the gully and through the "Kanones Loch," and with our hopes rising at every advance, we followed my old route to the top of the great gap. Here we fixed a hundred feet of rope, and the party went down one by one. As I was descending last, having just passed a perfectly smooth and precipitous section of the cliff relying exclusively on the rope, I rested a moment on a trifling irregularity in the rock. When I essayed to continue the descent, the rope came to me as I pulled. With a great effort I succeeded in keeping my balance on the insecure footing where I had been resting, but for a moment I felt supremely uncomfortable. The rope was apparently quite loose above, and there appeared to be no means of climbing down the rock to the gap without its aid. However, after about ten feet of it had been hauled in, no more would come, and it resisted the united efforts of my companions in the gap. Collie also managed to see an apparently possible line of descent, and skilfully coached by him, keeping the rope in my hand merely as a *dernier ressort*, I succeeded in reaching the welcome security of Hastings's grip and was landed in the gap.

So far as we could see, the rope had slipped off the top of the tower on to the Nantillon face, and caught in a hitch some ten feet down. We could not see whether this hitch was reliable or not, but we all agreed that the first man to go up from our present position would have an unpleasant task. As it was still doubtful whether we could scale the final peak, and thus get on to the C. P. route, this was not an impossible contingency, and we hastened forward to set the question at rest.

This final peak had nearly baffled Burgener and Venetz, and we scarcely hoped to be able to climb it by fair means. We had determined, in consequence, to try and win the summit by throwing a rope over the top. It is true Burgener and I had failed signally in so doing, but on this occasion we had a light rope with us, far better adapted for that purpose than the ordinary Alpine Club rope we had used in 1881. Collie, on the way along the ridge, selected two excellent stones wherewith to weight the rope and give it some chance of facing the furious gale. With much discomfort to himself and grave damage to the pockets of his coat, he conveyed these murderous weapons through various difficulties to the very foot of the final climb.

The preparations for a preliminary assault by fair and legitimate methods were in progress, when Pasteur joyfully shouted that we had already joined the C. P. route, and could ascend by a perfectly simple and fairly easy line. The crack, by which Venetz had climbed, is not the only one leading to the top. To the right, and rather on the Nantillon face, is a second cleft, precipitous at the bottom, where a friend can conveniently give you a shoulder but quite practicable above. M. Dunod, ascending from C. P., reached the base of this crack, and naturally utilised it for the ascent. We, in 1881, reached the base of the other crack, and Burgener dismissed the alternative line with a contemptuous "Es ist schwerer als dieses." He was, however, wrong. Pasteur gave me a shoulder, and in a few minutes we all crowded round the ice-axe and its fluttering flag.

The wind was howling across the ridge with such fury that we could only crouch under one of the stones, and we soon determined to go down to warmer quarters. We scrambled off the summit, and, sheltering under its lee, rejoiced in victory and lunch. Pasteur, who had been previously on this side of the mountain, now took the lead. He slipped a spare rope through a "piton" left by

M. Dunod, and we all quickly slid down to a broad shelf. When I say all, however, I must except Hastings, who unluckily inserted his foot into a tempting crack, and found that no effort could subsequently release it. All hands heaved on the rope, but it was of no avail, and he bid fair—save for the dearth of eagles—to rival Prometheus. Some one at last suggested that he should take off his boot. The idea was hailed with approval, and we all shouted and yelled the advice. When, however, one is supported on a steep, not to say perpendicular, slab by one foot jammed in a crack some twelve inches from the surface, it is a problem of no slight complexity to unlace and remove an offending boot. The task was, however, accomplished; but then a second difficulty arose, what was to be done with it? Happily a pocket was discovered large enough to contain the property, and the ledge was soon reached in safety.

A short ascent by an easy gully led us to the gap between the Pic Balfour and the summit. From thence easy ledges brought us down to the C. P. cleft. Our porters greeted us with shouts, and let down a rope for our help. It was obvious, however, that a rock bridge, not, perhaps, wholly easy of access, would have enabled us to turn the obstruction without extraneous aid. Since, however, the porters were at hand, we thought they might as well have the privilege of pulling us up.

Safely arrived in the neighbourhood of the knapsack, we "lay beside our nectar" till such time as the nectar was consumed. We subsequently raced down to the breakfasting rocks, descended to the lower glacier, and finally got back to the Montenvers about 5 p.m. Kind friends, who saw our approach, welcomed us with a vast pot—the pride and joy of the Montenvers Hotel—full of tea, and under its stimulating influence the crags became steeper and more terrible, until it seemed incredible that mere mortals could have faced such awful difficulties and perils.

A year later I was again at the Montenvers, and was taught the great truth that in mountaineering, as in all the other varied affairs of life, "l'homme propose mais femme dispose," and consequently a desperate assault on the Aig du Plan, that we had been contemplating for a week or more, had to give place to yet another ascent of the Grépon.

The horrors of the valley of stones on a dark night were vainly conjured in their most hideous form. The utmost concession that aged limbs could obtain was permission to gîte high on the rocks above the lower fall of the Nantillon Glacier. I am aware that youthful climbers scorn gîtes, and regard a night spent in plunging head first into deep and gruesome holes as an excellent restorative previous to a difficult ascent. With this view

A Crag on the Géspen with the Vcôt in the distance

I was once in full accord, but the rolling years have given strength to the arguments in favour of camping out; and now a shelter tent, a sheepskin mattress, and an eiderdown bag are resistlessly attractive, when compared with an early start, interminable stones, and the tortures of a folding lantern—that instrument from which "no light, but rather darkness visible," is shed.

Like everything else in the Alps, a night out is in itself a great pleasure. In no other way can one see such gorgeous sunsets, such " wind-enchanted shapes of wandering mist," such exquisite effects of fading light playing amongst fantastic pinnacles of tottering ice. To watch the night crawling out of its lair in the valley and seizing ridge after ridge of the lower hills till the great white dome of Mont Blanc towers alone above the gathering darkness, is a joy that is hidden to dwellers in inns, and is never dreamt of amidst the riot of the *table d'hôte*.

Few places can rival the narrow ledge of rock, with a precipice in front and an ice slope rising behind, where our tiny tent was pitched, and few setting suns have disclosed more gorgeous contrasts and tenderer harmonies than that which heralded the night of August 4, 1893.

Our party consisted of Miss Bristow, Mr. Hastings, and myself. Warmly wrapped in sleeping bags, we sat sipping hot tea till the smallest and laziest of the stars was wide awake. Only when the chill breeze of night had dried up the rivulets, and the roar of the torrent five thousand feet below alone broke the solemn silence of the night, did we creep into the shelter of our tent. Hastings then tightened the ropes, and ingeniously arranged the cooking stove and the various provisions required for breakfast, in places where they were conveniently accessible from the tent; and having crawled in, shut the door, and we settled ourselves amongst our luxurious mattresses and bags.

By 5 a.m. the next morning a sumptuous meal was ready. From rolls to hot bacon, from jam to tea and fresh milk, the all-producing bag of Hastings had sufficed, and we feasted in a "regular right down royal" style till six o'clock, by which time the rest of our party, Slingsby, Collie, and Brodie, had arrived. A second edition of breakfast was promptly provided, and, whilst it was being duly attended to, Miss Bristow and I started up the ice, hewing such steps as were necessary. We went extremely slowly, but the excellence of Hastings's culinary efforts so delayed the rest of the party, that it was not till we had halted ten minutes or more on the rocks at the foot of the couloir, that they caught us up. Slingsby then unroped and came with us, whilst the rest of the party swung to the right to attempt the ascent by the southern ridge, more commonly known as the C. P. route. Their object was to effect the climb, if any way possible, without the elaborate rope-throwing operations which have hitherto always been found essential on this side. In the event of failure they were to accept a helping hand from us, so soon as we should have reached the foot of the final peak and were in a position to give them one. As the only serious difficulty by the C. P. route is a section of about thirty feet, immediately below the platform underneath the summit rock, it was obvious we should be able to do this without much trouble.

Five consecutive days of evil weather had sufficed to plaster the couloir with ice and loose snow. We were, in addition, altogether over-weighted with luggage—a half-plate camera and a spare sixty feet of rope, in addition to food, &c., sufficing to bulge out the knapsack in a most obese and uncomfortable way. I also distinguished myself by getting too much to the right in the couloir, and, to avoid descending, we had to make a traverse which involved climbing of a merit fully equal to anything required above.

On reaching the point where the Grépon route diverges from that to the southern pinnacle of the Charmoz, we found the couloir in a most unsatisfactory condition. Not merely were the rocks as rotten as usual, but they were decorated with great frills and tassels of brittle ice, the interstices being filled up with the loosest and most powdery snow. It was impossible to tell what was sound and what was loose, though we found it a good working hypothesis to regard everything as loose. After a time the process of raking out the snow and testing the stones became so intolerably chilling to our fingers, that Slingsby and I agreed we had better traverse directly to the lowest of the gaps dividing the Charmoz and Grépon. It was tolerably easy to get along a big slab of rock, but the ascent of a vertical crack, perhaps fifteen feet high, required prolonged and severe effort. I ought, however, to add that my companions appeared to scramble up without difficulty, Slingsby even bringing my axe, which I had left forlorn, wedged in a crack, in addition to his own.

The Mer de Glace face was in full sunshine, and was delightfully warm after the bitter cold of the shaded western rocks. We traversed by easy ledges, amongst the slush of melting snow, to a broad-topped crag, that projected far over a precipitous gully, plunging down towards the Glacier de Trélaporte. On the top of this rock we unpacked our provisions, and made our first long halt. We excused our laziness, for it was getting late, by saying the "crack" cannot be ascended till the day is further advanced and the shadows less bitterly cold. Our ledge was of the most sensational character. The cliff above overhung, and the tiny streams from the melting snow on the ridge fell far outside us in sheets of sunlit rain. Below, the cliff still receded, so that the stones dislodged by us fell four or five hundred feet before they touched the grim walls of the gully. My seat was at the extreme end of the projecting crag, and somewhat destitute of foothold. I will own that, at moments, the appalling precipice exerted such an effect on my brain, that the very stability of our perch itself seemed doubtful, and I almost seemed to feel it rock as if it were starting on its tremendous plunge through space.

After three-quarters of an hour, we packed the knapsack and scattered ourselves over the mountain, seeking for a suitable place for the camera. A little ledge, barely wide enough to squeeze along, led to the flat-topped tower which forms the Charmoz wall of the cleft, and which, from the Mer de Glace, looks like a hole through the ridge. It is not in actual fact a hole, as the key-stone of the arch above has fallen out, leaving a narrow gap. The camera was brought round to this point and Miss Bristow promptly followed, scorning the proffered rope. On this aerial perch we then proceeded to set up the camera, and the lady of the party, surrounded on three sides by nothing and blocked in front with the camera, made ready to seize the moment when an unfortunate climber should be in his least elegant attitude and transfix him for ever. The result may be seen on the next page.

Slingsby and I then returned to the col, and, putting on the rope, I went down the couloir and traversed to the rock known as the "take off."

THE "CRACK."

AN EASY DAY FOR A LADY.

My first attempt failed, owing partly to the cold, which, the moment we got into the shade, was still excessive, and partly to the fact that the first reliable grip, some ten feet above the base, was glazed with ice and more or less masked with frozen snow. By the time this latter had been pulled off, my fingers were so chilled and so inclined to cramp that I was glad to get safely down again.

It being undesirable to repeat this performance, Slingsby left the hitch and scrambled on to the "take off."* His shoulder enabled me to do without the ice-glazed holds, and to reach the perpendicular, but happily dry, part of the crack above. On reaching the shelving ledge midway up, I saw that a good deal of snow had drifted into the crack and frozen on to the two wedged stones which are more or less essential to progress. It is needless to say that the removal of this frozen snow was a matter of great difficulty, and was only effected by using my elbow as an ice-axe—a painful process and one, moreover, apt to be injurious to the joint. However, after many efforts and much gasping for breath, I reached the top of the rock, and Miss Bristow then came round from the Camera tower and ascended the crack. I did not notice that she

---

* The "take off" is about eight feet below the bottom of the illustration. The point to which my hands are clinging is the half-way resting-place, and the most difficult part of the ascent is a few feet above the top of the picture. The rope is being paid out from the col, and in no way indicates the line of ascent. This latter lies straight up the crack.

had two ropes on, and carelessly untying her, I let the end slip, thinking that the other end of it was round my own waist. Unluckily it was the rope connecting her with Slingsby, and my carelessness thus cut him off from us. In consequence, the axes, camera, and other baggage, could not be hauled up direct from the col, but had to be carried round to the "take off," to which alone my rope could be lowered.

These rocks are, at the best, none too easy, and for a very heavily-laden man are hardly practicable. However, Slingsby proved equal to the difficulty, and in some extraordinary way managed to carry the piled-up baggage, including my coat, to the ledge below the crack. When the whole mass was duly tied on to the rope, and I had to pull it up, I was a good deal impressed with the weight.

The next stage in the ascent is usually easy, and I took the knapsack and proceeded to attack it, but on reaching the little gully that leads up to the "Kanones Loch," I found it plastered with ice. The walls are so narrow, and the gully itself is so precipitous, that it is scarcely possible to use the axe with effect, and I found the knapsack must be discarded. Free from its encumbrance, the obstacle was overcome, and stepping through the hole I reached glorious sunshine. The knapsack and other luggage were then hauled up, and the rest of the party followed. The ice-glazed ledges and wrinkles of the gully, to say nothing of having to constantly handle the snow-covered rope, had reduced our fingers to a degree of cold that was positively excruciating. We sat down on the warm sunny rocks, and bent and twisted ourselves into the various attitudes which seemed most conducive to mute suffering. Gradually the sensation of having one's fingers slit by a blunt knife, from the tips upwards, was replaced by a warm glow, and as we had no longer to deal with ice-glazing and the other similar abominations which render gloves an inadmissible luxury, we put them on and proceeded happily. Of one thing we felt satisfied, our sloth and laziness were justified; had we attempted to grapple with this part of the mountain earlier in the day, we must have been driven back by the cold.

From this point onward the sun was blazing on the ridge, and our spirits rose to the highest pitch. Miss Bristow showed the representatives of the Alpine Club the way in which steep rocks should be climbed, and usually filled up the halts, during which the elder members of the party sought to recover their wind, by photographic operations.

Reaching the foot of the final tower, we slung a rope down to the C. P. section of the party. They had been so overcome by sleep, tobacco, and a love of ease, that the ascent of the mauvais pas had not even been attempted! We then scrambled on to the highest point. We shouted to friends, who, we thought, might be watching us from the Mer de Glace; we congratulated the first lady who had ever stood on this grim tower; and then we listened to the voice of the charmer who whispered of hot tea and cakes, of jam and rolls, of biscuits and fruit, waiting for the faithful in the Pic Balfour gap. There we feasted sumptuously, and having bundled the cooking-stove and other luggage into the knapsacks, we hurried down the easy ledges to C. P., and were finally chased off the mountain by wind, rain, and hail.

It has frequently been noticed that all mountains appear doomed to pass through the three stages: An inaccessible peak—The most difficult ascent in the Alps—An easy day for a lady.

I must confess that the Grépon has not yet reached this final stage, and the heading of the last few pages must be regarded as prophetic rather than as a statement of actual fact. Indeed, owing to the great accumulation of ice and snow on the mountain, the ascent last described will always rank as amongst the hardest I have made. None the less, its chief defence—the sense of fear with which, till lately, it inspired the guides—has gone, and a few of them have actually screwed their courage to the " sticking point " and reached the summit. Last season another lady, well known in climbing circles, traversed the mountain in the opposite direction, and it bids fair before very long to become a popular climb.

Mont Blanc and the Dent du Requin

CHAPTER VII.

THE DENT DU REQUIN.

Four travel-worn men * arrived at the Montenvers at 7 o'clock one evening, after thirty-three hours of continuous railway and diligence, and, with the enthusiasm of inveterate climbers, immediately began to discuss what was to be done on the morrow. "Began"! do I say? It had formed the staple of their talk during all those weary thirty-three hours, and still no satisfactory conclusion had been reached. The walk up to the Montenvers had, however, convinced three out of the four that a start at 2 a.m. the next morning would be contrary to all the canons of mountaineering. On the other hand it was felt that perfect weather must not be wasted, and, as a concession to the youth and energy of the party, it was decided that we would camp the next night in the open, and assault the redoubtable Dent du Requin on the following day. Even the suggestion hazarded by

* Messrs. Cecil Slingsby, Norman Collie, G. Hastings, and myself. The ascent was made on the 25th July, 1893.

the aforementioned youth and energy, that we might spend a second night out and do a sort of right and left barrel arrangement — climb the Requin one day and the Plan the next—was regarded with distinct approval.

A consultation with the map, and our collective recollections of what may be seen on the way over the Col du Géant, decided us to camp on some nameless rocks a little below the Petit Rognon, where the more sanguine spirits averred we should find grass and other untold luxuries.

The next day we began our preparations directly after breakfast, and the elder members of the party, with the accumulated wisdom of years, chartered a porter to carry their share of the baggage, but Hastings, with the muscles of Hercules and the imprudence of youth, loaded a huge bag, and, in addition, easily showed us the way to the foot of the rocks leading up to our proposed bivouac.

From this point a remarkable desire to enjoy the view became manifest, both in the party as a whole, and in its individual constituents. On the rare occasions when we were not all seated on a flat stone admiring the prospect in concert, four scattered wanderers might be seen leaning on their axes, wrapped in serene contemplation of the glories of a steep slope of screes. Progress was consequently slow, and it was not till 2.35 p.m. that we straggled on to a pleasant little grassy valley. As each member of the party reached this tiny oasis in the desert of stones, he might have been seen to gaze wearily at the steep moraine above and then, throwing himself on the ground, begin to pour forth, with most persuasive eloquence, a series of convincing reasons for camping at this particular spot.

There being no dissentients, the porter was promptly paid off, and the afternoon tea was put in train; we then proceeded at our leisure to contemplate the formidable summit we were to attack. Seated in the shadow of a great rock, we examined it with the telescope, and came to the conclusion that it would be won if we could only reach the eastern ridge anywhere in the near neighbourhood of the summit. From a cleft in this ridge we could see there was a convenient crack or gully leading down to a great buttress that merged in the face of the mountain, about five hundred feet below the ridge. To the left of this was a considerable patch of snow, and it appeared to us that once on this snow, we should have a fair chance of success. Below this snow, however, the rock was, for a short distance, slabby and precipitous, and it seemed doubtful whether the ascent of this section could be effected. The optimists were confident that it could be done, but the pessimists were even more certain that we should be stopped. An alternative line was then suggested by Slingsby, who pointed out, that though the southern ridge of the peak concealed the western face, this face not only looked easy when seen from the Col du Géant, but had actually been climbed by parties seeking to make the ascent. So far then as this point, where the southern and western ridges join, an assured route was open to us. From thence it would, apparently, be easy to go down the southern ridge towards a remarkable rock tower, capped with a great stone which looked much like a three-cornered hat. Whether it would be possible to descend the face at any point on to the snow patch was not quite so certain, but the rocks looked distinctly more favourable than those below the snow patch, and there was, in addition, very much greater choice of route. The only objection to this line was the *détour* it involved, and the great extent of more or less difficult rock it would be necessary to traverse. It was, however, pointed out, that our main object was not an ascent, but a training walk, and it would, in consequence, be an advantage rather than otherwise to have a sufficient extent of rock on which to develop our muscles and burn out, what Professor Tyndall refers to, as the "effete matters" which English life lodges in the muscles. We were quite unable to resist the strength of these arguments, and decided in favour of the south-western face, the descent from the southern ridge to the snow patch, and the re-ascent to the eastern ridge.

Our next proceeding was to prospect for suitable holes to crawl into should the weather turn bad,

and for soft and dry grassy hollows, should it keep fine. We then made the tea, and enjoyed one of those sumptuous meals with which Hastings invariably treats his companions. It is needless to add that Slingsby and I once more gave the party a graphic description of the Aiguille du Plan, and the joy which its ice slopes afford the faithful.*
Meanwhile the sun " toward heaven's descent had sloped his westering wheel," and the cold breeze of evening suggested sleeping-bags, so we each retired to the lair of our choice, and, pitying the poor wretches cramped in stuffy inns, we were soon sleeping the sleep of the just.

About two o'clock Hastings stirred me out of a refreshing slumber, and we then set up a series of howls to wake Slingsby and Collie, who were concealed in certain remote and invisible hollows. At length they emerged from the gloom and, wrapped in our sleeping bags, we sought to eat our breakfast. But breakfast at 2.30 a.m. when you are totally out of condition, is not a successful meal. It requires much careful training before the stage is reached, when at that hour of the morning, you can eat three questionable eggs *and enjoy them.* While drinking our hot tea, Slingsby and I gave our companions further interesting details of the Plan, Collie now and

---

* This scramble has been described by Mr. Ellis Carr, one of the party, in a paper entitled " Two Days on an Ice Slope," *Alpine Journal*, vol. xvi., p. 422, *et seq*.

again breaking in with an unanswerable demonstration of the inferiority of the Alps, for climbing purposes, to Skye and other Scotch districts.

At 3.10 a.m. we started up the moraine, led by Collie, who had prospected this part of the route on the previous afternoon. We then crossed a level tongue of glacier to the foot of the steeper slopes. Here we found the ice just as steep as it was possible to walk on without cutting steps. More than once, I expected to effect an involuntary glissade to the bottom; but as the rest of the party seemed to be thoroughly enjoying themselves, I concealed my difficulties and pretended that I liked it. We then reached more level ice, and had the choice of either going to the left on to the open glacier, or keeping to the right along an apparently easy valley between it and the rocks of our peak. Unluckily I led off by the apparently easy valley, and soon found it would not do; it appeared, however, possible to cut up a sérac and reach the glacier, and thus avoid actually retracing our steps. The sérac proved long and hard, and both Hastings and I had a try at it before we succeeded in cutting our way to the top. The top proved to be merely a peninsula of ice with crevasses on three sides and a perpendicular wall from twenty to twenty-five feet high on the other. The lowest and only vulnerable part of this wall was at the left corner and immediately over a large and nerve-shattering crevasse.

Slingsby cut himself a step and made himself firm, and I essayed to ascend; but want of training made itself felt, and I suffered from the ridiculous idea that a slip would pull Slingsby out of his hold. Retreating for a moment, Collie was added to the anchor; then Hastings, firmly planted at the corner, gave me a lift, and after a short struggle the top was won. So soon as the next man was up, I unroped and went off to see whether we could reach practicable glacier. This proved perfectly easy, and a weary climber was soon reposing on the snow, offering devout and most heartfelt prayers that the progress of his companions might be slow. Not merely was a gratifying response to these aspirations vouchsafed, but on the arrival of my companions they promptly sat down, as if it were the most natural and proper thing for enthusiastic climbers at 5.30 a.m. to indulge in a protracted halt. Shame at length drove us on to our feet and we laboured solemnly up the slopes, each member of the party exhibiting a most pleasing and touching modesty in the matter of leading.

At 6.10 a.m. we struck the rock. I injudiciously jammed myself in a chimney, and had the pleasure of seeing the rest of the party, led by Collie, going up slightly to the left with ease and cheerfulness. Having extricated myself from the chimney I followed, and discovered the rest of the party. They said they were waiting for me, but the *abandon* of their attitudes suggested that this was not the whole truth. Seeing some signs of movement, I suggested lunch. Applause greeted this brilliant idea, and we all solemnly pretended to eat. At length we repacked the knapsack and climbed up for another half-hour, when we came to a little pile of meat tins. We promptly decided that as it was obviously the custom to lunch at this point it would savour of radical, not to say of anarchical doctrines, to break a rule evidently hallowed by time. We once more solemnly sat down and consumed ginger, chocolate, and similar light refreshment. By these and other devices we succeeded in bringing the pace down to a point that agreed with our lack of training, and it was not till 8.50 a.m. that we reached the ridge.

A steep chimney, partly blocked by a big stone at the top, had to be attacked next. We put on the rope, and Hastings shoved me up as far as he could reach. The big stone, however, appeared to be loose, and was otherwise unpleasant to climb over, so I sought to squeeze in between it and the rock. The space proved insufficient, and I had to retreat and take off my coat, after which it was just possible to get through. The coat was then stowed away in a secure hole and left till we should return.

A short distance further we reached the crest of the south ridge at the point where it joins the main ridge of the mountain. Immediately in front rose a perpendicular tower, and, directly behind it, but apparently cut off by a smooth step in the ridge, was the summit. The south face of the tower had been rent by frost into three great blocks one above the other. On the second of these dangled an end of rope, lashed round a more or less insecure stone, and it obviously denoted the high-water mark of previous attempts. It appeared barely possible to reach this rope by climbing a crack on the face in front of us, but the better plan was, presumably, to traverse into the gully between the perpendicular tower and the final peak. This latter, we subsequently learnt, was the line taken by Mr. Morse's party in their various attempts on the peak.

On consultation, however, we agreed that the final peak was probably inaccessible on this side, even if the tower could be climbed, and we were also inclined to think that the end of rope hanging down the rock suggested that the inside of the gully was a less convenient staircase than weary climbers might desire. Slingsby judiciously settled the discussion by leading along the southern ridge towards the "hat." This proved perfectly easy, and at the point noticed the previous afternoon he swung round to the left and led towards the snow patch. In a few minutes we were pulled up by a cliff, faced for the most part with a frost-riven veneer, so near falling that a very slight pull sufficed to detach very considerable quantities of *débris*. From this point of view our chances looked desperate. The crack we had seen overnight appeared precipitous, and it did not even look possible to get into it, the cliffs between us and it consisting of smooth and outward shelving slabs. After some consultation, in which Slingsby still held to the favourable opinion formed overnight, it was decided that I should be steadied down by the whole of our light rope (200 feet) and spy out the land on the further side of the snow patch.

The descent proved very much easier than I had anticipated, though the fact that no single hold could be trusted, even in those places where anything worthy of the name of "hold" was to be found, made me extremely glad of the moral support afforded by the rope. Immediately above the snow I found an easy and convenient traverse on the rock, leading across to the top of the buttress of which mention has previously been made.

From this point the opinion formed the proceeding day was seen to be amply justified; easy rocks led into the crack, and it appeared, though difficult, to be well within the limits of the possible. Shouting to my companions to hurry up, or rather down—an injunction they certainly did not obey—I selected a suitable hollow between two rocks and proceeded to indulge in a doze. My dreams were, however, somewhat frequently interrupted by shouts for directions from the next man. Some considerable time was then taken in finding a rock to which the rope could be fixed for the aid and comfort of the last man, and altogether at least an hour and a half were expended on this two hundred feet of cliff. Whilst Slingsby and Collie were tying the lower end of the fixed rope to a suitable stone, so that we might be sure of finding it on our way back, Hastings and I started up the easy rocks into the crack. We soon found this latter was not all that could be desired, and we again put on the rope. Our companions quickly caught us up, and we then began the attack in earnest.

The first serious obstruction was formed by a smooth slab quite destitute of hold except for a perpendicular crack between it and the precipitous wall on our right. This crack was in parts too narrow to admit one's fingers, and at no point did it afford really satisfactory hold. Hastings gave me the usual lift, followed by a shove, but owing to the extreme steepness of the slab it was a matter of some difficulty to keep oneself from toppling outwards. Unfortunately the utmost limit at which he could help me was still some six feet from the top, and it became evident that a very serious struggle would have to be made. Moreover, it was impossible to tell whether hold would be found at the top of the slab. Unless there was such hold nothing could be done, for a second perpendicular rock rose immediately above it, and the outward sloping ledge on to which it was necessary to climb was not more than eighteen inches wide. Hastings, with extraordinary daring and skill, managed to follow me up a yard or so, and gave a most welcome push to my feet with an ice-axe : so aided, I got a hand on to the ledge, and at its extreme upper limit found a deep and most satisfying crack ; even with its aid getting one's feet on to the ledge and subsequently abandoning the crack, and reassuming an upright attitude, was not wholly easy.

We then encountered the usual sort of chimney work, steep corners, occasionally wet rock, and a general tendency in everything to slope outwards with overhanging edges. At more than one place Hastings had to propel the leading man upwards for some eight or nine feet, but beyond trifles of this sort, which appeared to that same leading man a most convenient and restful method of getting up a hill, we met with no very serious obstacle. About 11.30 a.m. we reached the window in the eastern ridge and were within a short distance of the summit.

On our right a bold pinnacle cut off the view; on the left a knife-edge of granite rose steeply for some fifteen feet and then abutted against a square tower. Taken as a whole it looked very formidable, and we all agreed that a halt was desirable. It soon, however, became obvious that life is not worth living if you have to sit on a rock sloping outwards at an angle of forty-five degrees, retaining your position by clinging to inconveniently placed knobs; nor are matters materially improved if you exchange that position for one in which you sit astride in a V shaped gap. These discomforts speedily brought us to the conclusion that we had no time to lose and had better see what could be done with the sharp ridge and the tower beyond.

The ridge proved easier than we had expected. With the fingers on one side and the palms of the hand on the other, and the grip that could be obtained by holding it between the knees, progress, if not exactly elegant, was fairly easy so far as the foot of the tower. Beyond this a bit of very awkward scrambling was necessary. Supported exclusively by the grip of the fingers on the by no means horizontal knife-edge, the right leg had to be stretched, till, at its utmost reach, a small outward sloping shelf afforded some sort of support for the foot. The right hand had then to leave its hold on this edge and, at its longest stretch, grope along a very inferior perpendicular wrinkle in the tower. When the most desirable point of this wrinkle had been found, the knife-edge, the only reliable grip within reach, had to be definitely abandoned and the weight swung over on to the right foot. The whole proceeding was of much delicacy, for the foothold was so precarious that any miscalculation in balance would have inevitably involved a slip. The cliff immediately below is remarkably precipitous even for the Chamonix Aiguilles, and I hardly like to say how many thousand feet the scientist of the party declared it to be.

The next stage did not appear very much easier. The aforementioned wrinkle, with one or two other similar rugosities, afforded the only means of support. Clutching them between my fingers and thumb, and scraping my feet downwards on the rough granite, I succeeded in getting sufficient propelling power to work up inch by inch. Fortunately the rock was pleasantly warm, and Hastings ever shouted out most comforting assurances; so, little by little, the difficulties yielded and a gasping climber at length reached the square-cut top of the tower.

The rest of the party quickly followed, and we again indulged in a quiet bask. Starting once more, we were soon confronted by a profusion of that sort of split rock which is known to *habitués* of the Montenvers as a "letter-box." In the present instance the postal arrangements were represented by three of these boxes; that to the left being the most formidable and that to the right the easiest. I made a preliminary survey of the middle one as it did not appear wholly certain that that on the right led to the ridge above. However, it proved distinctly difficult, and the

Nestor of the party advised a preliminary investigation of the easy one on the right. Having ascended it, I found a long stride round a nasty corner placed me in the upper section of the central box, and from this point there was no serious difficulty in climbing once more to the ridge.

Immediately in front rose the final tower. It was obviously impregnable to direct assault, and, at first glance, it looked as if we were to be defeated within twenty feet of the summit. A second glance, however, disclosed a detached flake on the left that seemed to offer distinct chances of success, and, as we advanced to the attack, an easy and convenient route on the right was unfolded to our delighted eyes. This latter led up the edge of a great rent-off flake, from the top of which the edge of a second, steeper and sharper flake, gave access to the summit. It was only ascended at the cost of some damage to our fingers and nether garments, but the nearness of the summit made us callous to the minor ills of life, and a few minutes later we were shouting ourselves hoarse on the highest point.

Though we had left the provisions behind, Hastings turned out of his pockets the materials for a sumptuous repast, and we feasted on a great variety of dainties. One half of the party then proceeded to indulge in the sweet pleasure of tobacco, and the other half went perilously near sound and solid slumber. Having refreshed ourselves by these judicious methods, we constructed a cairn of the few stones that were available, and we then, feeling our labours were completed, gazed on the great peaks and rejoiced in the glorious mass of light reflected from the vast fields of snow which surrounded us on all sides.

Owing to the fact that we had distributed our ice-axes, knapsacks, spare rope, &c., on sundry and various rocks throughout the line of ascent, it was essential that we should return the same way, otherwise we should have been tempted to make a short cut to the point where the main and south ridges meet. The top of the great tower was, we could see, easily accessible, and, even if the gully between it and the mass of the mountain should prove impracticable, a "piton" and the rope would easily have solved that difficulty. Unluckily we could not abandon our various baggage, and we were, in consequence, bound to follow the route we had taken in ascending.

At 2.20 p.m. we left the peak and were soon on the top of the tower above the window. Hastings promptly produced a "piton," which we drove into a suitable crack to help the last man down. The window being regained, we took a farewell glance at the ridge and started down the gully. At the first bad pitch we carefully hitched the rope, and I was delighted to find the ease with which it could be descended. My delight, however, was somewhat modified when, after ten minutes spent in endeavouring to loosen the rope, I had to go up again to unhitch it. This procedure struck us as both fatiguing and likely, if repeated, to prove injurious to our tempers, so, on reaching the second mauvais pas, Hastings was once more utilised as a ladder, and the rocks descended by the simple methods of my youth.

We reached the snow patch at 4.5 p.m., and, to save time, we determined to go up on one rope and trust to luck and such shelter as the cliff afforded, to escape the stones certain to be sent down. I was happily accorded the post of leader. I say happily, because, where stones are concerned, I fully concur with the Biblical maxim that it is "more blessed to give than to receive." My liberality on this occasion was great, but, as frequently happens, this generosity did not evoke those feelings of enduring affection that were desired. I must, however, except Collie, who, as last man, not only enjoyed the missiles I sent down, but had in addition those scattered by the rest of the party; so far as I could judge, he thoroughly enjoyed dodging them, and when not so engaged, watched our proceedings with calm and benignant composure from loose and inconvenient ledges.

Regaining the southern ridge at 5.5 p.m., we raced along it to its point of junction with the main ridge, and, supported by Hastings, I slid through the hole and regained my coat, which the chill of evening made extremely welcome. We then opened the knapsacks and had a short halt. We re-roped with Slingsby as last man, and soon found that the snow was in such a sloppy state that the utmost care would be needful. Our hopes of "rattling down to the glacier" were consequently dashed to the ground, and it was not till 6.25 p.m. that we reached the Bergschrund.

Slingsby got well over, but as Hastings followed, the rickety sérac gave a groan and a shiver and a great mass fell from it into the depths below. Happily it quieted down after this little exhibition of ill-humour, and we were able to follow on to the glacier. The crevasses proved very badly bridged, and we were constantly forced to quit our morning's track to find a more secure route. Night came on apace, and the suspicion began to float across my mind that we were in for an impromptu bivouac on the snow. Slingsby, however, rose to the occasion; quitting our route of the morning which would have taken us down a long slope of ice on which snow, varying from three to nine inches in thickness, was lying, and which, in its present sloppy condition, would have involved grave danger, he struck boldly to the right, and unravelled a complex series of obstructions as readily as an ordinary mortal would have done in broad daylight. But he was, at length, pulled up by a perpendicular cliff, which apparently constituted the edge of the world and overhung space. There is something strangely impressive in gazing over a great ice wall into inky darkness and absolute silence. The sense of boundless depth and utter mystery seems to pervade one's whole being. The utmost light of our lantern failed in any way to pierce the gloom, and despondency was settling down on us, and we were making up our minds to a night on the snow, when a rift in the clouds let a glint of moonlight fall on the glacier and the existence of firm land, or rather glacier, was disclosed some fifty feet below, accessible by a sort of peninsula of ice. The moon having done us this good turn, very unkindly extinguished itself again and left Slingsby the pleasant task of cutting along a nearly perpendicular face of névé with an extremely wide crevasse underneath, aided only by such light as a folding lantern emits. Our leader, however, appeared to thoroughly enjoy the business, the chipping gradually got more remote, and one after another my companions disappeared over the edge into the darkness. At last it became my painful duty to follow. Cheery voices out of the gloom told me that it was perfectly easy, but on this point I most emphatically disagree. The large coal-scuttle-like steps which I was assured existed in profusion, appeared to me mere scratches in loose and rotten snow, while the highly extolled hand-holds broke away at the least strain and served no useful purpose, other than filling my pockets with their broken *débris*. However, I managed to reach a place where Collie on the other side of a crevasse, armed with an abnormally long ice-axe, could just manage to skewer me with its point, and in this painful and undignified way I was landed, in a snowy and damp condition, on a small ridge of ice between two deep crevasses.

Slingsby meanwhile had once more started off into the darkness along a narrow edge of ice with profound chasms on either hand. After we had followed and made a few more dodges round various obstructions, a short glissade put us on the more level glacier, and we began to rejoice in the sure and certain hope of sleeping bags and hot soup.

The combined memories of Slingsby and Collie took us off the open glacier on to the little moraine at exactly the right spot, and we avoided all the difficulties we had encountered about here in the morning. Feeling our work was nearly over, we halted a few minutes and tried to make out where we were to go next. To our right we could see great looming séracs, to the left was an ice slope plunging precipitously into utter night. By the process of exclusion we decided, therefore, that our way must be straight ahead, and, as we remembered that the ice tongue had been very steep, even by daylight, we utilised our halt by putting some long spikes into our boots.

On attempting to descend we found the ice rapidly steepened, and some of the party protested that it was not the way we had come up. Slingsby then unroped and demonstrated that there was no possibility of going farther in that direction.

We next crossed a little crevasse to our right, but soon scrambled back again appalled by the great towering séracs, séracs that we were all prepared to swear had never been passed in the morning. Slingsby, however, still unroped, again prospected amongst them, and this time shouted to us to follow. Promptly the great looming séracs were seen to be mainly fictions of the darkness, and were reduced to mere hummocks of ice, and the yawning chasms to water channels or streaks of sand-covered glacier!

Thanks to our screw spikes we descended the ice tongue with tolerable ease, reached the level glacier and tumbled helter-skelter back to the gîte, regaining our camp at 11.45 p.m.

Here Hastings and I, realising the discomfort of packing by lantern light, and the advantage of getting some one else to carry our luggage, made various deceitful remarks about the delights of sleeping bags. So entrancing was the picture we drew that Collie declared his intention of not going further, and Slingsby was brought to the same state of mind by my generously offering him the loan of my sleeping bag for use as a mattress. Having in this ingenious way got rid of the necessity of carrying my bag, I felt equal to the descent to the Montenvers, and Hastings having with equal kindness presented his bag to Collie, we started down the stones, screes, and waterfalls that lead to the glacier. Wishing to avoid the necessity for jumping innumerable crevasses, I suggested going down the Chamonix guides' route to the séracs of the Géant. The previous year had descended it without jumping a single crevasse, and both Hastings and I agreed that this was well worth half an hour's *détour*. Alas, on reaching the point where in 1892 an unbroken causeway led between the Tacul system of crevasses on the one hand and the Trélaporte system on the other, we found that the two systems had joined hands, and the next hour and a half were expended in jumping and dodging and running across knife-edges, so that our arrival at the Montenvers was only effected at 4.30 a.m. The door was shut, but the smoking-room window was open, and having accomplished that well-known problem we filled our pockets with biscuits and retired to our respective rooms.

Mont Blanc and the Aiguille du Plan

CHAPTER VIII.

AIGUILLE DU PLAN.

My first acquaintance with the Aiguille du Plan was made in company with Messrs. Cecil Slingsby and Ellis Carr, during two memorable days in 1892. On that occasion an evil fate drove us back beaten, battered, and hungry; and as we slunk wearily homewards, the huge séracs poised above the first wall of cliff, seemed in the uncertain light of dusk to be grinning and pointing the finger of scorn at our tattered and woebegone appearance. None the less, baffled and bruised as we were, Slingsby was strongly of the opinion that "we'n powler't up an' down a bit an' had a rattlin' day," or rather two days, and averred with enthusiasm that it was the finest ice-climb he had ever had the luck to be on.

I can still shut my eyes and see Carr toiling like a giant at the endless slopes of ice, and can still feel the blank chill that shivered through us when night chased the last lingering streaks of daylight from the slopes. The songs still ring in my ears

with which he sought to keep us merry and awake
through the icy hours, as we sat huddled on a
tiny ledge. And when, despite all efforts, sleep
stealthily approached, Slingsby's strong arm wrapping round me and holding me on to my narrow
perch—there was naught between my back and
Chamonix, eight thousand feet below—still seems
a sure defence from peril. It was not, doubtless,
unalloyed pleasure, yet in after years the memory
of trusty comrades who, when in evil plight,

> " . . . ever with a frolic welcome took
> The thunder and the sunshine, and opposed
> Free hearts, free foreheads . . ."

is an enduring gain which enters into one's life,
and which may, perchance, even dull the edge of
sorrow in those long nights when the platitudes
of the lowlands seem but dust and ashes.

Amid the flicker of the winter fire I can still see
the swing of Slingsby's axe, as, through the day
that followed, he hewed our way ever downwards
towards the sun-lit pastures where cow-bells
tinkle and where merry brooklets ripple amongst
the stones, towards friends for whose glad welcome
our very souls were pining. I can still hear him
saying, as we scrambled over the " bad bit "* at

---

* About fifteen feet at the head of this couloir actually overhangs. The ice has, in fact, been formed by water dripping
from the slopes above, and it has frozen into a sort of bulging
cornice. Happily this overhanging formation has caused the

the head of the long couloir—a more than perpendicular wall of ice, as ugly a place as aught ere chronicled in Alpine history—" It certainly is a glorious climb." And I can still listen to the joyful jodels and shouts, the popping of champagne corks and the riot of tumultuous pleasure with which our friends received us at the Montenvers Hotel. But these are memories amongst which I must not dally. A more skilful pen has recorded the various details, and as a wholly undue meed of praise has been allotted to me, it would be the rankest folly on my part to dispel the pleasing myths that Carr has woven round my deeds. I therefore pass over twelve months, more or less, of inglorious ease to a day when Slingsby, Hastings, Collie, and myself were once more making ready for the assault.

On the morning of the 6th of August, 1893, we sent two porters up to our Grépon gîte, charged with the labour of bringing down the tent, sleeping bags, and other belongings, left there after an ascent of that peak. We bid them, on their descent, go to the extreme left moraine of the Blaitière glacier—as the glacier that descends almost exclusively from the Plan is most confusingly called—and wait for our arrival. Meanwhile, in company with a large party of friends,

---

water to freeze in a more or less hollow fashion, so that here and there good hold may be obtained by thrusting the hand into a hollow cavity.

we strolled to the woods beyond Blaitière dessus, and had a festive lunch in the shadow of some great pines. We had an exciting time trying to boil soup in a flat dish, and at the critical moment the united skill of Hastings and myself sufficed to empty the precious fluid into the fire. Hastings, however, accomplished a veritable triumph in bacon frying, and Collie provided us with most

GOATS.

excellent tea. Under its soothing influence I slowly recovered that equanimity of mind which the disastrous loss of the soup had temporarily upset.

Having said good-bye to our friends, we made our way towards La Tapiaz, collecting on the way great bundles of sticks and branches for our camp fire. Slingsby and Collie then led us to a delightful little grassy hollow, evidently the bed of some ancient tarn, where, sheltered from all the winds that blow, we could pitch our tent and make ourselves thoroughly comfortable. We soon spied the porters high above us on the moraine, and in response to our shouts and signals they began to descend towards us. The younger members of the party being left to get the camp ready, Slingsby and I started off to inspect the peak. We met and passed the porters, but were soon disturbed by the horrid fear that they might miss our tiny hollow, so Slingsby, as usual, sacrificed himself and went back to see that our luggage did not stray. The way to the Glacier des Pèlerins was very much longer than I had anticipated, and even when I got there the face of the Plan was veiled in cloud. There seemed, however, a chance of rifts and rents in the barrier, so, making my way to a great boulder close under the lower slopes of the Midi, I laid down at my ease and watched the eddies and gusts of wind ever wreathing and swaying the clinging folds of vapour. My patience was rewarded; from time to time sections of the cliffs were disclosed, and it became evident that a way to the summit could certainly be found by keeping well to the right of the peak, and striking the ridge that falls away from it towards the col. This was not, however, the route we wished to attempt. Our first "*objectif*" was to be the

THE BLAITIÈRE AND PLAN.

snow col on the left of the peak, and perhaps a thousand feet below it.* This col is shut in on the Chamonix side by the precipitous Aiguille in which the great northern buttress of the Plan culminates. It is an obtrusively visible notch, and may be seen from the stone man on the Little Charmoz ridge just above the Montenvers, or even from the Chapeau, though of course when seen from these points of view it is on the right of the summit. Once arrived on this col we should reach the precipitous little Glacier du Plan, on which during the preceding year we had exerted much fruitless labour. At the point, however, at which we were now aiming, we should be above the great ice walls and threatening séracs, and fairly certain of being able to force our way to the summit. The way to this col lay up a long gully, which formed a sort of line of demarcation between the great northern buttress and the main mass of the mountain. Unluckily the mists obstinately clung to this gully, and after waiting two hours the lengthening shadows suggested the propriety of an immediate retreat. I got back to camp

* The col for which we were aiming is that to the left of the great rocky tooth, and is about 1¼ inches from the right side of the illustration opposite. The highest point of the Plan is concealed by the great tower, which is 1¾ inches from the same edge. It is very materially higher than the Blaitière, but owing to its greater distance is wholly dwarfed by it. Mr. Holmes's photograph is taken from the Little Charmoz ridge.

just as the twilight was deepening into the gloom of night, and found a blazing fire and hot soup, and a scene more strange and picturesque than ever delights the eye of the modern hut dweller.

Hastings and Collie had unearthed a ruined châlet and out of its *débris* had built a drain-like construction, which, skilfully roofed with the ground sheet of the tent, they averred would make splendid sleeping quarters. Slingsby and I, with our usual magnanimity, expressed our willingness to put up with the inferior accommodation of the tent. From various remarks at breakfast the next morning—or ought I to say the same night?—I inferred that our generosity had not been without its reward.

We started at 1.45 a.m. The sky was cloudless, and the stars shone with that steady light which is the surest sign of perfect weather. We picked our way along the slopes, skilfully led by Collie and Slingsby, till we reached an old moraine. Following this to its extreme head, at 3 a.m. we traversed on to the glacier just above the point where it makes a more or less unsuccessful attempt at an ice fall. In order to inspect our intended line of ascent, we bore to the right on to the open glacier, and then sat down to wait for sufficient light to see whether the unknown couloir was likely to give us passage. The great circle of cliffs rising for nearly four thousand feet above the glacier looked in the dim light of dawn extremely forbidding. Indeed there are few glaciers in the Alps walled in by so mighty and precipitous a rampart. After sitting in a filled-up crevasse for ten minutes, we found the breeze so excessively cold that without more ado we picked up our sacks and moved on towards the base of the couloir. The glacier soon steepened, but the thin layer of snow still lying on the ice sufficed to give us footing, and was so well frozen that the thinnest and most absurdly fragile bridges could be utilised for our progress. Higher up, however, this thin coating of snow ceased. Slingsby, with the cunning of an old climber, kept away to the left, where, under the shelter of the great buttress, streaks of snow were still intact. The rest of the party boldly marched up the glacier and were soon reduced to using the axe. Patience and hard work at length brought us to some rocks on the right of the entrance to the couloir, where Slingsby was waiting for us. Working to the right over glacier-polished and ice-glazed slabs, we reached an awkward, outward-shelving, ice-encumbered ledge, over which a tiny stream from the cliffs above was trickling.

Having with some difficulty packed ourselves away in secure nooks we proceeded to eat, drink, and be merry. After a halt of twenty minutes we started (5.25 a.m.) once more, keeping almost horizontally across the cliffs to our right, a broad and easy ledge affording an obvious and most tempting pathway. Traversing a short distance, we came to a fault in the cliffs leading almost straight up. The ascent of this was easy and rapid, and it was followed by other ledges and gullies that rejoiced the hearts of men, who, on the other side of this great wall, had been compelled to earn each foot of progress by hewing steps in hardest ice. Gradually, however, the ledges and gullies so dwindled in size that we were glad to take refuge in the couloir and advance, relying on the axe. The snow had been melted and refrozen so often, that it required almost as much effort to cut steps as in ice itself, and we began to look about for some means of escaping this labour. On the other side of the couloir the rocks were obviously practicable, and we made a determined effort to reach them. Down the centre of the snow, however, falling stones, ice, and water had cut a deep groove, the trough of which was ice and the sides deeply undercut. After many efforts, I managed to get into it and cut steps across to the further side, but there the snow wall proved too much for me. It was as hard and intractable as ice on the surface, yet no sooner was the surface cut away than soft snow was reached, affording no reliable hold for the fingers. As moreover the groove was obviously and obtrusively the channel down which the mountain shot all its rubbish, it did not appear desirable that two of us should be in it at the same time, a circumstance which precluded the help of a shoulder and a good shove. We decided at length that the rocks opposite were not worth the effort, and I scrambled back on to the open surface of the couloir.

Our next hope of escape from interminable step-cutting lay in a gully that opened into the couloir about 250 feet above. On reaching its base, however, we found that it was ice glazed, precipitous, and led to huge unbroken slabs. Some distance further ahead we descried more broken rocks, and, even before reaching them, were rejoiced by finding hold for our right hands on the rock-wall, and an occasional step between it and the slope (where the heat of the rocks had melted the snow in contact with it) that could be relied on to anchor the party. Reaching the more broken rocks we struck on to them, but were soon pulled up by a bare slab some twelve feet high. The only possibility o ascent was afforded by a small and inferior knob of rock that could be just reached by the fingers of the left hand, but which was so nearly out of reach that it was well nigh impossible to test its security. Twice I essayed to go up, and on each occasion my courage failed me; but an endeavour to find an alternative line proving fruitless, a last and more determined effort bridged the difficulty and landed us on easy rocks.

In order to avoid getting stranded on the huge slabs of which the face of the mountain here consists, we kept to the left on a sort of shelf of the couloir; further to our left was a still lower groove filled with ice and evidently the main channel for falling stones. Happily the slabs forming our shelf were separated from the great wall of rock closing in the couloir on our right by a narrow and almost continuous crack, just wide enough to admit the fingers. Aided by this crack we progressed steadily, though an occasional " bad pitch " proved impracticable till the Hercules of the party had lifted the first man over the obstruction. The angle of the shelf increased steadily, and the frequency and length of the bad pitches increased in like ratio till it became an almost perpendicular wall. As this coincided with such a reduction in the width of the friendly crack that fingers could no longer be inserted into it, we were brought to a stand.

It was now evident that we must get into the lowest compartment of the couloir and cut our way up the ice, but the traverse of the shelf towards this compartment was a problem of grave difficulty. Once away from the friendly crack, there was no hold of any reliable sort. Hastings, with much wisdom, suggested driving a piton into the crack as high above us as possible, so that, by passing the rope through it, the leading man might be secured from danger and enabled to take liberties that otherwise could not be thought of. Hastings, despite his extremely poor footing, with great skill and strength hoisted me on to his shoulders, and, from this aerial point of vantage, I whacked the piton into the crack with an ice-axe. Before the rope could be slipped through the ring it was, of course, necessary to untie, a process always of much difficulty, and especially so when only one hand can be spared for the work. These various operations must have lasted well nigh five minutes, and it was with a sigh of relief that Hastings lifted me gingerly down to the rock and tenderly rubbed those portions of his body that had been abraded by my boot nails.

We then found that the rope would not run in the piton, so, once more, the living pyramid had to be constructed and a noose of rope tied through the piton ring, in which our rope could run freely. After these arduous labours the traverse of the slab was effected with unexpected ease; though, possibly, in the absence of the protection afforded by the rope above, the hold attainable would have seemed perilously small. Reaching the edge of the gully, it was happily possible to just touch the opposite wall with an ice-axe, and this support enabled me to kick an inferior step in some hard-frozen snow still lying against the rock. From this footing I managed to cut a step in the ice itself, and the traverse into the couloir was accomplished.

The ascent of the ice gully was not wholly enjoyable; there was no possibility of escape should stones or other missiles see fit to fall, and the angle of the ice rapidly steepened till it verged on the perpendicular. This excessively steep part of the gully did not exceed ten or twelve feet in height, and, once above it, a slope of fifty degrees led upwards towards practicable rocks. Before, however, sufficient rope could be paid out to enable me to reach them, it was necessary that the rest of the party should advance. Unluckily, though good footing on firm rock, well sheltered from falling stones, was easily accessible on the right, it was impossible to reach it without cutting away the fringes and sheets of ice masking certain intervening slabs. To do this would have involved the rest of the party, who were immediately underneath and sixty or seventy feet below, in serious danger. For ice of this sort is extremely apt to flake away in large plate-like masses, and the cliff below being practically perpendicular, these masses would have alit with resistless force on Slingsby and Collie, who were exactly in the line of fire. Indeed, the tiny fragments of ice hewn out of the solid slope above the traverse called forth many remarks of a deprecatory character. From subsequent discussion it appears that whilst to those below these fragments appeared, each and all, larger than an average sérac falling with a velocity considerably greater than that which astronomers ascribe to light; to those above they seemed comparable to finest grains of sand drifting on the wings of softest breezes.

So soon as Hastings had come up, and was settled squarely in the big step, I began cutting once more, but was soon brought to a halt by volleys of abuse; amongst which I seemed to detect a term used in the tennis court to define the score of forty all. The rest of the party having reached the upper slope, a way was soon cut to the rocks. Above, the cliff rose in a steep and threatening precipice, but it was seamed with a series of deep cracks, and we decided that one or other of these would be almost certain to afford a practicable route.

We selected for our first effort the deepest and blackest of the group. At the outset this gully proved more formidable than we had expected. The walls were rather too wide for the wedging method of ascent, and the scarcity of hold made it extremely difficult to effect any advance. By the aid of Hastings's head and ice-axe, it was possible to reach a considerable height in the innermost recesses of the gully, but further direct progress was barred by overhanging rock, and it was essential to traverse outwards on the left wall of the cliff to a broad step which seemed a suitable basis for further operations. The traverse was undoubtedly practicable if this step afforded any crack or grip sufficient to enable a man, not merely to haul himself up to it, but to scramble on to it; a performance by no means always easy when the shelf is merely a narrow ledge with smooth precipitous cliff above it. After much examination, however, the attempt was made, and an excellent crack of most convenient and soul-satisfying dimensions was discovered exactly in the right place. To the left, easy rocks led upwards for a short distance, when we were forced into a gully and were soon pulled up by a number of great plate-like stones that were jammed side by side, forming a sort of protecting roof. Outwards, and up, and over this roof it was necessary to climb, and, to gain the requisite energy, we halted and were regaled by Hastings with ginger, biscuits, chocolate, and the other luxuries with which his pockets are invariably filled.

This difficulty appeared worse in prospect than in actual fact it proved to be, and beyond the mental discomfort induced by hanging on to doubtfully secure stones, and climbing outwards over a very high cliff in a semi-horizontal position—much indeed as a fly walks along the ceiling—the obstruction was passed without difficulty. Above them, the way to the col was obvious. Merely a short slope of ice intervened between us and that wished-for haven. On the other side the view was most dramatic. The cliff immediately below actually overhangs. The huge pinnacle to which reference has frequently been made, as shutting in this col on its northern side, towers upwards in smooth precipitous slabs that recall the relentless cruelty of the great precipice on the Little Dru;

and on the other side great ice cliffs dominate as wild and vast a wall of rock as the climber often sees. A wall which, sweeping round through well nigh 180 degrees, forms one of the sternest cirques the Alps can boast, and which, with its overhanging séracs, vast cornices and black, ice-filled couloirs, recalls some of the more savage recesses of the Caucasus.

We stormed the short wall still intervening, broke through a thin crest of snow, and shouted our welcome to the Blaitière, the Charmoz, and the Grépon. We had reached the upper slopes of the little glacier on which Carr, Slingsby, and myself had spent such weary hours the preceding year. Now, however, we were above the series of ice walls, and could delight our eyes by studying the graceful curves with which the snows swept over towards the cliff. Immediately opposite were the gaunt crags we had tried to scale, and we recognised, with a feeling akin to pain, that from our furthest point the ridge could have been reached, in two or three hours at most, and the summit won. Our present position was, however, far more favourable. The little glacier—cut off from the rocks opposite by an appalling couloir of bare ice, in which no living being could cut or hew a pathway—led upwards in wind-moulded bends and sweeps, and though steep enough to require the use of the axe, afforded no serious obstacle to our progress.

At 12.5 p.m., after a short halt, we started once more and found that ten hours of hard work had begun to make itself felt, and our pace was reduced to most sober and decorous limits. Half way up, a great Schrund barred our advance. Its overhanging lip, twenty feet above our heads, looked as if it would force us to descend a long distance, even if it did not stop us altogether. The idea of descending is always extremely distasteful to weary men, so we turned to our left to see whether anything could be done at the point where the little glacier curls over towards the huge ice couloir. Happily, a few feet before reaching the ice cliff, the upper lip drooped till it was not more than twelve feet above the lower. Collie was packed away into the inner recesses of the Schrund, where he anchored himself in soft snow and made ready for all emergencies. Hastings and Slingsby then considerately made themselves into the base of a pyramid, and I was skilfully hoisted on to their shoulders. From this point of vantage it was possible to cut inferior nicks in the overhanging ice below the lip, and, after many efforts, a good reliable step on the ice slope above it. Climbing from Hastings's shoulders to this step was by no means easy, and Collie was warned to look out for squalls. The lip so overhung that a man falling would have missed the Schrund altogether, and, if unchecked by the rope, would have started on a wild career down the steep slopes curving ever towards the huge ice couloir.

Just above the lip the ice was very steep, and it was not till seventy feet of rope had been paid out that such reliable footing could be cut, as would suffice to secure the next man's safety. Hastings was then hoisted up by the united efforts of Slingsby and Collie, and on his arrival at the big step I went on a short distance further, to a snow-filled crevasse in which was an admirable and pleasing seat. As, however, it was beyond the reach of our rope, a second lighter one had to be got out and to be tied to it. Slingsby came up next, and then the serious problem of Collie's ascent had to be tackled. So long as a man remained below to give a shoulder, the lip of the Schrund could be reached and the ascent effected in a reasonable manner, but the last man had, obviously, to be hauled up by main force. Unfortunately we were so far up the slope, and the projecting lip so deflected and cut off all sound, that we could not hear what Collie said. All we could do was to haul with one accord, but we soon found that our efforts ceased to have any effect. It appears that the rope unluckily failed to bring him to the steps, and jammed him under the lip a short distance to their right. Collie, however, proved equal to the emergency; finding that his head and shoulders refused to go over the lip, he stuck his feet against the ice and, forcing himself outwards against the rope, walked up the overhanging ice in a more or less horizontal position. This manœuvre brought him, feet uppermost, on to the slope, and it is needless to say caused both astonishment and mirth to the spectators. However, he soon resumed a more normal attitude and tracked up the slope to the little crevasse. As time began to press, and we were unroped, I started at once and began cutting the requisite steps to the ridge. A few hundred feet further, the slope eased slightly, and this laborious process was no longer necessary.

A huge cornice surmounted the ridge, overhanging the tremendous cliffs above the little Glacier d'Envers Blaitière. Well to its right I pursued my solitary way to the foot of the final tower. This is almost completely detached from the main ridge, being, in fact, the highest point of the secondary ridge lying at right angles to it. The south-eastern end of this secondary ridge culminates in the Dent du Requin. In consequence, the route we were following from the north-east brought us to the same, or almost the same, point as that which Mr. Eccles reached when making the first ascent by the south-western ridge. In either case one turns sharply to the south-east, and a few rock gullies and steep crags lead to the topmost pinnacle (2 p.m.).

We basked long on the warm rocks, and it was not till 3.30 p.m. that we turned to the descent.

The steep slopes leading towards the Glacier du Requin required care, as the snow was in that soft and watery condition which suggests avalanches. Hastings led us across the Bergschrund, and just as we were discussing the best line to take through the séracs, a chamois appeared. It dashed down the slopes in a wild and reckless fashion, keeping to the left towards the cliffs of the Dent du Requin. We were, as usual, the victims of old tradition, and thought we could not do better than follow its tracks. We soon had to take to the rocks, and scramble up and down slopes of screes, broken by short patches of steep rock. Ultimately we forced our way back on to the glacier by crossing a long and remarkably rotten sérac. It was a mere knife-edge, some eighty feet in length, exhibiting such a state of elderly decrepitude that we expected every moment the whole structure would collapse. However, it served our purpose, and a short glissade put us on to the track we had followed on our way to the Requin, a fortnight before. Though it was past 5 p.m., thanks to the endurance that two weeks' Alpine work stores in the muscles, we still hoped to reach the Montenvers. Returning from the Requin, we had consumed ten hours in gaining that home of the faithful, of which not more than one hour had been expended in voluntary halts. On this occasion, rather less than four hours sufficed to bring us to that welcome bower, and at 8.50 p.m. four hungry travellers were urging Monsieur Simond to provide a speedy and substantial dinner. Our entreaties, it is needless to say, received most cordial attention and numerous friends joined our party. In the early hours of morning, a warrior, contemplating doughty deeds, broke in on our revels. He had expected to find the dim light of a single dip candle and the dread solitude of a deserted room, but, to his astonishment, he beheld a numerous company, the illumination of many lamps, and the flitting to and fro of ministering angels—I mean waiters. For the moment he was utterly bewildered, and thought he had slept on throughout a whole day and just got up in time for the next *table d'hôte*. Finally we explained matters by inaccurately pointing out that we were dining in yesterday while he was just going to breakfast in to-morrow.

CHAPTER IX.

THE AIGUILLE VERTE—BY THE CHARPOUA GLACIER.

As Burgener and I were coming across the Col du Géant early in 1881 it appeared to us that the ascent of the Aiguille Verte might be effected by the south-western face; a convenient couloir leading right up to the western ridge of the mountain from the head of the Glacier de Charpoua. Burgener was, indeed, so struck with the possibilities of this route, that he could hardly believe such a promising line had not already been taken by some of the diligent searchers after new ascents. These fears were, I assured him, quite groundless, and on our arrival at Chamonix they were finally set at rest.

After a long discussion we decided to make a midnight start from the Montenvers, for I had not, at that early period, seen the folly of spending the hours of night in painful tumbles into holes and crevasses. Burgener with the wisdom of age, and skilled in the art of sleeping soundly at temperatures which would keep his Monsieur dancing a hornpipe all night, was in favour of a bivouac. He yielded, however, to the sound principle that "he who pays the piper has a right to call the tune."

During the afternoon of the 29th of July I walked up to the Montenvers, and at eleven o'clock the same night we got our ropes and provisions together and set out along Les Ponts. We lost a good deal of time coaxing our lantern, which refused to burn properly, and we subsequently entangled ourselves among the irritating crevasses by which the eastern side of the Mer de Glace is intersected. We then scrambled up the evil stones of the lateral moraine on to the slopes beneath the Glacier de Charpoua. Here Venetz had to acknowledge that he was unwell. I took his knapsack and he struggled on for about half an hour more. It was then perfectly plain that he would not be able to make the ascent, and it was consequently altogether useless to let him drag himself up the atrocious slopes of loose stones we were ascending. We held a council of war, and Venetz was submitted to searching inquiries as to the nature, source, and extent of his maladies, and these appearing to be limited to a sick headache and bad indigestion, we decided that he might safely be left to make his way home at daybreak.

Burgener was, however, doubtful whether we were sufficiently strong to make the ascent by ourselves, the more so as it would be impossible to return the same way and we should have to descend by Mr. Whymper's route. Unluckily, neither of us were exactly acquainted with it, though we knew in a general way that a big couloir led to the Talèfre glacier. Some one suggested as an alternative that we should try the Dru; but this did not find favour in our eyes, and we started upwards with no very definite plans. Reaching the Glacier de Charpoua, we struck on to the ice and discussed our plans in earnest, finally deciding to examine the merits of our couloir. We mutually disclaimed any intention of making the ascent, but still we would go far enough to see if it were worth a second attempt. Later in the day, having our hearts warmed by the near neighbourhood of the summit and a bottle of Bouvier, we confessed that some faint hope of climbing the peak had cheered us on our way. But to return to my story, Burgener, inwardly intending to do a good day's work, handed over the lantern to me as he did not wish to fatigue himself prematurely. We found the glacier a good deal crevassed, and many steps had to be cut, but by daybreak we reached the tongue of rocks which splits the Glacier de Charpoua into two arms. This tongue is now better known as the upper Dru gîte, and is frequently used by parties ascending that mountain. It is needless to add that our route to this point is not that which experience has subsequently shown to be the best and which is now invariably followed.

This latter does not touch the Charpoua glacier at all, the ascent being made by endless slopes of loose stones.

We halted for half an hour in order to see the sun rise and to have some breakfast. We also carefully hid away our lantern and otherwise made ourselves ready for serious work. As far as the first Bergschrund we met no difficulty, but on reaching this huge chasm at 5.30 a.m. it appeared as if further progress was absolutely barred. It stretched right across the glacier, and the rocks on either side were wholly impracticable. However, at one point we found that the thick covering of winter snow had not actually fallen, but had only sunk some fifty feet into the chasm, and being protected from the sun's rays, had not yet wholly melted. It was a fragile structure, in some places punctured by round holes from which depended long icicles, and in others was a mere glazing of ice a quarter of an inch thick. When an axe was thrust through these weak places, most soul-shuddering depths were disclosed. It so happened that the only point at which it was possible to descend on to this bridge was well to the right, whilst the only possibility of scaling the opposing wall of the Schrund was far away to the left. We were in consequence forced to pick our way along the rickety structure for a hundred yards or more. Once or twice the jar of our passage caused a few loose icicles to rattle into the darkness below, at which

Burgener emitted ejaculations of horror. Despite these shocks to our nerves, we reached the base of a detached sérac, the top of which was connected by a fantastic imitation of a flying buttress with the firm ice beyond the Schrund. After cutting a few steps, and aided by a shove from Burgener, I scrambled on to the sérac and hauled at the rope as the sheet anchor of the party followed. We then wormed our way like caterpillars along the flying buttress, distributing our weight as far as possible and expecting at every moment that the brittle structure would collapse. Happily, after the invariable habit of ice early in the morning, it proved as rigid as iron, and we tramped steadily up to the second Bergschrund, which we passed without difficulty. The third turned out to be even worse than the first. Its lower lip overhung in the most provoking manner and necessitated the utmost caution in even approaching it, whilst the upper lip rose in a clean, precipitous cliff of blue ice some seventy feet above our heads.

We unroped, and Burgener went to the right to prospect for a possible line, whilst I went to the left. After a while Burgener shouted that it would not go on his side, but by great good fortune I had caught sight of a spot on my side that looked as if it might be forced. After crawling along a sharp knife-edge dividing the Bergschrund from a wide crevasse, we reached this desirable spot. The extremely steep slope above had been cut into a deep gully by the constant fall of stones, ice, snow, and water. The floor of this gully was some twelve feet lower than the remainder of the slope, and the falling *débris* had built up a cone underneath, exactly where it was wanted. The overhanging ice-wall was reduced by this arrangement to a manageable height of about ten feet, and Burgener decided that it could be climbed. He promptly made me a good step on the top of the cone and cut some hand holes in the wall opposite. I found on reaching the cone that it was cut off from the cliff opposite by a gap about four feet wide; leaning across this and putting my hands into the holes cut ready for me, I formed an insecure sort of bridge. Burgener then proceeded to climb up my body and on to my shoulders. He did not seem to think much of the stability of the human edifice thus raised, and his step-cutting was correspondingly slow. Indeed, so hard were the nails in Burgener's boots, so cold the ice to my fingers, and so interminable the chipping, that to my disordered imagination it seemed as if eternity itself must be rapidly drawing to a close.

At length, three steps below the lip and one above, with all the necessary hand-holds, were duly completed, and Burgener, bidding me hold fast, gave a half-spring and scrambled up the steps over the lip and on to the slope. I was soon so battered by the lumps of ice hewn out by his axe that I withdrew from the cone and waited till such time as I should be wanted. The floor of the gully was exceptionally hard, and it was quite twenty minutes before the rope was taut and Burgener told me he was ready. The ascent of the lip was not easy, but once above it, an excellent staircase led me up to him. The gully in which we now stood being the track of stones and all the other good things the Verte keeps in store for the faithful, we decided to force our way out of it on to the slope. This was only effected after very great difficulty, the walls of the gully being so deeply eroded that it was impossible to stand on the steps without hand-hold, thus leaving only one hand to wield the axe. Once on the slope, we made straight for the nearest rocks, the ice being so terribly hard and steep that it was absolutely essential to get off it as soon as possible.

It was obvious that the easiest line up the cliff in front was well to our left, a line moreover that had previously been indicated to me by Mr. Eccles as affording the easiest route, but in the then state of the slopes it was impossible to reach it without most undue loss of time, and we struck into a rock gully hoping to be able to traverse higher up. We climbed this, finding the rocks very rotten and a good deal glazed with ice; it was also the track of falling stones, and an occasional hum warned us to look out. Higher up the ice-glaze thickened so much that we had to cut shallow steps, but we were able to make fairly rapid progress, and soon scrambled out of the gully on to a shelf of rock overlooking the great snow couloir.

I was glad to take off the two knapsacks I had been carrying, and, as an excuse for a halt, we both pretended to eat. Possibly the extraordinary appetite climbers appear to exhibit on mountains is in no small degree due to their desire for the halt involved. Food on the higher ridges and "the view" on the lower slopes appear to be much enjoyed by individuals short in wind and flabby in muscle.

After half an hour's halt we tied up again, and I paid out the rope whilst Burgener traversed to the left, in part along some big slabby rocks, and in part on the upper edge of a more or less treacherous crust of ice abutting on them. Eventually we had both to be on the traverse together. Burgener, however, succeeded in hitching the rope over a big splinter above us. As this operation seemed to afford him great pleasure, I thought it would be cruel to object, though, as the splinter wobbled most ominously with the slightest pressure, I prudently unhitched the rope before venturing below it.

Reaching the snow couloir, we began to go at a tremendous pace. Burgener's axe hewed out huge frozen lumps that acquired great velocity before they reached me, and one or two heavy blows from them suggested that it was desirable to have something less than one hundred feet of rope between us. I therefore closed up to my leader, and we shortened the rope. As the work of cutting steps at this rate was very severe, I took Burgener's coat in addition to the knapsacks.

On our left was the huge trench which innumerable avalanches had graven in the slope, and more than once Burgener led us to the edge hoping to see some vulnerable point where he might force a passage. For the couloir is shaped like a huge Y of which we now occupied the tail. Our only hope of success lay in ascending its left or northern limb, but the avalanche trench led up to the inaccessible southern branch, and we, being on its right, were edged ever away from our true line of ascent. Its walls, however, were so eroded and undercut that we dared not attempt the traverse, and in consequence, on reaching the point where the couloir divides, we found ourselves to the right of and beneath the right-hand branch. A moment's glance was sufficient to dismiss any lingering hopes that it might prove practicable, and we turned with one consent to the left.

The couloir had by this time ceased to be a great walled-in gully, and was little more than a slight depression in the face of the mountain. Owing, perhaps, to this, it was no longer filled with deep snow, but was merely plastered to the depth of a few inches; the alternations of sun and frost had converted this, for the most part, into ice. It is needless to say that here the avalanche trench thinned out to insignificant proportions, and we were able to effect its traverse without difficulty. The stones, however, being no longer deflected into a well-marked track, hummed past our ears in any but a pleasing manner, and one, which struck a crag just above us, burst into splinters, both Burgener and I being hit by the fragments. Under these circumstances my companion made most desperate efforts to get out of range, and, as usually happens when he exerts his strength to the full, the axe gave way, its handle breaking in two. I promptly handed over mine, but unfortunately it was blunt and called forth many uncomplimentary remarks concerning amateurs and London-made axes. None the less it did its work, and we got into the northern branch of the couloir, where we were comparatively safe.

This proved to be filled almost entirely with ice, so we struck on to the rocks on our right as soon as it was possible to effect a lodgment. Burgener, being greatly excited by an almost-won victory, and being, moreover, unburdened by any luggage, and free from the chest-contracting bondage of a coat, dashed up at a pace that called forth pitiable gasps from his Monsieur. The latter began to realise that a porter's "lot is not a happy one, happy one," and that two knapsacks, with a coat as a superstructure, are apt to jam between projecting rocks and impale themselves on every sharp splinter that exists within a radius of six feet, in addition to the steady drag exerted by their weight. Burgener, however, was not to be checked, and his only reply to my entreaties was to jodel with fierce derision at the easy cliff which still rose before us. Our racing pace soon brought us to a little snow ridge which led, in about three minutes, to the great ridge connecting the Dru with our summit. This gradually broadened into a wide, hard-frozen causeway, up which we tramped arm in arm to the summit.

My first impulse was to shake myself free from the load I had been carrying, Burgener's was to run along the ridge leading towards the Aig. du Moine in order to examine the route by which we were to descend. He returned in great glee, saying that it was all "bares Eis," and that I should be remarkably stiff next day, referring to a solemn compact I had made to do such step-cutting as might be requisite on the way down.

Meanwhile I had unpacked the knapsacks, and we stretched ourselves on the snow to eat our lunch and revel in the glorious view which this rarely visited peak affords. Burgener then attempted to splice his broken axe. Though his efforts in this direction dismally failed, he succeeded in making as deep and ugly a cut in the fleshy part of his thumb as one could wish to see, and the remainder of our time had to be expended in its repair. Owing to these various operations we spent one hour and twenty minutes on the summit, and it was not till 1.30 p.m. that we started on the, to us, wholly unknown descent to the Jardin. We began, rightly or wrongly I hardly know, by descending towards Les Droites, and, on reaching the head of the great couloir, we swung round and cut our way down extremely steep ice to a patch of rocks that gave us footing and enabled us to look about. Below us a line of rock broke at intervals through the ice of the couloir, and as the slope was not very steep, and time pressed, Burgener suggested a novel method of procedure. First I lowered him on the rope to the next patch of rock, and then, with the confidence of youth, I glissaded down, Burgener skilfully "fielding" me when I got within his reach. In sections where this process was not admissible, we hitched the rope and slid to the next suitable rock. By these and other similar methods, and almost without cutting a step, we descended the whole length of the great couloir to the point where the rocks of the Moine ridge project far into the couloir, nipping it till it resembles a fashionable lady's waist. The outermost series of these rocks is separated from the main mass by a narrow gully partly glazed with ice, but so precipitous that any falling stones would keep well beyond the heads and other belongings of enthusiastic climbers. Down this gully we now proceeded to climb, and after one or two rather awkward scrambles we emerged on the broad slope which lies between the lower part of the two huge buttresses forming the walls of the great couloir. We found the slope covered with well compacted, hard frozen snow, and proceeded cheerily, chipping little steps, till at 4 p.m. I was pulled up by an appalling Bergschrund.

Burgener, who was sixty feet above me, advised cutting right down to the very edge of the chasm to see whether the *débris* of the broken axe and a looped rope would enable us to baffle the enemy. When I got to the extreme verge of the cliff, I found it overhanging to such an extent that, beyond seeing that no rope in our possession would reach to the bottom, no useful information could be obtained. Burgener, with his usual resource, then made himself a large step, and bid me make my body rigid and allow him to lower me out to such a distance as would enable me to see whether any convenient method of turning the obstruction was within easy reach. With the exception of some séracs far to my right and almost close to the great buttress, the overhanging ice wall was unbroken; to the left a promontory of ice hid everything from view. Having made these observations I yelled to Burgener to pull me back, and we proceeded to consider what was to be done. The séracs on the right were only to be reached by a prolonged traverse, which, with a single axe in the party, was not exactly pleasant. So we decided for the invisible slope on the left. After cutting about two hundred steps, I reached a small crevasse intersecting the slope at right angles to the Bergschrund, and Burgener, who was close behind me, shouted, "Es geht."

We then proceeded to bury ourselves in this small crevasse, and having descended by steps cut on one side and our heads resting against the other as far as its ever narrowing walls would admit, we squeezed along, wedged between the icy walls, till we emerged on the face of the great cliff. At an inconvenient distance in front a great flake of ice had parted from the main mass, leaving a sharp knife-edge of weathered ice, parallel to the cliff but rather below our present position. Burgener promptly decided that the intervening space could be jumped, and that he could hold me even if I failed to effect a lodgment on the sérac. The method to be adopted was to jump in such a way as to land on the knife-edge with the hands, whilst the feet were to scrape down the inside of the sérac, trusting that its rotten and decayed surface would afford sufficient hold to the boots to materially reduce the strain on the hands.

Having, with grievous damage to my hands, accomplished this jump, I cut a big step for

Burgener to alight on. Owing to his greater girth he found he could not squeeze so far down the crevasse as I had been able to do, and had, in consequence, a longer jump to make. However, he landed in the neatest way possible, and we went along the knife-edge to the extreme end of the sérac. There was still a drop of at least forty feet before we could reach the open glacier, and we turned to the crevasse between the sérac and the ice cliff to help us down. Whereas the first crevasse had been too narrow for comfort, this erred in the opposite direction, and the first ten feet had to be descended by cutting steps and hand-holds. It then became possible to reach the opposing wall with one's head, and descent could once more be made with reasonable facility. Reaching the level of the glacier, a long sideways jump landed me on the open snow, and our troubles were over. Without wasting time—for the passage of the Bergschrund had cost us two hours' work, and it was now six o'clock—we raced down to the Couvercle as fast as our legs would carry us. We reached that desired haven in ten minutes! It is needless to say that in those places where we could not glissade, we ran at our top speed. The excitement of the climb being over, a rapid increase in the decorum of our march took place, and on each of the moraines of the Mer de Glace we found it desirable to rearrange the luggage, contemplate the view, or engage in some other equally important occupation that involved a five minutes' rest on a flat stone. Owing to these various delays it was nearly eight o'clock before we re-entered the Montenvers. Venetz met us at the door and bitterly bewailed the loss of the expedition, but we poured balm into his injured soul by promising that he should climb as much as he liked on the Grépon.

CHAPTER X.

THE AIGUILLE VERTE—BY THE MOINE RIDGE.

The ascent of the Verte just described is open to the objection that almost at every step the texture of one's skull is likely to be tested by the impact of a falling stone. Though this lends much interest and excitement to the climb, it is of a sort that altogether loses its power of pleasing so soon as the mountaineer has passed the first flush of youth. A similar objection, though in a very modified form, may be taken to the ordinary route; indeed, various parties have been so battered and harassed by falling missiles, that the ascent has, of late years, been very rarely effected. Oddly enough the Dru, which so appalled the early explorers and which they unhesitatingly described as absolutely inaccessible, has become an everyday ascent, and is regarded as comparatively easy. A third route, leading from the Argentière glacier discovered by Messrs. Maund, Middlemore and Cordier, is yet more exposed to avalanches and stones, and, so far, no one has ventured to repeat it.

Under these circumstances it obviously behoved climbers to discover a safe and convenient way on to the summit. It might, of course, be argued that where so many and various parties had each and all been forced into stone-swept couloirs, no safe method of reaching the top could exist. But Collie, with resistless logic, demonstrated the falsity of such a conclusion. "Is it not," he said, "universally admitted, is it not written in the Badminton and All England series—and if it isn't it ought to be—that every peak can be ascended by a properly constituted party in absolute safety? Now, since the known routes are all dangerous, it necessarily follows that a fourth, the strait and narrow path, must exist." Converted by this teaching, we determined to elucidate the problem at the earliest opportunity.

During the summer of 1893 we had, more than once, examined the mountain, and the result of these observations, backed up by the study of many photographs, purchased with reckless extravagance during the autumn of that year, had led us to the belief that the true path would be found to lie along the Moine ridge. It appeared that this ridge could be safely and conveniently reached from the Talêfre by means of a secondary ridge dividing two couloirs in the near neighbourhood of the great rocky buttress which projects far into that glacier. This rib would bring us to the arête at a point immediately to the right, or on the Verte side, of the tower known at the Montenvers as the "Sugar Loaf." So confident were we that this was the true line of ascent, that we wondered why none of the guides and travellers who haunt the Mer de Glace had taken this most obvious route, but we ascribed it to that lack of initiative which is fast becoming the main characteristic of the Alpine guide and his ever roped Monsieur. Little did we dream that buried in an early number of the Alpine Journal is a full description of an ascent made by this very ridge twenty-nine years ago. Curiously enough, Messrs. Hudson, Kennedy and Hodgkinson did not realise the many advantages of their climb, and advised future travellers to give the preference to the uninteresting and stone-swept slopes by which Mr. Whymper had effected the first ascent. The mountaineering fraternity accepted this erroneous teaching, and for thirty years have wearied their muscles and imperilled their skulls on the longer, less interesting, and far more dangerous southern face. Since the memory of Mr. Hudson's ascent has so completely died out, and since the scenery and the ridge are all that the keenest enthusiasts could wish, I may perhaps be pardoned for relating our experiences, even though they may constitute but a twice-told tale.

Immediately on our arrival at the Montenvers last year we engaged a porter, and early the next morning we stretched our cramped and railway stiffened legs in a slow and decorous march to the Couvercle. Though the early climbers used to start from Chamonix or other equally low-lying valleys, and walk steadily, and so far as one can learn without any symptom of fatigue, to the top of their peaks, we moderns are cast in a less robust mould—at least some of us are—and I freely confess that as I floundered and slipped on the last slope of loose stones leading to the Couvercle, exhaustion had laid hold of me as its victim, and even Hastings . . . . But the love of veracity must not be pushed too far. Truth, at all events outside its symbolical representations, requires decorous garments and draperies; even one's belief in an overruling Providence is strengthened and upheld by the wise ordinance that not merely is Truth ever appropriately habited and veiled, but usually compelled to lie hidden at the bottom of deepest wells. Moreover, it is always unwise to excite retort. Hastings, raging at the shameless goddess, might even hint that a few days later, as we were slowly plodding up the calotte of Mont Blanc, weary with a long struggle amid the mazes of the Brenva slopes, the rope tightened between us till its function seemed rather that of a tow-line than a mere protection against concealed crevasses. But these are incidents which, even in this age of brutal realism, are too painful for written words, and I will, therefore, merely chronicle the bare fact that we, all of us, did actually reach the Couvercle. Sinking on various angular stones, we pointed out to each other's admiration the splendid overhanging roof, the perfect shelter of the gîte, and the admirable underground apartment wherein it appeared one could rest in warmth, dryness, and security, even though old Æolus broke his sceptre and sent all the tempests howling through the hills. At this juncture a white squall swept down upon us. Our hats and other loose properties were torn rudely from our grasp, and we ourselves were literally blown out of the lower or cellar apartment. We immediately agreed that this lower apartment was a fraud, and made our way back to the customary gîte. We soon, however, discovered that the huge overhanging roof constituted an excellent fan and drove the whole force of the icy blast, sharpened and edged with hail and sleet, into and through every corner and crevice that could be found.

The rain and melting snow which fell on the top of the rock ran down inside it, and the more important trickles were promptly captured and imprisoned in sundry bottles and tin boilers, thus enabling our cooking operations to proceed without any painful and protracted search for springs or tiny rivulets. When, however, an unexpected stream ran down one's neck, or the stone on which one was sitting became suddenly submerged, our altruistic feelings carried us away, and led us to express earnest and heart-felt prayers, that these varied blessings might be promptly removed and placed within convenient reach of Dives and other suffering humanity.

As the night wore on the rain ceased, and fog wrapped us in a dense, black obscurity. About 4 a.m. this obscurity began to get luminous, and by five o'clock the opaque wall by which we were surrounded emitted sufficient light to enable tea brewing and other culinary operations to proceed. Cheered by the varied pleasures which a breakfast under Hastings's auspices invariably grants, we decided that the weather might not be as bad as it looked—it was quite evident that by no manner of means could it be worse. In consequence, we determined to go up the glacier on the chance that sun and wind might sweep away the all-pervading fog.

The search for axes and knapsacks was carried on under great difficulties, it being absolutely impossible to see two yards in front of one's nose. Indeed, outside our great and glorious Metropolis, the just source of pride to every Briton, it has never been my fate to grope in a thicker and more utterly opaque atmosphere. After scrambling over many stones we found the glacier, and, feeling our way through a few crevasses, reached a fairly continuous snow slope, which, for all we knew to the contrary, led in the right direction. At this point, however, Collie wisely suggested a pipe, and as we squatted on the snow, we quickly came to the conclusion that, under some circumstances, even mountaineering is vanity and vexation of spirit. Firmly founded on this dictum of antiquity, Collie and I expressed an unalterable determination that when next we moved, it should be downwards. But Hastings, a scoffer at tobacco and otherwise wholly unregenerate, was insensible to the arguments with which a steep, wet, snow slope appeals to weary limbs, and was equally resolved to continue the ascent.

"Have we not," he said, "toiled through the crevasses, filling our pockets with snow and shaking our digestive organs by long jumps and unexpected tumbles into concealed holes, and now, that we have reached an obvious and easy line, is it not the height of absurdity to turn back?"

His eloquence, however, was as nothing compared with the mute oratory of the slope. We could realise in every limb the pain of lifting a leg till the knee almost touches the chin, then the agony of tightening the various muscles till one's weight is fairly raised upon it, followed by the heartbreaking squash as the snow gives way, and a hole eighteen inches deep remains almost the only result of the effort. We were, in consequence, not to be persuaded, and as we fully recognised the grand truth that "language is given us that we may conceal our thoughts," we advanced fictitious arguments based on the text-books, and backed them up with various sentences from the advice of wise and august personages—Presidents of the Alpine Club and the like—to the effect that climbers should always turn back in bad weather. Hastings, gazing on the two yards of slope visible in front, with the same sort of joy that inspired Cromwell's Ironsides when a troop of cavaliers came in sight, was difficult to convince, and appealed to the actual examples of the heroes and demi-gods we had quoted. Expedition was piled on expedition, demonstrating that the authors of this excellent advice, those in whose brains it was best understood and appreciated, had invariably and consistently disregarded its teaching; showing, as he alleged, that in this, as in other departments of human life, "the rule is better honoured in the breach than the observance."

The argument here touched on the larger question, whether it is better to follow the advice or the example of great men, and recognising with pleasure that much time would necessarily be consumed in grappling with it, I lit a fresh cigarette. Collie, accentuating his points with a hand extended and made more emphatic by his pipe, was just briefly reviewing the outlines of the problem when a smart shower of hail, snow, and rain terminated the discussion in our favour. With our coat collars turned up, and our hats secured with lashings of various and picturesque appearance, we hurried back to the shelter of the stones, and soon regained the Couvercle.

IN THE VAL D'AOSTE.

We packed up our sleeping-bags and other belongings, and, the rain having partly ceased, we crossed to the Pierre à Béranger. By this time the sun was making a few partially successful efforts to break through the clouds, so, spreading out our coats to dry, we made various perilous ascents of the great rock against which the hut is built.

During the afternoon we strolled back to the Montenvers pursued by sundry showers and ever darkening weather. Arrived at the hotel, we shook off the mud from our boots and the rain from our clothing, at the desolate ice and rock, and vowed that our next walk should be amongst the pine trees and meadows of the L'Ognan, and thence away to the rich fields and luxuriant vegetation of the Val d'Aoste.

A week later we returned to the Montenvers, but unfortunately a spirit of laziness seized hold upon us, and in company with some friends we wasted the precious hours scrambling on rocks and séracs well within reach of the dinner-bell, and not wholly beyond shouts and other signals indicative of afternoon tea and similar mundane pleasures. Indeed, our occupations were graphically described by a foreign friend as consisting of " an eternity of breakfast and an everlasting afternoon tea."

Hastings at length rescued us from this ignoble sloth, and drove us forth along "Les Ponts" to the Pierre à Béranger. Though the hut has reached the pig-sty stage of existence characteristic of the Chamonix district, we preferred it to the Couvercle, remembering that a roof, like charity, covers a multitude of sins.

BY THE MOINE RIDGE.

At 2 a.m. the sleepers were awakened, the fire was lit, and a somewhat extensive breakfast consumed. Then the knapsack was overhauled and all surplus baggage ruthlessly ejected. These various proceedings consumed much time, and it was not till 3.15 a.m. that we left the hut and began the monotonous ascent of the moraine. Crossing the glacier just as the first signs of dawn became apparent, we once more reached the long bank of loose stones and struggled slowly upwards.

The advent of daylight was a good deal interfered with by the dense masses of vapour that filled the glacier basin and gave much effective aid to the powers of darkness and night. However, before we got much higher, the huge towers of unsubstantial mist were touched by glints of sunshine, and the last lingering gloom was put to flight. We hailed the lifting of the clouds as a good augury, and set ourselves more resolutely to breast the slope. Reaching the high glacier shelf close under the wall-like ridge extending from the Moine to the Verte, we halted for a quarter of an hour hoping that the swaying of the mists would enable us to see something of our mountain. But the great dark curtain clung steadfastly round it, and nothing was visible on that side. In the other direction, however, we had a marvellous vision of the Grandes Jorasses, half veiled in films of floating cloud. Far on high we could even see the lighter and loftier streamers sailing before a gentle northerly wind. Cheered by this hopeful sign we tramped along the glacier shelf till we were pulled up by a short but steep step in the ice. After a little work with the axe we gained its upper level, and were rewarded, the mists having meanwhile somewhat lifted, by a clear view of the rocks by which we hoped to gain the ridge.

At the point where the true peak of the Verte begins to tower up above the long turreted ridge of the Moine, a great buttress projects far into the Taléfre glacier. Between this buttress and the Moine ridge is a semicircular hollow, divided from top to bottom by a long rib of rock. On either side of this are snow-filled couloirs, and we trusted that by one or other of them, or the dividing rib, we might make our way to the ridge. So far as we could see, no very serious difficulty was likely to be encountered, though as all the upper rocks and all the ridge were still obstinately shrouded in a fog we could not be absolutely certain. We crossed the Bergschrund, and, after a sharp struggle with some frozen rubble, effected a lodgment on the cliff at 6.45 a.m.

We then unanimously decided that the weather was not very bad, and that we were as good as on the summit of our peak—" wherefore," we said, " let us eat, smoke, and be merry." Half an hour later, after these duties had been thoroughly performed, we began to scramble up the slabs, each taking that particular line which seemed best.

THE VERTE FROM ABOVE THE TALÈFRE GLACIER.

* Point where we struck the ridge.

Meanwhile the mists closed round us once more. The cliffs above looming through the rushing vapour, looked ever bigger and more precipitous, so, to avoid the possibility of being cut off by some insuperable step, we worked to our right into the couloir. We were at first able, from time to time, to use the rocks on our right as a ladder, and thus save the labour of step-cutting, but as we got higher the slabs became too large and smooth, and we were forced to proceed relying on the axe alone. We soon got tired of this, and crossed back to our rib and found that its appearance was delusive, and that in fact it was a perfect staircase. Reaching the near neighbourhood of the ridge, we swung across easy slopes to our right, traversing the head of the couloir, and making for the top of the great buttress.

I took this line fearing that otherwise we might waste valuable energy in climbing to the top of the "Sugar Loaf"; it being, in the dense fog, quite impossible to tell just where this pinnacle was. Collie, it is true, was quite sure that we were on the Verte side of it, but the blight of a sceptical age was upon me and we kept to the right. Just as we scrambled on to the crest of the buttress, an eddy of wind swept the arête bare of cloud, and we halted a few minutes to inspect our mountain. Swinging back to our left, a short diagonal ascent landed us on the main ridge at 8.20 a.m., and we were able to look down on to the

Charpoua glacier and across to the great south-western face of our peak. With a weakness which is not, perhaps, altogether unusual amongst mountaineers, I pointed out to my companions the various crags and gullies, ice slopes and slabs, by which Burgener and I had made our way to the summit thirteen years before.

A rush of cloud, bearing with it more than a suspicion of snow, hurried us from our seats, and we scrambled merrily along the ridge. As we advanced, however, a few jagged towers began to give us some trouble. Whilst turning one of these on the Taléfre side, we were surprised to see a broken bottle. Soon after we discovered the remains of a broken stick wedged into a cleft of the rocks, and made immovable by a mass of ice frozen round it. Its ancient appearance led us to suppose that it marked the limit of some early exploring party, and dated from the time when the Verte was still an unclimbed peak.

Almost immediately after this the work became more serious. I tried a turning movement on the left, and was soon brought to the opinion that if another way was available it would be desirable to use it. Whilst extricating myself from these difficulties, Collie led round to the right, and after a short struggle stormed the obstruction. A few yards further we were pulled up by a precipitous step, which could not be turned, and which defied all unaided efforts. Hastings, however, lifted me bodily upwards till I could get a grip on the top of the block, and after a few spasmodic struggles, I was able to reach firm footing. This sort of thing then continued for some time.

One delightful little traverse is, however, worth recording. A great gendarme barring direct assault, we turned over on to the Charpoua face. Above our heads a mass of overhanging rock prevented the adoption of any decorous or upright attitude, and we were forced to wriggle, worm-like, along an outward-shelving ledge. At the end of this it was possible to regain a normal posture, but this advantage was more than compensated by the necessity of abandoning all hand-hold and making a long stride across an ugly gap on to a narrow, ice-glazed, sloping rock. It was not difficult to do, but I find in such places that the mind is apt to dwell unpleasantly on the probable consequences of any trifling error or lack of balance. Safely over, I found myself at the bottom of a precipitous tower, plastered and piled up with snow and ice. Direct ascent was out of the question, but by craning one's neck round the tower a ledge, partly rock and partly ice, could be seen running round the head of a great gully that falls away towards the Charpoua glacier. To reach this shelf it was necessary to traverse the snow-plastered face of the tower. Happily, Hastings found a hitch for the rope, and relying to some extent on the doubtful security so afforded, I leant round and, with the axe in the left hand, made some slight notches in the wall. A gap was then hacked out of the snow and ice above, into which the rope was carefully tucked, so that it might be above me should anything unforeseen occur. For one step my adhesion to the cliff was somewhat doubtful, and I have a very clear remembrance of my inability to get the right leg round an awkward bulge without throwing what seemed an undue strain on a hand-hold carefully carved out of the fragile snow above. However, cheered by encouraging remarks from Hastings, who always knows how to inspire the leader with confidence, the bulge was passed, and a comparatively simple piece of step-cutting brought us to the shelf. This in turn led us back to the ridge.

We were soon again forced off it, and had to descend a short distance on the Talèfre face. Climbing back, we were met by a great cornice fringed with a long row of icicles. We crept along between the snow wall and the icicles, fearing to touch the latter lest the whole structure should come down bodily on our heads. A small gap was at length reached, and after a few remaining tufts and tassels of ice had been hacked away, it was possible to crawl through. Good anchorage for the rest of the party being here available, I scrambled on to the cornice, and from that point of vantage was able to effect a lodgment on the next rocky tower. These various traverses and scrambles, interspersed with halts whenever the ingenuity of laziness could invent a tolerable excuse, consumed much time, and we were still without any very definite sign of the top.

Suddenly we stepped out of the cloud into brilliant sunshine, below us stretched an unbroken sea of billowy mist, from which Mont Blanc and the Grandes Jorasses alone emerged. Pressed for time as we were, we could not resist yet another halt to gaze at this extraordinary and most beautiful spectacle. Before us a short snow ridge led to what was obviously the top, and setting resolutely to work, a quarter of an hour or twenty minutes of step-cutting placed us on the summit (2 p.m.).

A biting northerly wind swept across the ridge, and kept the huge expanse of cloud below us in constant movement. At moments vast masses would be upheaved, and, caught by the wind, sailed away, throwing extraordinary shadows on the fleecy floor below. This, like some previous halts, was brought to an end by a sudden uprush of icy cloud and a sprinkle of snow. At 2.15 p.m. we left the top and sped hastily down the slope. In ever worsening weather, we sprawled and scrambled along the ridge as fast as we could go. Collie, despite the changed appearance of the mountain caused by the rapidly falling snow, followed our route of the morning with unwavering certainty. At exactly the right point he turned off the ridge (5.10 p.m.), and led us through the wet slush of new snow, down the rib, to the point where our tracks of the morning could be seen in the couloir. He preferred, however, to keep to the rib, and after a little winding and dodging we once more got on to our morning's line below the part where we had taken to the couloir, and followed it to the glacier and the Bergschrund. This latter was in a very soft and dangerous state, and required careful engineering. Once over (6.5 p.m.), we ran along the snow fields and down on to the stony slopes above the Couvercle.

Making our way across to the Pierre à Béranger we picked up our traps, and after a short meal we started at 7.40 p.m. for the Montenvers, through a persistent drizzle. We had intended to go down to Chamonix that night, and in consequence had sent on our baggage, but on our arrival we found it was far too late to do so. Friends, however, most kindly arrayed us in various garments, and about 11 p.m. we did rare justice to the efforts of Monsieur Simond's cook.

It is needless to say the ascent was made under very unfavourable conditions. We were constantly compelled to halt in order to wait for a break in the mist, and it is probable that the impossibility of seeing what lay in front occasionally prevented our taking the best route. The climb is, however, most interesting, and is, throughout, absolutely free from all danger of falling stones.

CHAPTER XI.

A LITTLE PASS — COL DES COURTES.

THE great cliffs closing in the head of the Brenva Glacier had long attracted my hopes and aspirations, but a series of untoward events had, for three consecutive seasons, prevented any attempt being made to convert these hopes into accomplished facts. Last year, however, our whole party was resolved that, come what might, we would ascend the Mont Blanc from that glacier. In consequence, when we found the weather inclined to be unpropitious, we abandoned for the moment the attack on the Verte which has just been described, and determined to cross to Courmayeur, so that we could, if need were, devote our whole season to waiting for a favourable day.

We did not, however, wish to repeat the somewhat too well-known Col de Géant; or, for that matter, any of the passes leading from the Mer de Glace basin. It appeared to us that Mr. Whymper's route from the Glacier d'Argentière to Courmayeur was by no means the shortest or most direct that could be taken, and, with that altruism which Mr. B. Kidd tells us is the dominant note of our civilisation, we wished to confer on our fellow-creatures the inestimable boon of a better and easier way from L'Ognan to the unparalleled delights of Mons. Bertolini's Hotel. It

COURMAYEUR.

must not be supposed that this was merely a momentary burst of the altruistic feeling; on the contrary, it had, as attentive readers of "Social Evolution" would infer, been surging and working in our minds for years. We had, indeed, in 1893, made a journey to the Col Triolet for the sole and express purpose of studying whether the pass could be made, and had come to the conclusion, so dear to Uncle Remus, that, " it mout, but then again it moutn't."

As the maps are all incorrect in this district, it will, perhaps, be as well to explain that the Aiguille de Triolet does not, as therein represented, rise at the point at which the Courtes ridge joins the watershed. At this particular point is a small nameless peak, between which and the Triolet is a col, probably lower than the Col Triolet. On one side of this col is a steep gully leading down to the Glacier de Triolet, and on the other are scarped ice slopes that fall away to the Glacier d'Argentière. Whilst this col, if feasible, would offer many advantages, an alternative and easier way was evidently to be found by ascending the great snow and ice wall to the north-east of Les Courtes, and known in the Conway Guide series as the Col des Courtes. From the top of this wall it would, presumably, be possible to traverse the ridge to the curious upper basin of the Glacier des Courtes and reach the ordinary Col Triolet.

With these two strings to our bow, we felt tolerably certain of getting across the ridge, and on the 2nd of August, 1894, left the Montenvers about 9 a.m. and tracked down and across the glacier to the Chapeau. On the way from the ice to the little refreshment booth, Hastings and I refused to follow the path where it descends slightly, and preferred to scale some wet and slimy rocks. After many efforts and much perching of ice-axes, we managed to force our way on to the path known as the Mauvais Pas above the obstruction, Collie meanwhile gazing on our performance with mild sorrow, his attitude suggesting the question, "Why should men with dry and fairly

GOING TO CHURCH.

decorous knickerbockers sacrifice them on the altar of water and slime, when fifteen feet of descent would have enabled them to follow a dry and convenient road?"

François Simond met us with a hearty welcome, and hearing that we were ignorant of the ways of the forest path to L'Ognan, insisted on ascending a steep series of zig-zags till, reaching the open hillside, he could point out blasted pines and great rocks to serve us as safe landmarks and guides. After exchanging farewells with our good friend Simond, Hastings deposited the knapsack on the turf and we adopted those attitudes most conducive to rest and comfort. Two of the party, however, soon discovered that their ascent of a watercourse had made them too wet for a prolonged indulgence in repose. Collie, from amongst the wreathing pleasure of tobacco, protested in vain. We were deaf to his assertions that the chief delight of mountaineering is to be found in the skilfully selected halt; that the great dome of the Gouter, whitest snow above purple valley, the jagged crest of the Charmoz, the ice cliffs of the Plan with their piled-up memories of scorching sun and bitter night, were worthy of a longer halt. But we were obdurate, and, turning to the hill, we scrambled up amongst the pines and crags. A pleasant ramble brought us, some hours later, to the châlet inn of L'Ognan.

Sitting in the sun, we drank deep draughts of milk, thus recalling those far-off years when a long pull out of great wooden bowls constituted no inconsiderable part of the climber's food. A cross-examination of our hostess having elicited comforting assurances relative to the possibilities of dinner, we gave ourselves up to the contemplation of the shining sun and the knotted ridges of the Buet. Gradually the harder lines and sharper contrasts were softened and etherealised by those vague mists and wondrous visions that ever hover on the verge of sleep. Some of us, indeed, fell utter victims to the drowsy god.

The next morning we started at 12.40 a.m., our party being strengthened by the addition of a full-grown porter to carry the sack, and a small boy to instruct the full-grown one in the mysteries of the path. We ascended mule tracks and foot tracks, moraines and ice, these latter being varied by an occasional deflection on to the slopes at the side of the glacier. After a somewhat weary pilgrimage we emerged on to the smooth and even ice, and were able to tramp quickly towards the great wall by which it is enclosed. Lowering clouds, sailing swiftly before a south-westerly gale, aroused painful thoughts, and we declaimed on the vanity of early starts and the ignominy of returning to the Montenvers a second time wet and beaten. Soon after daybreak, a suggestion concerning breakfast was received with enthusiasm. We accordingly made our way to a small sérac, behind which we were partly sheltered from the wind.

It is needless to say we had many courses; beginning with Yorkshire bacon, we pursued our way amidst the delights of rolls and butter, of jam, of biscuits, of preserved fruits and ginger, of chocolate, and all the varied comestibles which our prince of caterers had provided. The two porters, after gazing with astonishment at the progress of this grand "gastronomic symphony," said good-bye, and quickly rounding a shoulder of Les Courtes, were lost to sight.

The pipe of peace being once more lit, we deputed Hastings, who, not being a smoker, had no particular duties on hand, to pack the knapsack, and subsequently, from the cold and wind-swept summit of the sérac, to prospect for an easy and convenient way across the Schrund. All idea of making the col immediately under the Aiguille de Triolet had been abandoned, owing, partly to the difficulty of finding a possible route, and partly to the fact that any such route would of necessity be exposed to many and various falling missiles. We fell back, therefore, on the alternative plan of climbing up to the Glacier des Courtes, and thence traversing on to the ordinary Col Triolet. Before, however, these operations could be begun, it was necessary to get over the very formidable Bergschrund, by which access to the slopes of Les Courtes is defended.

At 5 a.m. we left the friendly sérac, and walked slowly up to the great yawning chasm. Two courses were open to us. We could either assault the Schrund at a point where, once across, the ascent would be merely an ordinary piece of step-cutting work; or we could keep more to the right, where an occasional sérac and more than an occasional stone were in the habit of falling, and ascend by a series of séracs piled one on the other, till an avalanche groove, high above the Schrund, was gained.

According to our usual practice, we decided on the shorter and temporarily more difficult line, and bore towards the open Schrund with the overhanging lip. As we approached, however, it became obvious that this lip was too high to be practicable, so we altered our course, and swung round to the right towards the piled-up *débris* of séracs. When we had got to this rather rickety structure, we halted a moment to put on the rope and pull ourselves together before beginning the attack.

We had at the outset to climb on to a fragile, egg-shell sort of arrangement that bridged the crevasse, and led to the lowest of the séracs. Steps worthy the name could not be cut, as it was obvious that a very trifling interference with the structure might send it crashing into the open chasm below. After some preliminary efforts, Hastings hoisted me on to his shoulders and shoved me on to the top of the bridge. Its upper edge was peculiarly insecure, and so loaded with powdery snow that its passage suggested unpleasant possibilities. At the point where it abutted against the precipitous face of the first sérac, loose snow was piled high upon it, and much labour was required to beat and tread it down into the semblance of foothold. A first attempt to scale this obstacle proved abortive, and Hastings had to be once more summoned to give the needful aid. So soon as Collie had anchored himself as well as circumstances would allow, our second man entrusted himself to the bridge. Happily it proved of stronger virtue than we had expected, and, despite all temptations, did not stray into the downward path.

The advent of Hastings soon altered the appearance of affairs; planting himself on the highest reliable step, he once more lifted me up the slope, and when I had got beyond his reach, still gave me that moral support which the knowledge of his resource and extraordinary skill in "backing up" always affords, and which in many cases is as valuable as an actual shove. The short perpendicular cliff being ascended, a narrow and very steep gully, lying between a great sérac and the ice slope on our left, was reached. This gully being loaded with incoherent, dusty snow, no really reliable hold could be obtained. However, as all our rope was now out, it was necessary for Collie to come up on to the bridge. This being effected, Hastings untied, and thus gave me rope enough to crawl round on to the top of the sérac. From this point one looked down a hundred feet or more of overhanging ice cliff into the blue-black depths of the Schrund. The top of this cliff, which forms the upper lip of the Schrund, still towered high above our heads, but the piled-up séracs gave us a means of circumventing the obstruction, and we could see that the first serious obstacle was overcome. With ever lessening difficulty, though not without much hewing of steps and an occasional wrestle with loose snow, we gained the well-swept avalanche groove, and were able to cut really reliable foothold in its icy floor.

The hum of one or two small fragments which spun merrily over our heads soon directed our thoughts and aspirations toward some rocks shutting in the ice slope a short distance on our right. A first effort to cross was, however, foiled by the layer of dangerous new snow lying on all the slope outside our well-brushed avalanche slide. Fifty feet higher up the snow seemed slightly more compact, besides which we were not so terribly near the edge of the great overhanging ice cliff. Though the actual peril may not be affected by the nearness of such a cliff, none the less the human mind is so constructed—at least mine is—that one feels much happier when a reasonably long slide would precede the final and concluding drop.

By much careful anchoring, and by treating the new snow as Isaac Walton advises the angler to treat the frog he is impaling, " use him as though you loved him," we got across without material risk. A sharp scramble up and round a precipitous corner brought us to a secure ledge, on which we promptly sat down to recover our wind and to indulge in a few minutes of well-earned repose. The sacrificial fires being lit, Collie, soothed by their pleasant restfulness, was fain to admit that even Ben Nevis has nothing to quite equal this Schrund. A quarter of an hour later he took the lead, and climbed to the left round a peculiarly awkward corner. Beyond this, a little splinter of rock lures the cragsman forward. I found, however, that it could only just be reached by the tips of the fingers of the left hand, whilst the right was doomed to imitate the "evil one" and wandered up and down the face of the rock. This place was distinctly awkward, but the sight of Hastings, firmly planted on a broad ledge, braced my courage, and I gave a bold spring, and, after sundry wriggles, landed successfully on the splinter.

The rocks now became easy, and we could see that our way to the ridge was assured. The weather, perceiving that we were more or less independent of its vagaries, gave up making any further efforts to bother us, and moved off its clouds, winds, and other engines of torture towards the Bernese Oberland. We felt that these varied and satisfactory circumstances ought to be celebrated by a halt. I regret to say it was by no means the only halt; indeed our progress from this time forth was interrupted by such frequent pauses for rest and refreshment that our ultimate arrival on the ridge called forth the utmost surprise from each and all of the party. We felt, however, that our first view of the crevasses of the Glacier des Courtes must be honoured by a lunch, and a more than usually protracted halt was unanimously decided on.

To our right an extraordinary needle of rock blocked the ridge, whilst to the left a series of jagged spires suggested that we might, possibly, still find work to test our mettle. Happily it is one of the strong points of amateur parties that no fear for the future ever interferes with their enjoyment of the present, and we basked in sundry nooks, a whole world of glorious form and colour delighting our half-closed eyes, with never a thought beyond the restful beauty of the scene. Gradually, however, it became apparent that sharp stones and occasional cold blasts of wind interfered with that perfect bliss which it is the invariable object of the climber to attain, so we hailed with enthusiasm a suggestion of Collie's that we should make our way along the ridge to a wide shelf of broken rock, where perfect shelter and luxurious resting places could evidently be discovered (9.15 a.m.).

A sharp descent, followed by a hard climb up the precipitous flank of a needle-like spire, brought us to this delectable table-land. It is doubtful whether we should have ever been able to make up our minds to start—possibly we should have remained there even to this day, wrapped in all the pleasure of sun and air and sky—had not a consuming thirst laid hold upon us. Driven unwillingly forward by this fiend, we grappled in succession with the few obstructions still remaining. At no point did they become at all serious, though once or twice neat little problems in rock-climbing presented themselves for solution. At length the upper snows of the Glacier des Courtes rose to our level, and we tramped across their sun-softened surface till we reached the Col Triolet (10.30 a.m.).

We discovered a pool of delicious water, formed in a tiny hollow between the névé and the rocky ridge of the pass, and forthwith knapsacks and all encumbrances were discarded, and we drank our fill with the keen enjoyment of thirsty men. Hastings, as usual, extracted unimagined luxuries from his knapsack, and we proceeded to enjoy an aldermanic banquet with far more than aldermanic appetites and digestion. At the conclusion of this feast, which of necessity took place on the margin of our pool, we repaired to the Italian side of the col, where we were sheltered from the wind, and warmed by the full blaze of the sun.

Sleep soon nestled among the party, and it was not till 11.40 a.m. that a stern sense of duty drove us down the rocks. The first Schrund or two did not give us very much trouble, but the final chasm, which cuts off this bay of the glacier from the main snow field, proved to be of a most formidable character. We had only a single circumstance wherewith to console ourselves, at one place alone was it possible to attempt to cross; those tiring traverses and vain searches for a better line so usual in such circumstances were, in consequence, wholly avoided, and we set ourselves determinedly to the passage.

After a few preliminary efforts, I got down on to a curious flake of ice that had been split from the upper lip of the Schrund, and, carefully held by Collie and Hastings, examined its stability. The great flake appeared perfectly sound and secure, so the others came down on to it, and after careful inspection agreed that if we could reach a small notch in the edge of the ice flake some distance to our right and some twenty feet below our present standing ground, the last man could lower the two others and then jump across the chasm on to some convenient snow.

The edge of the flake was too thoroughly disintegrated and rotten to be of any use, but we were able to cut our way down and along, inside the crevasse separating it from the parent ice. By this means the gap was reached without undue delay. As, however, we, one after another, stepped into it, a somewhat blank look settled on our features. It was evident that below the snow on which we wished to jump, were large blocks of broken ice excellently suited for the fracture of any legs or other similar objects which might happen to fall on them; moreover, the difference in height was considerably more than we had judged from above—certainly not less than thirty feet. A strong and irresistible feeling of modesty now invaded each individual of the party, and no one would consent to accept the usually coveted distinction of descending as last man. This humility of mind seeming wholly proof to the blandishments of the most artful flattery, we had to seek another method of grappling with the difficulty.

On the inside of the flake, and about six feet below us, was a small ledge from which it appeared that a staircase might be constructed leading obliquely down the crevasse, till it emerged beyond the edge of the flake at the level of the lower snow field. Whether it would be possible to cross the Schrund at this point was not very certain, but in mountaineering something should always be left to luck. It adds such zest and interest to the proceedings!

No sooner had I scrambled down to the ledge and begun work on the staircase than the general opinion of the party veered round till it once more favoured the jump. Collie went so far as to offer to lower us down and then risk the thirty feet. But there are few pleasures of the muscular sort keener than that afforded by cutting down a crevasse—even the joys of rock climbing pale before those of perpendicular ice—the remonstrances from above remained, in consequence, unheeded, and I hewed my way down into the blue depths. It was at first possible to descend with one foot in a hole in the flake and the other resting on the parent mass; so long as this was possible the axe could be wielded with both arms, and excellent holes and cavities could be cut out of the opposing walls. Somewhat lower, the crevasse widened very materially, and, despite considerable length of limb, I could no longer reach across the chasm. I was, in consequence, reduced to cutting the staircase exclusively in the flake. It was impossible to stand in the steps so cut without holding on with at least one hand, the other being alone available for the axe. The steps soon began to show signs of scamping, and my companions above were urged to give due heed to the rope. Fortunately the axe held at full length still reached the opposing wall, and its support materially aided the otherwise most perilous business of getting from one step to another.

The flake, near its outer edge, curved in toward the great upper wall of the Schrund, and, having fought my way to this part of the crevasse, secure standing ground could once more be constructed. Here I halted a moment to recover from the effects of the struggle. One foot was supported on the flake and the other was wedged into a notch in the parent ice, while all eternity yawned between, and in this attitude I had to consider what should be done next. The flake was becoming very thin, indeed the difference of light and shade in the distant landscape could be clearly detected through its mass; the texture of its substance also left much to be desired, and it was evident that extreme care would have to be taken in dealing with it. Besides all this, a most objectionable lump of ice, weighing several hundredweights, was suspended by a curious and apparently most insufficient stalk of the same fragile material, exactly in the place where I wished to pass. To send the lump thundering down into the crevasse with a single blow of my axe would have been easy, but the very delicate health of the flake seemed unequal to the strain of so drastic a remedy.

I decided, at length, to pass below this "impendent horror," and to wholly avoid touching it. After several ineffective attempts, and not till the patience of those above had been sorely tried, did I succeed, by wedging my axe across the chasm, in swinging round the corner of the flake in such sort that I could grasp the edge of a second and lower flake that formed a sort of extension of our first acquaintance and friend. A moment or two later I scrambled on to its rotten and decaying surface and picked my way across a good and solid bridge to the firm glacier beyond.

The knapsack was lowered and Collie soon followed. Hastings, descending last, showed a contemptuous disregard of the great lump of ice, and putting his back against it, squeezed round the corner with great facility. Being thus at a

A STREET IN COURMAYEUR.

higher level, he was able to step on to the axes that Collie and I held wedged across the chasm, and thus avoided the main difficulties of the passage.

Two years previously I had crossed the Col Triolet and passed this same Schrund almost without difficulty, but two snowless winters had altogether altered its character. Lower down, remembering splendid slopes of avalanche snow on the right bank of the glacier, I led our party across, but in place of a glissade of a thousand feet or more on hardest snow, we had to flounder down loose stones and rocks, the same exceptional winters having failed to make good the waste of the summer sun. As a consequence the bridge, which used to cross the torrent in the Val Ferret, had been allowed to disappear. Presumably no one now ever goes near this endless waste of desolation and hideousness. Having waded the stream we tramped down to Courmayeur, where we arrived amidst the deluge of a thunderstorm at 9.15 p.m.

CHAPTER XII.

DYCH TAU.

Though the faithful climber is, in his essence, a thoroughly domesticated man and rarely strays from his own home, the Alps, a spirit of unrest occasionally takes hold upon him and drives him forth to more distant regions. Seized with such a fit of wandering, the first days of July, 1888, found me camped on the right bank of the Bezingi glacier, where, in the cool air of the snow fields, on slopes white with rhododendron and with the silent unclimbed peaks above, I could rest from the rattle and roar of trains, the noise of buffets and the persecutions of the Custom-houses.

My sole companion was Heinrich Zurfluh, of Meiringen. The experience of ten days' continuous travel, culminating in two and a half days on the peculiarly uncomfortable Tartar saddle—we had ridden from Patigorsk to Naltcik, and thence to Bezingi and the foot of the glacier—had sufficed to make him a confirmed pessimist.

"Es gefällt mir nicht" was the burden of his song, and though this phrase may, perhaps, be regarded as summarising the conclusions of modern philosophy, it struck me that it was scarcely a fitting watchword for the mountaineer face to face with the hugest of unclimbed giants.

Our camp was of a most Spartan simplicity, for we had outwalked our baggage, and Zurfluh's knapsack, which I had fondly imagined contained sleeping-bags and soup-tins, proved to be mainly filled with a great pot of most evil-smelling boot grease—brought with much labour all the way from Meiringen—a large hammer, an excellent stock of hobnails and a sort of anvil to assist in their insertion. These various articles were doubtless of great value, but hardly useful as bedding, for, whatever may be the case with rose-leaves, a man need scarcely be a sybarite to object to crumpled hobnails as a mattress. Luckily various portions of a sheep, a large loaf of Russian bread, and a load of firewood had been piled on an active native whom we had met and appropriated before leaving the rest of our caravan.

The night proved remarkably cold, and we were glad to turn out at 4 a.m. and start on a preliminary examination of our peak. I soon discovered, however, that Zurfluh had more ambitious views, and was possessed of the wild idea of taking a mountain 17,054 feet high, as a training walk! It was, however, desirable to see what lay behind the Misses glacier, so I limited my protests and followed the rapid advance of my leader. We kept up a long couloir which was separated from the Misses glacier by a low ridge of rock. Reaching its head we ought to have crossed over on to the glacier, but we disliked the long snow slopes leading up to the ridge amongst which we thought, I believe erroneously, that we detected the sheen of ice. In consequence, we kept up the rocks to our left, and, about eight o'clock, reached a point where it was, perhaps, possible to traverse on to the great slope, but the whizz of the train was still in my ears and the limpness of English life still ached in my muscles, and I failed to give my leader the moral support that was needed. He looked at the traverse and did not quite care for its appearance. He looked at the slope above and thought it very long. He gazed at the ridge leading to the summit and denounced it as interminable. A confident Herr and he would have hurled himself at the difficulties, and his great skill, quickness and strength would, I verily believe, have enabled us to reach the summit; but for the nonce I adopted the destructive rôle of critic. I pointed out that it was already late, that a night on the ridge would be chilly and that the traverse and the slope beyond had every appearance of being stone swept. My mind, however, was as flabby as my muscles, and instead of declaring for a prompt and imme-

diate retreat, I followed Zurfluh languidly up the cliff to see whether a second and easier traverse could be found. There proved to be no such possibility, and about 9 a.m. we abandoned the ascent.

On the way back we glissaded the couloir, spinning down a thousand feet or more in a single slide. A few weeks later when Messrs. Woolley, Holder, and Cockin reached the Misses kosh, the Caucasian sun had stripped almost every atom of snow from this gully.

We found to our sorrow that the camp had not yet arrived, and a second cold and comfortless night ensued. The next morning, as a consequence, Zurfluh was too unwell to start, so with the energy of an amateur I explored the approaches to the southern face of the mountain. In the course of my solitary wander I scared a herd of seventeen Tur, and subsequently reached the extreme south-western buttress of the peak, a point almost worthy of a distinctive title, as it is separated from the mass of the mountain by a broad col, and is only to be reached by a long and not wholly easy ridge. Its height is about 13,500 feet, or possibly more, and one looks over the Zanner pass into Suanetia and across the Shkara pass to the mountains on the further side of the Dych Su glacier. The face of Dych Tau, however, had all my attention. The peak seen from this side has two summits, and I found it quite impossible to decide which was the higher, the great tower to the right and apparently behind the main mass of the mountain looking as if it might be the culminating point. This doubt, and the fact that much snow was still lying on the huge rock face, determined me to cross the passes I was anxious to see before attempting the ascent, so that by distant views the doubt as to the true summit might be settled, and by the lapse of time and the Caucasian sun the snow might be, in a measure, melted from the rocks. On my return to the Misses kosh I found that fortune was smiling on me, the camp had arrived and Zurfluh was once more ready for work.

The next two weeks were devoted to excursions in the valleys of Balkar, Suanetia, the Bashil Su, and Chegem.* Returning from the latter by a grass pass to Tubeneli, we once more made our way toward the Bezingi glacier. Near the foot of this latter a thick and wetting mist, combined with the offer of new milk, induced us to halt at a cow kosh and we pitched our tent by the side of a great boulder. During the night a goat mistook the tent for a stone and jumped off the boulder on to the top of it, subsiding amongst its startled inmates. Though I am quite willing to guarantee the behaviour of this make of tent on an

---

* Our experiences in these valleys and on these passes are described in the next chapter. It has appeared more convenient to describe my Dych Tau wanderings consecutively.

exposed ledge in a gale of wind, it must be admitted that it is wholly unequal to the attack of a daring goat. After many efforts Zurfluh and I succeeded in extricating ourselves from the tangled *débris* and rebuilt our mansion, though, when morning dawned, it exhibited a miserably baggy and disreputable appearance. During breakfast our Tartar porter gave us to understand that a palatial kosh, replete with all the luxuries of life, was to be found on the left bank of the glacier nearly opposite the Misses kosh. The weather looked so threatening that Zurfluh urged me to go to this Capua of the mountains where, as he wisely said, we could wait till sufficiently fine weather set in for our great expedition. This seemed so excellent a proposition that we at once packed up the camp and started. Zurfluh and the Tartar soon began to exhibit symptoms of rivalry, and gradually lapsed into a walking match for the honour of their respective races, creeds, and foot-gear. I had no ambition to join, and the men quickly disappeared from sight. Injudiciously following some directions which Zurfluh had given me, and which he averred were faithful interpretations of the Tartar's remarks, I tried to get along the left moraine. This latter, heaped up against the cliffs and scored by deep water-channels, soon demonstrated Zurfluh's inefficiency as interpreter. After some trouble, not to say danger, I succeeded in reaching the glacier, and tramped merrily over its even surface. Before long, however, a thick mist settled into the valley and suggested the possibility that I might fail to find the kosh, for, unluckily, I had only the vaguest idea of its whereabouts. Fearing to miss it, I felt my way through some tangled crevasses to the left bank and explored a tenantless alp. Beneath a great boulder I found a most excellent cave. Where natural walls were lacking, it had been skilfully built in with stones, and the whole was roomy, clean, and dry. It undoubtedly affords the best shelter to be found anywhere above Bezingi. However, there were no sheep on the pasture and no sign of Zurfluh, shepherd, or porter, so I had to betake myself to the ice again, here crumpled and torn into the wildest confusion. After some protracted struggles and much hewing of steps I reached a second oasis. This likewise appeared tenantless, and I was beginning to think I should have to return to my previously discovered cave when, rounding a big rock, I heard the welcome bleating of sheep and walked almost into Zurfluh's arms. He had been much alarmed for my safety. Owing to more erroneous interpretation, he had gone considerably out of his way to take the séracs at exactly their worst and most broken point. Believing this worst passage to be the only one practicable, he not unnaturally concluded that I should come to untold grief.

Having mutually relieved our anxieties, I asked

Zurfluh to take me to the much vaunted kosh. We found at first some difficulty in locating it, but the shepherd came to our help and led us to a black mark against a perpendicular cliff; this black mark defined the place where he lit his fire on the rare occasions when he had any firewood. At the present moment, he explained, he had not got any. Other pretence of habitation or shelter there was none. Even our small tent which had formed part of the Tartar's load had disappeared, and the Tartar himself had vanished into space, Zurfluh, indeed, was inclined to think a crevasse his probable resting place, but my experience of his skill made me pretty confident that he had not chosen that particular method of joining the houris in Paradise. The misty rain pervaded everywhere; the lee side of the rocks was as wet as the weather side, and we gradually lapsed into that soddened condition which depresses the spirits even of the most cheerful. Moreover, we had depended on one or other of the active sheep we saw around us for our dinner; but the conversion of live sheep into cooked mutton is difficult in the absence of firing. We bitterly regretted the Misses kosh, where a Willesden canvas tent and a good store of wood were securely packed in the cave. I even suggested crossing, but Zurfluh absolutely refused to have anything more to do with the séracs while the fog lasted. An hour later, however, our mourning was turned into joy, for we beheld the broad shoulders of the hunter, buried beneath a pile of wood, struggling up the grass slope. He had, it seems, on learning that there was no wood, concealed his baggage in a dry hole under a stone and crossed to the Misses kosh to fetch our supply from thence. A bold and kindly action, done without thought of reward, for men who had little or no claim upon him.

A lamb was promptly pursued and slain, and soon we were sitting round a roaring fire watching portions of the aforesaid lamb sizzling on long wooden spits. The contemplation of these succulent morsels shrined in a halo of dancing flame rapidly raised my spirits, and I regarded as inspired the hunter's favourable reply to my query as to the weather. Zurfluh, however, was not to be comforted; he repudiated my translation of "Yak shi," and cast bitter contempt on my efforts to speak the Tartar tongue.

The next morning his pessimism seemed justified, for the mist was thicker and wetter than ever. Yet the hunter still replied "Yak shi" to all inquiries, so, somewhat contrary to Zurfluh's wishes, the camp was packed, and about mid-day the hunter led us through the mist along an excellent path. The shepherd had also consented to join our party, so I had the rare and delightful privilege of walking unloaded. As we ascended, the source of Zurfluh's troubles on the previous day became obvious. The hunter had evidently wished him to ascend the glacier till beyond the séracs, and then to return to the kosh by the path we were now following. Zurfluh, however, recognising the fact that he was getting too far up the glacier, had turned to the right, and in the impenetrable fog forced the passage at the worst possible point. The hunter naturally refused to show the white feather before an unbeliever, and followed.

We walked past the séracs and reached the level glacier without difficulty. On the way across we picked up some fine horns—which had once belonged to a Tur—and which I believe now ornament Zurfluh's abode at Meiringen. After ascending the short slope that leads to the long level moraine which here forms the most convenient pathway, we halted whilst the hunter sought to rearrange his foot-gear. This latter was, however, hopelessly worn out by our previous expeditions, and the contemplation of his bleeding feet roused him to much wrath. Finally he chucked the *débris* of his hide sandals into a crevasse and expressed his intention of returning home. I confess he had reason on his side; I have known a moraine try the temper even of a well-shod member of the Alpine club, what then could be expected from a " poor benighted heathen"? We endeavoured to coax him forward, but he was obdurate to the most artful flattery— possibly because he could not understand a word we said. The suggestion, conveyed by appropriate gestures and an occasional word, that he would not be paid if he did not do the work merely elicited the reply, also expressed by gestures and a large mass of wholly unintelligible sound, that he did not at all expect to be. These conversational efforts proved unsatisfactory to all concerned and consumed much time. It was in consequence a good deal past four before the luggage was redistributed. Happily the mists were by now obviously clearing, and through rifts and rents we could see the long ridges of Shkara glittering in cloudless sunshine.

Quitting the moraine, we swung round to our left and began ascending interminable slopes of séracs and stones. The shepherd here took pity on my struggles, and seizing my knapsack, insisted on adding it to the vast pile of luggage he was carrying. Despite his burden, he was still able to show us the way and strode upwards, a splendid picture of muscle and perfect balance. About six o'clock we reached the highest point at which it appeared likely we should find water. Above, long slopes of snow and screes led up to the little glacier which lies below the col separating the peak from the great buttress I had climbed two or three weeks before.

We dug out the screes with our axes and made an excellent platform for the tent, then the fire was lit and we rejoiced over hot soup, English biscuits and Caucasian mutton. Before us was the great ice-embattled wall of Shkara and Janga, rising high into the warm tinted air, whilst below the silent glacier gloomed dark and cold, as the gathering mists of evening crawled slowly along its slopes. Behind our tent towered the great cliffs of Dych Tau. There is something in huge unclimbed peaks, especially when seen by the light of ebbing day, which is strangely solemn. Jest and joke are pushed aside as profanation, and one gazes on the tremendous cliffs with feelings closely akin to those with which the mediæval pilgrim worshipped at some holy shrine. The lengthening shadows fell athwart its face and showed deep gullies and jagged ridges, ice-glazed rocks and vast pitiless slabs of unbroken granite. From crack to gully and gully to ridge we traced a way till it emerged on a great smooth precipitous face where, as Zurfluh piously remarked, we must hope that " Der liebe Gott wird uns etwas helfen." We watched the last flicker of sunlight play round its topmost crags, and then crept into the shelter of tent and sleeping bags. The hardier Tartar refused the proffered place beside us, and, having washed his head, his feet and hands, in due accordance with the ritual of his creed, laid down in the open beside a great rock (not impossibly the same as that beside which Messrs. Woolley, Holder, and Cockin camped a few weeks later). Zurfluh regarded these proceedings with much

sad interest, feeling certain that the bitter wind would freeze him to death before morning.*

At 1 a.m., Zurfluh, who had kept awake to bemoan the Tartar's slow and pitiable decease, crept out of the tent to investigate how this process was getting on. A few minutes later, with his teeth chattering, but none the less with real delight in face and voice, he told me that not merely was the Tartar still alive, but, bare feet and all, appeared to be enjoying a refreshing sleep! Zurfluh's mind relieved on this point, he engaged in a protracted struggle with the fire. The Bezingi wood always requires much coaxing, but at 1 a.m. it would try the patience of a saint and the skill of one of his Satanic majesty's most practised stokers. Unluckily the little stream, on which we had counted for a perennial supply of water, was frozen to its core, and the weary process of melting ice had to be undertaken. My boots were also frozen, and putting them on proved to be the most arduous and by far the

* Our camp was on the screes at a point one inch from the bottom, and one and three-quarter inches from the left side of the illustration opposite. We ascended to the snow col still further to the left, and then ascended the mountain diagonally to the great secondary ridge on the left of the long couloir lying between the two summits. Owing to great foreshortening our traverse of the face appears almost horizontal; in actual fact it was nearly a direct ascent. The same cause makes the slopes look materially less steep than they really are. Even the snow slopes in the immediate foreground are very steep.

most painful part of the expedition. However, these preliminary difficulties were at length overcome and we were able to rejoice over hot tea and biscuits in the warm shelter of the tent.

Soon after half-past two we began the ascent and tramped steadily up the crisp snow to the little glacier. We crossed it, and ascended the slopes to the col by the route I had previously taken when on the way to the south-western buttress. Reaching this we turned sharply to the right, and, scrambling round one or two crumbling towers, were fairly launched on the face. Working upwards but bearing ever well to the right, we reached a shallow couloir still plastered in places by half-melted masses of snow. One of these, smitten by Zurfluh's axe, broke away bodily, striking me very severely on head, knee, and hand. Luckily I was almost close to him, but even so, for a minute or two, I scarcely knew what had happened. Had there been three or four of us on the rope the results could scarcely have failed to be serious. I am aware that two men are usually regarded as constituting too small a party for serious mountain work. None the less, on rotten rocks, or where much frozen snow loosely adheres to the ledges and projecting crags, it has advantages which, so far as I am able to judge, make it almost an ideal number.

Happily, five minutes' rest restored my scattered senses, and we quitted this ill-behaved gully, bearing still further to the right over disintegrated rocks and loose stones. Going fairly fast, we reached the great mass of red rock, referred to by Mr. Donkin as marking the limit of his and Mr. Dent's attempt, at 7 a.m. Without halting we still pushed on, bearing ever to the right in order to reach the smaller of two long couloirs that had been very conspicuous from our camp. This couloir runs up the face of the peak towards the south-western ridge in the near neighbourhood of the summit. Zurfluh had, the previous evening, diagnosed its contents as snow, and the rocks being mostly ice-glazed and distinctly difficult, we thought it desirable to reach it as soon as possible. When we at length gained its brink we saw at a glance that it was much steeper than we had imagined, and that, if I may be pardoned the Irishism, the snow was ice. In consequence we clung to the rocks as long as any sort of decent progress could be made, and it was only when each foot of advance was costing precious minutes that we turned into the gully.

Hypercritical climbers have occasionally suggested that I am in the habit of cutting steps rather wide apart. I only wish these cavillers could have seen Zurfluh's staircase. He has a peculiar habit of only cutting steps for the left foot, his right having the faculty of adhering firmly to absolutely smooth ice and enabling him by a combination of jump and wriggle to lift his left foot from one secure step to another six feet above it. He kindly showed me how it was done and urged me to imitate his procedure, pointing out the great saving of time thus rendered possible. Since, however, any trifling error would have resulted in an undue acquaintance with the glacier below, I preferred to cut intervening steps; even then it was a most arduous gymnastic exercise to climb from one to another. Happily, some twenty minutes of these violent athletics brought us to a point where we could quit the gully for the slope on our right. Hard, solid rock then led us merrily upwards to a great secondary ridge. This ridge divides the south face of the peak into two well-marked divisions, to the east is the great couloir which reaches from the col between the two summits to the very base of the mountain, and beyond are the interminable series of buttresses and gullies that stretch away towards Mishirgi Tau; whilst to the west is the less broken cliff reaching to the south-western ridge. We worked up the secondary ridge, now on one side, now on the other, till we were pulled up at the point where it bulges outwards and towers up into the great crag which, like the hand of some gigantic sun-dial, throws long shadows across the face of the mountain. It was evident that the work would now become very much more serious, so we halted and made a good meal. We packed the remainder of the provisions into the knapsack and stowed it away under a large stone.

After prospecting the cliff on our right, Zurfluh came to the conclusion that nothing could be done on that side. We therefore turned our attention to the rocks on our left, and were soon traversing a huge slab by the aid of various minute wrinkles and discolorations. Happily it soon became possible to turn upwards, and, trusting mainly to our finger tips and the sides of our boots, we forced our way back on to the ridge at the very top of the sun-dial projection. For a short distance it was almost horizontal and extraordinarily sharp. So much so, indeed, that we were fain to adopt the attitude much affected by foreign climbers in foreign prints, and progress was made on our hands whilst a leg was slung over each side as a sort of balancing pole. A gap fifteen feet deep separated this razor edge from the mass of the mountain beyond. Zurfluh jumped down on to a convenient bed of snow and cheerily went on his way. Shortly afterwards I reached the gap, and, as I fondly imagined, similarly jumped, but the bed of snow did not take the impact kindly and slid away into the little couloir on my left, a more or less breathless Herr being left clinging to a sort of banister of rock which projected from the gap. Happily this incident escaped the notice of the professional member of the party. I say happily, because the *morale* of the leader is frequently a plant of tender growth, and should be carefully shielded from all adverse influences.

We were now on the final peak. Gestola Tetnuld and Janga were well below us, and even the corniced ridge of Shkara did not look as if it could give us much. Unluckily, over this great ridge an evil-looking mass of cloud had gathered, and from time to time shreds and strips were torn from it and whirled across the intervening space by a furious southerly gale. Some of these shreds and strips sailed high over our heads, shutting out the welcome warmth of the sun; others less aerially inclined now and again got entangled in the ridges below, blotting out their jagged spires and warning us that at any moment the cliffs around might be veiled in impenetrable mist.

The wall immediately above was evidently very formidable. Though I sought to keep up an affectation of assured success, I was quite unable to see how any further advance was to be made. Zurfluh, however, is a man who rises to such emergencies, and is moreover an exceptionally brilliant rock climber. He proved equal to the occasion, and vowed by the immortal gods that we would not be baffled a second time. Whilst he was looking for the most desirable line of attack, I replied to the shouts of the shepherd who had climbed to the col early in the morning, and, greatly interested in our proceedings, had spent the rest of the day on that bleak spot in a biting and furious wind.

Zurfluh, after a careful survey, determined that we must again traverse to our left. We crawled along the face of the great cliff, clinging to outward shelving and most unsatisfactory ledges, till we reached a place where strenuous efforts just enabled us to lift ourselves over a sort of bulge. Above this the angle was less steep, and a few cracks and splinters enabled us to get reliable hold. A short distance further, however, a second and, if possible, nastier bulge appeared. After contemplating Zurfluh's graceful attitudes and listening to his gasps as he battled with the desperate difficulty, it was " borne in upon me "—as the Plymouth Brethren say—that the second peak in the Caucasus ought not to be climbed by an unroped party. Would it not be contrary to all the canons laid down for the guidance of youth and innocence in the Badminton and All England series? Might it not even be regarded as savouring of insult to our peak? I mildly suggested these fears to Zurfluh. He asked me whether I would come up for the rope or whether he should send the rope down to me. For some hidden reason a broad grin illuminated his face as he strongly recommended the former course, pointing out that the ledge on which I was huddled was not a convenient place for roping operations. Despite this advice I unhesitatingly decided on the latter alternative, and when the rope came down, successfully grappled with the difficulty of putting it on. And now a strange phenomenon must be recorded: a moment earlier I could have sworn before any court—and been glad to do it, provided the court was, as courts usually are, on level ground—that the cliff in front was absolutely perpendicular. Yet no sooner was the rope firmly attached than the cliff tilted backwards till it barely exceeded a beggarly sixty degrees!

We were now able to get round the square corner of the peak on to the face fronting the lower summit, and could look across to the ice-swept cliffs of Koshtantau. The gap between the two peaks was well below us—indeed, we were almost level with the lower summit. I had always had misgivings about this section of the ascent, and it was, therefore, with no small delight that I perceived a long crack up which a way could almost certainly be forced. Apart, however, from the accident of this crack or fault, I am not sure this wall could be ascended. With our elbows and backs against one side and our knees against the other, we worked our way quickly upwards. The lower peak sank rapidly, and the appearance of distant snows above its crest was hailed with triumphant shouts. Then Zurfluh dived into a dark hole behind a stone that had wedged itself in our narrow path, and desperate were the wriggles and squeezings necessary to push his body through the narrow aperture. Then we had to quit the crack for a yard or two and scramble up a great slab at its side. Once more we got back into our crack and on and ever upwards till at length we emerged on the ridge. On the ridge do I say? No; on the very summit itself. Every peak in Europe, Elbruz alone excepted, was below us, and from our watch-tower of 17,054 feet we gazed at the rolling world. Turning to the left, a few steps brought me to the culminating point, and I sat down on its shattered crest. Huge clouds were by now wrapping Shkara in an ever darkening mantle, and the long ridge of Janga was buried in dense, matted banks of vapour, white and brilliant above, but dark and evil along their ever lowering under-edges. Koshtantau shone in its snowy armour, white against black billows of heaped-up storm. Elbruz alone was clear and spotless, and its vastness made it look so close that Zurfluh laughed to scorn my statement that our passes from Mujal to the Bashil Su were between us and it. He maintained and still believes that Elbruz is situated close to Tiktengen, and I defy all the surveyors of the Holy Russian Empire to convince him of error. A yellow look about the snow suggested, it is true, considerable distance, but the huge size and height of the enormous mass so dwarfed the intervening space that I am not surprised at his mistake.

As I declined to give up my seat on the highest point, Zurfluh was constrained to build the cairn, on which his heart was set, on a point slightly lower. Under his fostering care this point grew and waxed strong till it proudly looked over the crest of its rival that, for the last few thousand years, had topped it by a foot. After three-quarters of an hour's halt the furious blasts of the hurricane made us quite willing to move, and at 11.30 a.m. we left the summit. We rattled down the crack, and got back on to the south face without much trouble. Then, however, I distinguished myself by losing the way, and was relegated to the nominally more important post of last man. Zurfluh with brilliant skill picked up the line of ledges and cracks by which we had ascended, and we duly reached the horizontal ridge. Elated by our success, we strode boldly along its narrow edge instead of adopting the undignified procedure of the morning. Shortly afterwards Zurfluh imitated my bad example and lost the right line of descent. We could see the rock by which our knapsack was securely stowed, and our footprints were on a small patch of snow just above the wall, but we could not discover the line by which we had connected these two points. Ultimately we were compelled to make a sensational descent by a tiny cleft or crack just wide enough for toes and fingers. Its lower end opened into space, and a long, sideways jump was requisite to reach footing. Zurfluh, aided by the rope, got across, and said he could catch and steady me as I came over. I have a keen remembrance of descending the crack, of leaning forwards and down as far as I could reach, and just being able to rest the point of my axe on a small excrescence; then leaning my weight upon it, I swung over sideways towards Zurfluh. An instant later he was clasping my knees with such devout enthusiasm that I felt like a holy prophet ejected from the shining mountain into the arms of some faithful devotee.

This practically ended our difficulties. A few minutes later we reached the knapsack and soon demolished its contents. Our porter was still sitting on the col watching us, and Zurfluh, mindful of the habits of the Swiss when in high places, averred that he would certainly have finished every scrap of provision in the camp. None the less we greeted his shouts with loud jodels and much triumphant brandishing of iceaxes. Our lunch being brought to a summary conclusion by the total exhaustion of the supplies, we stuffed the rope into the empty knapsack and turned once more to the descent. We got on rapidly till we reached the couloir. The ice was here so rotten, and much of it so ill-frozen to the rocks and underlying ice, and the whole gully was so obviously swept by falling stones, that we unanimously refused to follow our morning's track. My own impression is that, apart from other objections, even Zurfluh did not quite like descending the remarkable staircase by which we had scrambled up. Crossing the couloir we struck on to the rocks, and soon discovered some precipitous iceglazed chimneys down which we managed to crawl. Regaining our route of the morning, we sped merrily downwards to the belt of red rocks. The summit of a new peak in one's pocket lends strength and swiftness even to the clumsy, and I shuffled after Zurfluh in most active fashion. Our porter soon came to the conclusion that the interest of the play was over, and we saw him pick himself up and go warily down the slopes. A little later, Zurfluh, perceiving that even a Herr could not go much astray, was seized with a desire to show the Tartar how easy slopes should be traversed, and dashed towards the col with the speed and graceful ease of the well-practised chamois hunter. When a man is being hopelessly outpaced by his companion, he always experiences great pleasure in seeing that same companion miss the easiest line of descent. This pleasure I experienced on seeing Zurfluh, after reaching the col, keep to the line by which we had come in the morning. My previous exploratory climb had made me aware of a convenient snow-filled gully in which an exceedingly rapid standing glissade was possible. Reaching this highway, I spun down to the little glacier. Having run across this, I sat myself comfortably on my hat, and slid down the long slopes almost into the tent, where Zurfluh was still busy emptying the snow from his pockets.

The porter met me with loud shouts of "Allah il Allah! Minghi Tau, Allah, Allah!"

We soon discovered that, instead of consuming the whole of our provisions, the porter had not even had a crust of bread. We urged him to take a preliminary lunch, or rather breakfast, while the soup was cooking, but he refused, and seemed in no hurry for dinner. He manipulated the fire with much skill, making the vile wood burn in a really creditable manner, and only pausing from his efforts to award me an occasional appreciative slap on the back. It being early, 4 p.m., Zurfluh expressed a strong desire to strike camp and descend; but the delights of the kosh did not rouse my enthusiasm, and I refused to move. Indeed, it is one of the great pleasures of Caucasian travelling that the weary tramp over screes, uneven glacier, the horrors of the moraine, and, too frequently, the reascent to the hotel, are unknown. A camp at one spot is practically as comfortable as at any other, and in consequence, so soon as one feels inclined to sit down and laze, the day's work is over and one postpones the screes and moraines to the sweet distance of to-morrow. It is, indeed, a rare delight to sit at one's ease in the early afternoon and gaze at the huge cliffs amongst which one has been wandering, free from all the thought of hurry, of moraines, or of darkness.

Towards evening the gathering clouds burst in thunder, and the screes below us, right down to the glacier, were powdered with hail and snow. As the moon rose, however, the curtain was rent apart, and the great ridges, shining in the brilliant whiteness of fresh-fallen snow, gazed at us across the dark gulf of the Bezingi glacier. The evening, being windless, was comparatively warm, and it was nearly midnight before Zurfluh's peaceful slumbers were disturbed by the struggles of a shivering Herr with his sleeping bag.

The next morning we went down the glacier to the Misses kosh, packed up our belongings, and tramped to Tubeneli. Fresh stores had arrived from Naltcik and the old chief feasted us on chicken and cakes, but these delights failed to comfort the melancholy Zurfluh, and he flatly refused to do aught but return straight home. On Dych Tau the excitement of the climb had aroused all the vigour and strength he possessed, but now that the spurt was over he broke down completely. He was undoubtedly very poorly, and looked the mere ghost, and a most thin and melancholy ghost, of his former self. "Es gefällt mir nicht," may be good philosophy, but it undoubtedly tends to a pre-Raphaelite condition of body.

CHAPTER XIII.

SOME CAUCASIAN PASSES.

Having recovered from the effects of the two cold nights described at the beginning of the last chapter, we made up our minds to cross on to the basin of the Dych Su glacier and see whether any convenient and easy route could be found thence to the summit of Shkara. At 4.30 a.m. we left our camp and walked up the Bezingi glacier, halting occasionally to examine the face of the mountain. The endless series of hanging glaciers suspended on its cliffs seemed to threaten so much risk and danger on this side, that we were not in any way tempted to modify our plans. We subsequently saw, however (when ascending Dych Tau), that great glacier plateaux were concealed by the foreshortening due to our position, and that, in reality, the ascent may be effected from this side without venturing on to any sérac-swept position. But this knowledge was hidden from us as we tramped up the glacier and passed its endless

JANOA FROM THE REGION OF GLACIERS.

terraces of glacier cliffs on our way to the Bezingi vsek.

Zurfluh suggested keeping along the ridge from the col to the summit—a route which has since been demonstrated to be feasible; but I was impressed by the enormous length of the ridge, and ultimately decided in favour of our original plan. We accordingly plunged down to the glacier at our feet, and half an hour later reached a tangled ice-fall. We could see, below us, the deep trench of the Dych Su glacier, but our Tartar porter evinced a strong objection to a direct descent by the séracs. Zurfluh accordingly clambered up to a little notch in the ridge on our right, and after a brief inspection called on us to follow. Without much trouble we found a way down the rocks, and about 4 p.m. reached a tiny shelf of grass a few hundred feet above the great Dych Su glacier. The Tartar cheerily emptied his knapsack and tramped off down the ice to Karaoul, charged with the duty of buying and cooking a sheep, and getting such bread as the resources of that tiny hamlet afforded. Zurfluh and I, after putting up the tent and setting our soup to boil, prospected for the best way to the top of our peak.

The great glacier down which we had come from the Bezingi vsek, falls into the main Dych Su stream at approximately right angles. Between these two glaciers rise the huge rock buttresses which form the north-eastern pedestal of Shkara.

A long couloir, or the rocks at the side of it, obviously gave access to a great glacier region from which we considered the higher ridges of our mountain might be attained. On the whole we thought our prospects fairly good, and returned to our camp in the best of spirits.

Early the next morning the camp fire was lit, tea was brewed, and our frugal meal of brown bread duly consumed. Leaving the camp securely packed in the watertight knapsacks, we tramped and scrambled up the slopes towards the plateau we had marked as our first *objectif*.

The cliffs proved very easy, and our hopes rose as we saw the facility with which we were topping the neighbouring crests. Arrived at the plateau, we found ourselves below a huge wall of ice-bound rock that forms the ridge dividing the shelf we were on, from a vast glacier flowing almost from the summit of Shkara down to the glacier we had descended the previous day. Keeping along our shelf, we advanced merrily till a great buttress of black rock, projecting from the ridge, partially broke its continuity. Either we must round this buttress, a process involving a considerable descent, or we must climb on to the ridge and follow it. We appeared to have covered a great deal of ground, and were obviously at a great height; we concluded, therefore, that we must be somewhere in the neighbourhood of the summit. Acting on this, as it turned out, wholly erroneous supposition, we turned to the cliff, and were soon engaged in really serious work. Ice-glazed rocks, rotten slopes of stones only held in position by a cement of ice and snow, were alternated by steep slabs that tested my leader's skill to the utmost. Nearing the ridge we reached an ice slope, up which we had to hew our way with much toil and a great expenditure of time.

A huge cornice overhung the glacier to the north-east of the ridge, and it was with much trepidation that I advanced, carefully held by Zurfluh low down on the other slope, to its very crest, so that we might obtain some knowledge of our whereabouts and the capabilities of our ridge. My position was superb; through a big hole in the cornice I could look down three thousand feet or more on to the vast unbroken glacier referred to above, whilst on every side the giant ridges stretched away below me to the regions of trees and grass-grown uplands. Far away to the south two cones of snow, a larger cone with a smaller one to the left, could have been naught else than Ararat itself. Never have I looked through clearer air, or been able to trace so distinctly each fold and buttress that bent and twisted the white lines of foam, marking the rushing torrents in the valleys deep below me.

Zurfluh, however, who does not usually appreciate the pleasures of noble scenery, and who failed to realise the extreme solidity of the cornice, or the fact that it was frozen till it could rival the tenacity of iron, urged me to examine the route and come down from my aerial perch. To follow the ridge was easy, and, if one trusted to luck and the cornice, would not have involved an impossible amount of time; but we did not care to take this risk, and to hew steps in hard ice, along the steep face below the cornice, would have been the work of days rather than hours. It was evident we had struck the ridge far too soon, and could only escape defeat by the reckless expedient of using the cornice as a high road.

Prudent councils prevailed, and we determined to retreat. From a convenient ledge, formed by a projecting rock, we mapped out various promising routes to the top of our peak; but the extraordinary clearness of the atmosphere, the absence of all wind, and the intense heat, were signs infallible of approaching bad weather. The day, indeed, was ours, but the morrow evidently belonged to the tempests and the snow storms. We ate our lunch in that state of modified happiness which is induced by failure on the one hand, and exquisite scenery, warmth, comfort, and sunshine on the other.

Much care was needed to regain the glacier shelf. The heat of the sun had loosened the bonds of ice by which the crumbling slope was held together. Swift and resistless was the rush of the dislodged rocks now and again upset, and it was always necessary to descend with one's head over one's shoulder to see what little jokes the mountain might be seeking to play at our expense.

The last slope, consisting of a most objectionable mixture of loose stones, ice, and snow, we declined to have anything to do with, and, after much labour and search, discovered a precipitous line of rock leading into a tiny couloir. Once in it, we sped through a cloud of snow-dust to the welcome field of névé. Tramping back to the top of the steep slopes that led down to our bivouac, Zurfluh made for the head of the great couloir, and boldly proposed glissading to the bottom. The couloir was bent, and a deep groove, cut by water and falling *débris*, crossed it from side to side; to glissade the open couloir would, in consequence, have involved a sudden drop into this deeply eroded channel. Zurfluh, to obviate this difficulty, suggested that we should glissade in the groove itself. Its exaggeration of the great bend of the couloir and a variety of minor sinuosities and wriggles, materially reduced the angle of its slope, and compensated, in some measure, for the icy character of its floor.

Zurfluh shot off down the channel, and whisked away round the first corner; he emerged into sight some few hundred feet lower down, and was again lost in another curve. He appeared, however, very comfortable, so I committed myself to the groove. I was swung round corners at a furious pace, and more than once was knocked off my feet by a stone frozen into the floor of the gully. Happily at the small bends it was usually possible to check the speed of one's flight, and regain an attitude suited to the self-respecting mountaineer. The final swoop on to the snow face was simply delightful, and I rejoined Zurfluh feeling that an unsuccessful day is not without its compensations; though, doubtless, the company of a daring chamois hunter, and the enjoyment of the methods and dodges appropriate to that sport, had something to do with my feelings of satisfaction.

Reaching our camp, we found the Tartar had not returned, and Zurfluh, depressed by the emptiness of the larder, fell a victim to melancholy. The Tartar, he insisted, had fallen into a crevasse, and was probably at that very moment slowly freezing to death between its icy walls. In vain I pointed out that the Tartar was in the habit of hunting the "big horns" on the glacier, and could, as we had witnessed, see a concealed crevasse with an ease that the best of Alpine climbers might envy. The decease of the Tartar, and the consequential absence of dinner, remained the dominant ideas in his mind, and care and sorrow sat in the deep furrows of his face. Just as it was getting dark, however, he espied a moving spot on the glacier, and our shouts were answered by a voice which did not in any way sound as if it belonged to the dead. About 9 p.m. the Tartar arrived, burdened with the many joints of a lamb, some extraordinary rye cakes, and a great bundle of firewood. We pinned a lantern to the roof of our tent, and made a sumptuous meal on cold boiled meat and the most objectionable cakes.

The morning broke with every symptom of coming storm. Long wisps of cloud formed above the ridges, and fitful rushes of wind swept, howling, down the glacier gorges. The Tartar shook his head and said "Karaoul?" and, when we demurred, wrapped his burka round him, and gave us to understand that wind and snow would be our portion on the Bezingi vsek.

Having ascended the steep rocks by which we had previously turned the ice fall, we began the short but very steep descent on to the upper glacier. The ice itself was cut off from the rocks by an incipient, well-bridged, Schrund, and through one of the holes in this bridge the Tartar managed to drop his iron-shod stick. Zurfluh and I regarded the weapon as hopelessly lost, but the Tartar insisted on being tied to the end of our rope and lowered into the chasm. We knocked away the frozen snow, and thought the black depths would prove more eloquent than our speech. Not a bit of it, he seemed to rather enjoy its dark terrors, and we lowered him down till he disappeared from sight. After some twenty feet, a joyful shout suggested that his quest had been successful, and we hauled and pulled till the Tartar, with his black hair and beard well powdered with snow and ice, reappeared. He was much delighted at the recovery of his weapon, and gave me several sound slaps on the back, indicative of his affection and goodwill. His satisfaction then took a more pleasing form, and he insisted on taking my knapsack in addition to his own.

Instead of returning by our pass of two days since, we struck up a small glacier leading to a gap a few hundred yards further from Shkara, and perhaps 500 feet higher. Access to it is rather easier for a loaded Tartar, and the descent on the Bezingi side is admirably suited for a glissade.

As we reached the crest a fierce blast of wind buried us in a cloud of frozen snow and flakes of ice, torn from the slopes behind us. We fled before its resistless rush, and, glissading, running, and tumbling head over heels, shot down to the glacier below. Arrived on the moraine, which runs like a path along the side of the glacier, the porter unloaded the firewood, and the bundle was carefully concealed beneath a great stone. The storm, by this time, had enveloped all the ridges in masses of dirty, evil-looking cloud. Portentous growls and long reverberating peals of thunder issued from the impenetrable gloom, suggesting the near advent of rain. We sped along the moraine, or rather Zurfluh and I did; the Tartar seemed to be usually seated on a rock waiting for us, so easily could he outpace the representatives of the Alps!

Breathlessly we raced up the short ascent to the grassy oasis where stood our camp, and at that very moment a waterspout swept down on us.

In the Alps a wetting is not of much account, but in the Caucasus it is extremely inconvenient, at all events in settled bad weather. The only means of drying clothes is to hang them on the tent ropes, or spread them on warm rocks, methods which are not applicable during the continuance of rain.

We congratulated ourselves loudly over our most opportune return, and then proceeded to overhaul the stores of provisions. It became obvious that a journey to our supplies at Tubeneli in quest of biscuits, chocolate, tea, and soups was essential. The Tartar expressed a cheery readiness to start at once, and we saw him disappear in the deluge. Meanwhile, the shepherd from the pastures opposite rubbed his dagger on a hone, which the careful Zurfluh had brought from Switzerland, as a desirable preliminary to lamb cutlets. The luckless victim, the destined banquet, was still browsing on the luxuriant grass, regardless alike of torrential rain and swiftly-striding doom.

During the afternoon a serious defect in our Whymper tent made itself apparent. At each end, in this make of tent, there is a small hole in the roof, through which the poles supporting the structure project. Though these holes are very small, the rain fell in such torrents that enough came through them to form ponds on our waterproof floor. We drained these ponds by cutting holes in our flooring, but, in the narrow space available, it was somewhat inconvenient to have two damp and uninhabitable regions. Zurfluh, in a moment of inspiration, sallied out into the deluge and stuck a boot on the top of each pair of poles. By this ingenious device we were restored to comparative comfort.

Late the next afternoon we saw our porter reappear. A complex arrangement of knapsacks—one in front and one behind—a big load of firewood stuck on anywhere, and a burka skilfully draped round his shoulders and packages, gave him the appearance of an overgrown umbrella, enjoying a quiet constitutional in peculiarly fitting atmospheric conditions.

Shortly before dark a furious south-westerly wind drove the clouds down the valley, and the great peaks emerged resplendent in whitest snow. During the night the wind veered to the north, and terrific blasts threatened the security of our tent. More than once we were forced to adopt drastic measures to save it from total ruin. Happily the clouds and mist were put to utter rout, and at daybreak we could see the last fragments of their beaten host hurrying, helter-skelter, across the Zanner pass.

When I sought to put on my climbing boots, I found one of these valuable properties had wholly disappeared. With true wisdom, Zurfluh had used my boots for the ornamentation of the tent-poles, and during the night a more violent gust than usual had carried one bodily away. Subsequent search discovered it submerged in a slimy pool!

The shepherd from the pastures opposite had promised to come over and act as second porter; so, whilst waiting for him, my boot was duly washed and as much of the internal moisture wiped out as possible; we also utilised Zurfluh's hammer and anvil and drove in hobnails where required. We then passed under review the various remaining joints of boiled lamb, selecting those which had the least offensive and damaged appearance. The knapsacks were at last all packed and ready, but still the shepherd tarried. Finally, at 6 a.m., there being no signs of his arrival, we re-distributed the baggage and started without him.

Our interpreter, almost hidden beneath a gigantic burka, struggled along bravely till we had ascended two or three thousand feet of the screes leading towards the Zanner pass. We began, however, at this point to feel the full strength of the gale, and his allusions to the God of Abraham, of Isaac, and of Jacob became constantly more frequent, till at length he sank down in a heap and expressed his intention of promptly giving up the ghost. Our party grouped itself in picturesque and recumbent attitudes, and watched his proceedings with interest. Gradually, as we recovered our wind, we began to perceive the vanity, not to say chilliness, of this course of action, or rather inaction, and we, in consequence, deputed the Tartar, who always enjoyed a little addition to the day's work, to see the interpreter sufficiently far on his way down to be out of all risk or danger. Zurfluh and I then tramped steadily towards the pass. Before a great time we were overtaken by the Tartar, who reported that the interpreter had quickly recovered so soon as his feet were turned towards the valley.

At 10 a.m. we reached our pass, and saw that though the wind had driven every vestige of mist and fog from the northern slopes, the whole of Suanetia was a sea of matted cloud, out of which the great peaks towered into the sunshine. The wind was terribly cold, so we plunged at once into the damp, heaving vapour below us. It soon became apparent to a fatigued Herr that we were going up hill instead of down. Zurfluh, after I had made sundry protests of continually increasing strength, admitted this fact. He appeared, however, to think that in this topsy-turvy country, where all things go by contraries, that very possibly the best way down was to walk up-hill. My muscles protested against this doctrine, and we retraced our steps some distance. Further investigations showed that by going to the north-east, parallel to the main ridge, a gentle descent was begun. As we paced through the mist the angle steadily increased, and crevasses and gigantic pinnacles of ice began to loom through the fog. Zurfluh, forgetting the air of sorrow that befits the Swiss guide in a foreign land, began to rejoice in the struggle. An unknown ice fall shrouded in impenetrable cloud is, indeed, enough to rouse the sporting instinct in any mountaineer.

At one point we were nearly stopped. The sérac, on which we stood, overhung a rock cliff, the bottom of which was lost in the fog. Direct descent was impossible, but the side of the sérac evidently gave access to the rock slope slightly to our right. Zurfluh, however, averred that he had felt the sérac give a premonitory movement, and that the slightest jar, such as that caused by step-cutting, would inevitably send the whole structure in one thundering avalanche to the mist-filled depths below. Zurfluh and the Tartar accordingly retreated to solid footing, whilst, tied to the end of our rope, I managed to cut the steps and scramble on to a smaller sérac, more securely anchored to the slope. The men followed, and we climbed down the rocks to the glacier, urged to our best speed by the knowledge that a sérac might take it into its head to come trundling after us.

The fog, which had been getting thinner, now began to break into detached masses, and every now and again we saw the ridges and deep valleys of Suanetia. As we advanced, the great walls of the glacier began to close in on us, leaving merely a narrow gorge, through which the broken ice plunges to the world of grass and flowers and forest.

Thanks to Mr. Freshfield's description of this pass we now knew where we were, and, cheered by the rapidly improving weather, we traversed on to the rocks on the left of the ice fall, and by their aid turned the obstruction. Reaching the lower glacier, we tramped merrily along it, till, about 4.30 p.m., we stepped off the ice into the luxuriant vegetation of the southern slopes.

Our Tartar, having no longer mountaineering difficulties wherewith to occupy his mind, gave us his opinion of the Suanetian race. There was real fury in his voice as he described the wild delight of a hand-to-hand encounter; though on the whole he was clearly of opinion that a more enduring and artistic joy is to be found in skilfully stalking your adversary, and taking pot-shots at him from behind convenient stones. The conversation was illustrated by such wealth of gesture and mimicry, that our almost complete ignorance of his language did not materially interfere with our comprehension. I will confess that my mind was somewhat disturbed by the doubt whether it was prudent to take a warrior of such furious mood into the crowded villages of his hereditary foes.

We made our way through the thickly wooded slopes of the valley, now and again being almost forced into the boiling torrent in our efforts to avoid the entanglement of the underwood. Gradually the valley opened out, and towards evening we wended our way down rich pastures, shadowed by noble clumps of beech and pine.

Arriving at the first houses, my fears about the Tartar's demeanour were set at rest, his request for direction to the Starshina's residence, if not conciliatory in tone, being shorn of any expressions indicative of his real feelings. By the time we had reached this worthy's house at Mujal it was quite dark. We battered at his door, and, after some delay, rendered exciting by the fierce onslaught of sundry dogs, he appeared and accorded us a ceremonial welcome. Attired in his best clothes, and with an absurd chain, much like an English mayor's, festooned around him, he led the way to the guest-house.

The inky night was made brilliant with eight flaring torches of split pine. In the long procession figured a steaming samovar, and we noted with satisfaction a large basket, within which the eye of faith and hunger detected many good and nutritious substances. As we proceeded, sundry fleet-footed youths were shed from the caravan into the darkness. These youths, we subsequently discovered, had been despatched in quest of Russian bread, fresh butter, and milk—dainties

which the natives had learnt are appreciated by
the hobnailed western. At the end of a somewhat protracted walk we reached the guest-house,
and found that one of the fleet-footed youths had
preceded us and lit a blazing fire. The cheery,
dancing flames fell on the strange faces and
curious dresses of our hosts, while the dark, weird
shadows that lurked in the remoter corners
afforded pleasing cover from which the younger
and more bashful natives could watch the proceedings.

Tea, unleavened cakes, and eggs were immediately forthcoming, supplemented, on the arrival
of the various breathless youths, by fresh milk,
butter, and leavened bread. During the progress
of this meal we learnt that the female members
of the Starshina's family were engaged in the
preparation of a banquet of much complex magnificence. Knowing from past experience that
this banquet would probably be ready about
1 a.m., we begged the Starshina to excuse us,
alleging fatigue and the need of sleep. One of
the active youths was accordingly hurried into
the darkness, and I trust succeeded in stopping
the culinary efforts and enabled the ladies to
obtain their due allowance of beauty sleep.
Various elaborate preparations were then made
for our comfort; the crowd of visitors were unceremoniously ejected; the mysteries of the
bolts and bars were explained; elaborate farewells

were taken, and we were left to our well-earned rest.

The sun was blazing through the shutters when a tentative rapping at the windows aroused us. Emerging from our sleeping bags, we opened the door and found breakfast awaiting us in the verandah. The guest-house was beautifully situated, well away from the village, and in an open, park-like country. Splendid trees and rippling watercourses were all around us, whilst above towered the great white pyramid of Tetnuld. In the other direction the rocky crest of Ush-ba just showed above the lower ridges. The flickering sunlight through the leaves suggested a delicious feeling of freshness and home, which was further accentuated by a plunge in a neighbouring stream. I then joined Zurfluh in his attention to the good things supplied by our host.

Our quarters were so peculiarly tempting that after breakfast we despatched the Tartar to purchase chicken, bread, eggs, potatoes, and such other luxuries as the resources of Mujal might afford. Meanwhile a native, knowing a few words of French, appeared and told us of the wonders of Ush-ba and the wealth of the Ingur valley. However, our plan was to cross to Chegem, so we deputed our friend to engage two porters to take us to the recognised camp for the Twiber pass.

Two years later I walked and rode along the crest of the low ridge which divides the district

of Mujal from the main valley of the Ingur. For
delightful scenery this ridge has no equal. Grassy
lawns shaded by stately trees and watered by
delicious springs, offer perfect camping-grounds.
Away to the northward rises the great range
dominated by the most majestic peak in the whole
region—the double-headed Ush-ba; whilst to the
south are the forest-clad valleys and walled villages
where the native still looks with suspicion on the
stranger. At Scena the oxen may still be seen
treading out the corn, and rude winnowing effected
by throwing up the grain in the open air, the
wooden shovels used for this purpose being carved
out of a single pine-log. The women may still
be seen grinding the corn in quaint hand-mills, and
all the associations of the village carry one's mind
back to the earliest pioneers of civilisation. So
delightful is this region of dense primeval forest,
of valleys where the torrents carve their way
through the roots of huge pines, of tiny oases of
grass, and banks buried in raspberry-canes loaded
with delicious fruit, that the mountaineer is apt
to lose sight of the path of duty and abandon himself to lazing on the grass and watching the tiny
specks of sunlight dancing amongst the foliage.

But my enthusiasm is leading me away from the
matter in hand. Early in the afternoon we said
good-bye to our host, and strolled up a lateral
valley through well-timbered slopes. About 4 p.m.
we reached a grassy glade surrounded by fine trees

and intersected by brawling rivulets. It was an ideal camping-ground, and both Zurfluh and I felt our day's work was ended. Tall fern suggested luxurious mattresses, and decaying trees a roaring camp-fire. The Suanetian porters, however, protested. The proper place to camp was, they said, an hour further up. I went a few yards along the path and emerged on a great open alp. Along the steep slope of the gorge the path could be seen winding upwards through a region of grass, unrelieved by shrub or tree. The delights of the lower camp were irresistible, and I returned to our sheltered glade. The Suanetians still objected. They evidently thought that as they had not got to the regular gîte a corresponding part of their pay would be deducted. Finding this was not the case, they drew their long knives and cut the fern for our mattresses. They then lit a huge fire, and collected such a store of logs and sticks that it would have lasted a frugal Swiss the whole winter.

Next they prepared the chicken, severing the breastbone longitudinally and opening them into flat plate-like objects; these were impaled on long wooden spits and set to cook. As the supplies were abundant, we gave the Suanetians an invitation to dinner. Squatting round the fire we had a merry time, and wound up in true Caucasian fashion by an examination of each others' weapons. On their departure, the faces of the Suanetians were illumined by a "schönes Trinkgeld," and after a last shout of farewell they disappeared silently in the forest.

Zurfluh and the Tartar then agreed that chicken are a vain and frivolous food to pack into knapsacks, and that consequently it would be well to consume the remainder of our store. In consequence the rest of the birds were got ready and similarly impaled on the spits. The fire by this time had grown into a vast furnace, more suited for the pedestrian exercise of Shadrach, Meshach, and Abednego than for the toasting of diminutive chicken. A furious onslaught with our axes, however, sufficed to tear up the decaying roots and other combustible material amongst which the fire was making its way, and to reduce it to such limits that the forest itself was no longer endangered. We then pitched the tent, and felt ready for our supplementary dinner.

When we turned in for the night we found our quarters so luxurious that we half made up our minds to assault a small rock peak at the head of the valley, and thus have an excuse for a second night in this most exquisite glade. Slumber, however, overtook us before these ideas had crystallised into solid resolution, and the next morning we were too sleepy to do aught but adhere to our original plan.

Starting before daybreak, we left the forest behind and tramped over the grass and along the right bank of the Twiber torrent. We passed the customary gîte amidst many self-congratulations. A less pleasing camp it would be difficult to imagine, and it was more than doubtful whether water, that first necessity of camp life, could have been obtained. Then the path either gave out or we hopelessly missed it, and we had to scramble along a steep grass slope till, in utter desperation, we clambered down on to the glacier. We broke the monotony of our walk up the ice by violent efforts to scare two chamois that were watching our movements; but they refused to be alarmed by our yells and gesticulations, and were still strolling about the slopes when we lost sight of them in the distance. Reaching the upper glacier, we found that the snow had been drifted into high ridges. The furrows between were at least fifteen inches deep, and walking across them proved so desperately tiresome that we determined to quit the great glacier and make for a very obvious gap on our left. It is true the Suanetians had expressly warned us against doing so. Possibly this partly prompted our decision, for there is always pleasure in running counter to the piled-up knowledge of the wise.

After a considerable ascent over screes, we reached a snow slope which led us to the pass. In front was a glacier basin, shut in, to the north, by a low wall of jagged rock. This wall evidently swept round further to the east, and enclosed the head of the glacier. Zurfluh and the Tartar turned to the left, never doubting that our route must lie in that direction. For a moment I could not quite understand where we were, and accordingly a halt was decreed. A few minutes' contemplation then convinced me that the mighty peak, blocking the whole width of the gorge down which the glacier before us wound its way, could be none other than Ush-ba, and that the glacier itself must be the Leksur. It was evident, therefore, that our route must lie to the right, and that we must force our way across the ridge in front if we wished to sup that night with the shepherds of the Bashil Su.

To avoid losing height, we skirted the slopes on our right, and a merely trifling descent led us on to the open glacier. We then began the ascent of a steep wall of frozen snow, which brought us to the uppermost reservoir of the Leksur. It proved, though extremely narrow, to be of considerable length, and we did not reach the ridge till 11 a.m.

A strong wind drove us from the crest of the ridge, and we made a halt on some rocks, a few feet below the pass, on the Chegem side. After half an hour's rest, we climbed down the rocks as far as they were practicable and then took to an easy ice slope, covered with some fairly adherent snow, six inches or more in depth. The Tartar found no difficulty in following in Zurfluh's steps, but, unluckily, he waxed impatient at our slow progress, and, without a hint of what he was about to do, stepped boldly out on to the slope. The result may be imagined. In an instant he was on his back, slithering, snake-like, amongst a mass of hissing snow, leaving a long streak of gleaming ice behind him. Immediately in front yawned the open Bergschrund, and Zurfluh's " Herr Gott! er ist verloren " seemed inevitably true. By some extraordinary luck he was shot head over heels across the chasm and came to a stop in the soft snow beyond. We then saw him, much to our relief, pick himself up and begin to dust the snow from his clothes—from which we rightly inferred that he was neither frightened nor hurt. He afterwards sat down contentedly on the snow and enjoyed a quiet rest while we laboriously hacked and hewed our way down to him. Once on the névé, Zurfluh took out the rope and the Tartar was put into efficient leading-strings.

Crossing the smooth basin of the glacier, we found ourselves above a great ice fall. As the native pass of the Bashil led on to this same basin, it was obvious that an easy route must lie on one or other of the banks of the glacier. Unluckily we decided to try the left bank. We got on to the rocks without difficulty, and followed a shelf for a short distance. The next step in the descent was less simple. For about seventy feet the cliff was quite precipitous, but it looked as if, this step once surmounted, we could force our way down and regain the glacier below the ice fall.

After some consultation, we determined to face the descent. We knew, of course, that it would save time to retrace our steps, cross the glacier, and descend by the right bank, where it was evident the native path must be. Both Zurfluh and I, however, felt the need of a little real climbing. The knapsack, coats, and axes were accordingly discarded, and we made ready for a piece of work of a sort rarely met with away from the Chamonix Aiguilles. The rocks had been worn smooth by glacier action, but had since weathered along the line of a perpendicular fault. This process, however, had proceeded a little too far, and the rocks at the top of the fault were extraordinarily loose, whilst lower down they had fallen away bodily. After an endeavour to force the descent by this line, we decided it would be too perilous. On the other hand, the glaciated rock on our right was hopelessly impracticable. Dividing these two impassable lines, however, was a precipitous corner. A few of the rents and fissures by which frost and sunshine had shattered the rock in the fault had extended thus far, and by their aid it seemed barely possible to descend. I managed to get down about sixty feet, but immediately below this point the rock was undercut, and it was, therefore, necessary to traverse into the gully or fault. This traverse was of a very sensational kind, and had to be made on excrescences well rounded by glacial action. Though they just sufficed to maintain one's equilibrium, they left nothing over for emergencies, and the slightest slip with a foot, or any miscalculation of the frictional resistance of fingers on smooth rock, would have involved my swinging free on the rope. The latter would have been extremely unfortunate, for I must necessarily have swung round the corner and dangled six feet or more from the cliff. It may not be beyond the strength of two men to pull a third up sixty feet, but the experimental determination of this problem did not commend itself to me. By the exercise of much care, I succeeded in safely reaching the fault, and was able to just squeeze into a fairly secure cleft.

I then tied my end of the rope on to a piece of strong string, in order that, by so lengthening it, the lower end could always be held by me, and I could thus check any pendulum movement should the Tartar slip. He showed, however, the utmost skill and resolution, and came down without requiring help of any sort. Indeed, his references to Shaitan were of as trifling and perfunctory a sort as is compatible with a sound and unimpaired belief in a future state. Zurfluh next lowered the axes and other luggage, but we found it impossible to store all this impedimenta in the gully. The Tartar, in consequence, had to continue the descent so as to make room for it.

Zurfluh had now to descend. He first tried the line by which we had come, but on closer acquaintance it did not prove very attractive to him. He then tried the fault, but, having sent various fragments unpleasantly near my head, he reverted to our original opinion that the rocks were altogether too rotten. After some further delay, he adopted the expedient of taking off his boots, and these precious articles were lowered with loving care, and I was exhorted to stow them away in absolute security. Bracing his nerves for the final effort, he committed himself to the cliff. He succeeded in descending fairly easily, though on the traverse into the gully he did not reject a proffered hand—an indication of a modest attitude of mind rarely attained by the professional mountaineer.

Owing to all the room available being occupied with knapsacks, axes, burkas, boots, and the like, I was obliged to follow the Tartar down the crack to give Zurfluh room to sit down and put on his boots. Accordingly, taking the Tartar's knapsack, I began the descent, much encouraged by cheery assurances that the cleft was "ganz leicht." I soon found, however, that the knapsack bulged out so far that it was impossible to descend face outwards. An endeavour to go with my face to the rock proved equally perilous. The size of the sack made it quite impossible to look over one's shoulder to prospect the next step, and its weight was so great that the exigencies of balance precluded all possibility of leaning one's body far enough out to see between it and the cliff. Turning round once again, I saw the Tartar on a convenient shelf below, giving me a pantomimic performance, suggestive of the velocity acquired by falling bodies, and of the squashy conditions induced by the sudden impact of the human frame on hard rock or ice. As it appeared just possible to throw the sack down to the Tartar's ledge, I determined to risk that course. So, slipping my arms out of the bondage of detestable straps, and deaf to the urgent entreaties, I might almost say tears, from above, I entrusted the precious sack to the tender mercies of the law of gravitation. The sack reached the ledge with great facility. It strove to check its further fall, stretching its straps over the rock like long sinuous hands, but to my horror I saw its efforts were fruitless, and amidst a lamentable howl from Zurfluh our tent, bedding, and soups disappeared over the cliff. My appreciation of the discomforts involved by its loss was temporarily overbalanced by the delightful ease of movement so attained. The Tartar, wholly indifferent to tents, bedding, or other western luxuries, smiled approval, and I gathered from various remarks and gestures that he had ceased from contemplating the lurid horrors of that nether world allotted to the infidel, and was pleased that one more chance was to be granted me of embracing the teaching of the true

Prophet and basking through eternity in the delights awarded the faithful.

Zurfluh, I am bound to say, made nothing of the difficulties; with a huge piled-up load on his back he descended in the most brilliant and finished style. Doubtless the wish to point a moral had something to do with the easy grace of his movements. Any way, on his arrival at our ledge, he enlarged in glowing terms on the facility and convenience of the highway by which we had come down.

Reaching the edge of the glacier, we were met by a tangled labyrinth of crevasses. Whilst Zurfluh was studying their peculiarities, I made a short *détour* to see if the sack was anywhere visible. Greatly to my delight, I soon espied it, high seated on an isolated sérac. My companion, ignorant of the vision that had blessed my eyes, and ever pessimistic in his thoughts, urged me to waste no time in a useless search, "for," said he, the sack is not merely knocked to atoms, but it is of necessity buried in the depths of a crevasse." Needless to say I persisted, and, after some strenuous effort, succeeded in reaching our stored-up treasures. I bore it back in triumph, to the confusion of pessimism and the utter rout of all prophetic lamentations. A halt was unanimously decreed to welcome the return of the prodigal; the treasured store of tobacco was extracted from its recesses, and, soothed by the sacred fire, we agreed that all things tend to happiness in this best ordered of worlds.

Preparing to resume the descent, we found ourselves in a position of some difficulty. It would obviously be very dangerous, even if possible, to cling longer to the left bank of the glacier. Immediately below, a tributary ice stream from the great snow-fields that lie on the ridge dividing the Adyr and Bashil valleys, dropped over a low rocky wall in a series of almost incessant avalanches, threatening the traveller with very complete annihilation. On the other hand, any attempt to reach the centre of the glacier seemed scarcely possible. The ice in front of us was riven in the most extraordinary way, the merest knife-edges, and flakes of rottenest ice, alone intersecting the blue depths of vast crevasses. Unlike the ordinary broken glacier, where the crevasses may be regarded as merely dividing and breaking up the solid ice, here it seemed as if one great chasm had been frailly partitioned and separated by a shattered network of frozen foam. So unpleasing did these crevasses appear to Zurfluh, that he set off by himself to examine the cliff under the hanging glacier. The Tartar, evidently thinking him ignorant of the danger involved, expostulated in loudest tones, calling alternately on Allah and Shaitan to testify to the truth of his warnings. Zurfluh, however, did not go very far. The wall of cliff was too long for a rush, even if it had not been impracticably smooth and steep. We turned perforce to the ice, and after some most thrilling performances of the tight-rope and long-jump character, emerged on the level glacier. I am bound to admit that during this passage the follower of the Prophet moved with a freedom, certainty, and ease, a perfection of balance and an utter disregard of danger, that the unbelievers could not pretend to emulate.

Our difficulties were now over, and a short distance further down, we saw, in the far distance, undoubted cows grazing on the slopes above the glacier. Zurfluh at once broke into a run, pointing out that the cows were evidently on the way to be milked, and unless we could arrive in time to interrupt this process we should find all the milk turned sour. About 6.30 p.m. our frantic efforts were rewarded, and we reached the kosh whilst the milking was in full progress. We succeeded in securing some gallon and a half of delicious milk in our indiarubber water-bag. The pails used by the natives are always sour, and from Zurfluh's point of view entirely spoilt any milk that went into them. It is needless to remark that milking a restive cow into a somewhat narrow-mouthed, collapsible, indiarubber bag is a performance requiring much patience and tact, and only to be accomplished by the help of the whole available staff.

These shepherds had so far fallen victims to

the spread of luxury, that they had built themselves a rough hut of unhewn stones, roofed with great branches of pine. With the unvarying courtesy of the Tartar, they spread their burkas on the floor and bid us rest beside their fire.

The porter, meanwhile, engaged in negotiations preliminary to the purchase of a lamb, a duty I found it advisable to leave to him, as I am somewhat doubtful about the identification of a lamb, unless duly accompanied by mint sauce and other suitable adjuncts. The only purchase I made on my account was not successful. It was at Bezingi, and the subject of purchase was a chicken. The whole feathered population of the village, each individual held legs uppermost in the hands of its fair proprietress, was passed in review before me. The proper method of selection was indicated by the chief, who prodded the shrieking victims with his finger, occasionally causing such convulsive effort and wing-flapping that, amidst a halo of floating feathers, the subject of purchase would escape, filling the whole village with its cries. Ultimately, after much careful prodding, I decided on three birds, apparently of the most youthful and succulent description. Subsequent sad experience, however, demonstrated the vanity of my efforts. But the porter was never at fault. In the present instance he acquitted himself splendidly; he explained to the shepherds how we had faced many desperate perils together, and behaved in a way almost worthy of true believers, and the price of the lamb, in consequence, was fixed at one rouble, which is I fancy the customary local price amongst the natives—at all events the foreigner usually has to pay from two to three and a half roubles.

Invitations were formally issued to the shepherds and one or two odd natives who had strolled up the valley for a chat. Altogether eight or nine of us squatted in front of the fire and watched the hungry flames licking round the big cauldron in which the larger joints were jumping and kicking as if still possessed of life. The thinner portions, impaled on spits, were skilfully roasted in red cavernous hollows below the great sputtering pine logs. The leaping flames lit up the faces of the bearded followers of the Prophet, while our porter gave them a graphic account of the precipitous cliffs and towering séracs amongst which the strange foreigners seemed to delight in wandering. At length the feast began to be ready. In accordance with some strange law of nature, feasts of this description always begin with parts of the interior economy of the victim, the revellers slowly working their way outwards through the ribs and winding up with the larger limbs. The extraction of these latter from the boiling cauldron, surrounded as it was by scorching flames, was a work requiring much skill, and was watched with breathless excitement by the party.

We slept till late, and found the good-hearted shepherds had once more filled our water-bag with milk. Breakfast under these circumstances was a lengthy business, as Zurfluh felt it a duty to allow none of the precious fluid to be wasted. In deference to this necessity we abandoned the idea of making a pass across the mountains to the Gara Aouzu Su, and determined to merely walk down the valley to Bulungu, where we hoped to find a store of baggage.

We soon reached a small forest, where we indulged in a long siesta in the grateful shadow of the pines. I subsequently had a delightful bathe in the icy waves of the torrent. Lower down we met a native cooper, who was constructing clumsy pails by the laborious method of digging out the inside of a round block of pine till only a hollow tube was left. A groove was then cut round the lower inside edge to hold the bottom. In order to insert this the tube had to be split down one side and pulled slightly open. The bottom being duly fitted, the tube was squeezed together again and rude wooden hoops nailed round. The cooper regaled us with some milk, and seemed much pleased at the interest with which we watched his proceedings.

We found that the upper valley of the Bashil Su still boasts a fairly extensive forest, but the ring of the axe sounds ceaselessly amongst it, and the sheep and goats destroy every young tree, so that the forest is shrinking rapidly, rotting stumps attesting its former limits. Passing through the forest, we emerged suddenly on open country, and, shortly after, passed a ruined tower, which, if I understood the Tartar rightly, marks the point where the Suanetian sheep and cattle raiders used, in the old days, to be held in check; presumably, therefore, it marks the point above which sheep and cattle were not, in those old days, ever pastured. Below this point one may seek in vain, not merely for a tree, but even for the smallest bush. As I walked down the valley, I could not resist the conclusion that the presence or absence of forest in the Bashil valley had been determined by the presence or absence of sheep and goats. And though I am doubtless generalising on very insufficient data, I am much inclined to attribute the extraordinary contrast between the treelessness of some of the northern valleys and the dense forests of the southern, less to climatic differences than to the form in which the wealth of their respective inhabitants exists. In the one case oxen, horses, sheep, and goats; in the other, well-tilled and neatly-fenced fields and orchards. Though at first sight it appears difficult to believe that sheep and goats can destroy the forest over great stretches of country, a careful examination of the upper Bashil Su shows that the cause is sufficient to produce a continuous contraction of the forest area, and leaves it a mere question of time when the last tree in that valley shall be cut down and burnt.

At Bulungu we found our hoped-for baggage had not arrived, and we were in consequence forced to cross to Bezingi, as our scanty wardrobe was in sad need of replenishment. The next morning we accordingly rode across the low grass pass which connects the two villages. We found on our arrival that the village was *en fête*, and I promptly received an invitation to join in the festivities. I followed the tall native who had asked me, and we made a fairly straight line to his residence, occasionally scaling one side of a house, walking over the flat grass-grown roof, and dropping down on the other side. Arrived at the scene of the festivity, I was led to a seat provided with great down cushions of a gaudy colour and pattern, and left to watch the proceedings. The youth and beauty of Bezingi, attired in silk dresses and trousers of various and brilliant hues, were gathered in force, but, as sometimes happens nearer home, dancing men were very scarce; a strong tendency to lean up against convenient doorways and shirk their duty having to be combated with much vigour by the stewards of the ceremony. The chief's son, and an individual who appeared to be his cup-bearer, proved, however, indefatigable in their exertions. The ladies disappeared between each set of dances, and, during these intervals, we had the Daghestan sword-dance and other similar performances.

At the conclusion of these festivities we rested ourselves preparatory to once more assaulting the great pinnacle of Dych Tau. Our experiences thereon have already been described.

CHAPTER XIV.

THE PLEASURES AND PENALTIES OF MOUNTAINEERING.

WELL-KNOWN climbers, whose opinions necessarily carry the greatest weight, have recently declared their belief that the dangers of mountaineering no longer exist. Skill, knowledge, and text-books have hurled them to the limbo of exploded bogies. I would fain agree with this optimistic conclusion, but I cannot forget that the first guide to whom I was ever roped, and one who possessed—may I say it?—more knowledge of mountains than is to be found even in the Badminton library, was none the less killed on the Brouillard Mont Blanc, and his son, more recently, on Koshtantau. The memory of two rollicking parties, comprising seven men, who one day in 1879 were climbing on the west face of the Matterhorn, passes with ghost-like admonition before my mind and bids me remember that of these seven, Mr. Penhall was killed on the Wetterhorn, Ferdinand Imseng

on the Macugnaga Monte Rosa, and Johann Petrus on the Fresnay Mont Blanc. To say that any single one of these men was less careful and competent, or had less knowledge of all that pertains to the climber's craft, than we who yet survive, is obviously and patently absurd. Our best efforts must sometimes be seconded by the great goddess of Luck; to her should the Alpine Club offer its vows and thanksgivings.

Indeed, if we consider for a moment the essence of the sport of mountaineering, it is obvious that it consists, and consists exclusively, in pitting the climber's skill against the difficulties opposed by the mountain. Any increase in skill involves, *pari passu* an increase in the difficulties grappled with. From the Breuil ridge of the Matterhorn we pass on to the Dru, and from the Dru to the Aiguille de Grépon: or to take a yet wider range, from the Chamonix Mont Blanc to the same mountain by way of the Brenva glacier and the Aiguille Blanche de Peuteret. It can scarcely be argued that Bennen and Walters were less fit to grapple with the cliff above the "Linceul" than we moderns to climb the Grépon "crack"; or that Jacques Balmat was less able to lead up the "Ancien passage" than Emile Rey to storm the ghastly precipices of the Brenva Peuteret. But if it be admitted that the skill of the climber has not increased relatively to the difficulties grappled with, it would appear to necessarily follow that climbing is neither more nor less dangerous than formerly.

It is true that extraordinary progress has been made in the art of rock climbing, and that, consequently, any given rock climb is much easier now than thirty years since, but the essence of the sport lies, not in ascending a peak, but in struggling with and overcoming difficulties. The happy climber, like the aged Ulysses, is one who has "Drunk delight of battle with his peers," and this delight is only attainable by assaulting cliffs which tax to their utmost limits the powers of the mountaineers engaged. This struggle involves the same risk, whether early climbers attacked what we now call easy rock, or whether we moderns attack formidable rock, or whether the ideal climber of the future assaults cliffs which we now regard as hopelessly inaccessible. Doubtless my difference with the great authorities referred to above is, in the main, due to a totally different view of the *raison d'être* of mountaineering. Regarded as a sport, some danger is, and always must be, inherent in it; regarded as a means of exercise amongst noble scenery, for quasi-scientific pursuits, as the raw material for interesting papers, or for the purposes of brag and bounce, it has become as safe as the ascent of the Rigi or Pilatus was to the climbers of thirty years since. But these pursuits are not mountaineering in the sense in which the founders of the Alpine Club used the term, and they are not mountaineering in the sense in which the elect—a small, perchance even a dwindling body—use it now. To set one's utmost faculties, physical and mental, to fight some grim precipice, or force some gaunt, ice-clad gully, is work worthy of men; to toil up long slopes of screes behind a guide who can "lie in bed and picture every step of the way up, with all the places for hand and foot," is work worthy of the fibreless contents of fashionable clothes, dumped with all their scents and ointments, starched linen and shiny boots, at Zermatt by the railway.

The true mountaineer is a wanderer, and by a wanderer I do not mean a man who expends his whole time in travelling to and fro in the mountains on the exact tracks of his predecessors—much as a bicyclist rushes along the turnpike roads of England—but I mean a man who loves to be where no human being has been before, who delights in gripping rocks that have previously never felt the touch of human fingers, or in hewing his way up ice-filled gullies whose grim shadows have been sacred to the mists and avalanches since "Earth rose out of chaos." In other words, the true mountaineer is the man who attempts new ascents. Equally, whether he succeeds or fails, he delights in the fun and jollity of the struggle. The gaunt, bare slabs, the square, precipitous steps in the ridge, and the black, bulging ice of the gully, are the very breath of life to his being. I do not pretend to be able to analyse this feeling, still less to be able to make it clear to unbelievers. It must be felt to be understood, but it is potent to happiness and sends the blood tingling through the veins, destroying every trace of cynicism and striking at the very roots of pessimistic philosophy.

Our critics, curiously enough, repeat in substance Mr. Ruskin's original taunt, that we regard the mountains as greased poles. I must confess that a natural and incurable denseness of understanding does not enable me to feel the sting of this taunt. Putting aside the question of grease, which is offensive and too horrible for contemplation in its effects on knickerbockers—worse even than the structure-destroying edges and splinters of the Grépon ridge—I do not perceive the enormity or sin of climbing poles. At one time, I will confess, I took great delight in the art, and, so far as my experience extends, the taste is still widespread amongst English youth. It is possible, nay even probable, that much of the pleasure of mountaineering is derived from the actual physical effort and from the perfect state of health to which this effort brings its votaries, and, to this extent, may plausibly be alleged to be the mere sequence and development of the pole and tree climbing of our youth. The sting of the taunt is presumably meant to lurk in the implication that the climber is incapable of enjoying noble scenery ; that, in the jargon of certain modern writers, he is a "*mere* gymnast." But why should a man be assumed incapable of enjoying æsthetic pleasures because he is also capable of the physical and non-æsthetic pleasures of rock climbing?

A well-known mountaineer asserts that the fathers of the craft did not regard "the overcoming of physical obstacles by means of muscular exertion and skill" as "the chief pleasure of mountaineering." But is this so? Can any one read the great classic of mountaineering literature, "The Playground of Europe," without feeling that the overcoming of these obstacles was a main factor of its author's joy? Can any one read "Peaks, Passes, and Glaciers" and the earlier numbers of the Alpine Journal without feeling that the various writers gloried in the technique of their craft? Of course the skilful interpolation of "chief" gives an opening for much effective dialectic, but after all, what does it mean? How can a pleasure which is seated in health and jollity and the "spin of the blood" be measured and compared with a purely æsthetic feeling? It would appear difficult to argue that as a man cultivates and acquires muscular skill and knowledge of the mountains, he correspondingly dwarfs and impairs the æsthetic side of his nature. If so, we magnify the weak-kneed and the impotent, the lame, the halt and the blind, and brand as false the Greek ideal of the perfect man. Doubtless a tendency in this direction may be detected in some modern thought, but, like much else similarly enshrined, it has no ring of true metal. Those who are so completely masters of their environment that they can laugh and rollick on the ridges, free from all constraint of ropes or fear of danger, are far more able to appreciate the glories of the "eternal hills" than those who can only move in constant terror of their lives, amidst the endless chatter and rank tobacco smoke of unwashed guides.

The fact that a man enjoys scrambling up a steep rock in no way makes him insensible of all that is beautiful in nature. The two sets of feelings are indeed wholly unconnected. A man may love climbing and care naught for mountain scenery; he may love the scenery and hate climbing; or he may be equally devoted to both. The presumption obviously is that those who are most attracted by the mountains and most constantly return to their fastnesses, are those who to the fullest extent possess both these sources of enjoyment—those who can combine the fun and frolic of a splendid sport with that indefinable delight which is induced by the lovely form, tone, and colouring of the great ranges.

I am free to confess that I myself should still climb, even though there were no scenery to look at, even if the only climbing attainable were the dark and gruesome pot-holes of the Yorkshire dales. On the other hand, I should still wander among the upper snows, lured by the silent mists and the red blaze of the setting sun, even though physical or other infirmity, even though in after æons the sprouting of wings and other angelic appendages, may have sunk all thought of climbing and cragsmanship in the whelming past.

It is frequently assumed, even by those who ought to know better, that if mountaineering involves danger of any sort, it should never be indulged in—at all events by such precious individuals as the members of the English Alpine Club. Before considering this most pernicious doctrine, it is well to remember, that though the perils of mountaineering may not have been wholly dissipated into space by the lightning-like flashes of the Badminton and All England series, yet, nevertheless, these perils are not very great. With a single exception, the foregoing pages contain an account of every difficulty I have experienced which has seemed to render disaster a possible contingency. As my devotion to the sport began in 1871, and has continued with unabated vigour ever since, it will be evident that the climber's perils—in so far as a modest individual may regard himself as typical of the class—are extremely few and very rarely encountered. Such, however, as they have been, I would on no account have missed them. There is an educative and purifying power in danger that is to be found in no other school, and it is worth much for a man to know that he is not "clean gone to flesh pots and effeminacy." It may be admitted that the mountains occasionally push things a trifle too far, and bring before their votaries a vision of the imminence of dissolution that the hangman himself with all his paraphernalia of scaffold, gallows, and drop, could hardly hope to excel. But grim and hopeless as the cliffs may sometimes look when ebbing twilight is chased by shrieking wind and snow and the furies are in mad hunt along the ridges, there is ever the feeling that brave companions and a constant spirit will cut the gathering web of peril, "forsan et hæc olim meminisse juvabit."

The sense of independence and self-confidence induced by the great precipices and vast silent fields of snow is something wholly delightful. Every step is health, fun, and frolic. The troubles and cares of life, together with the essential vulgarity of a plutocratic society, are left far below—foul miasmas that cling to the lowest bottoms of reeking valleys. Above, in the clear air and searching sunlight, we are afoot with the quiet gods, and men can know each other and themselves for what they are. No feeling can be more glorious than advancing to attack some gaunt precipitous wall with "comrades staunch as the founders of our race." Nothing is more exhilarating than to know that the fingers of one hand can still be trusted with the lives of a party, and that the lower limbs are free from all trace of " knee-dissolving fear," even though the friction of one hobnail on an outward shelving ledge alone checks the hurtling of the body through thin air, and of the soul (let us hope) to the realms above.

I am of course aware that it is an age which cares little for the more manly virtues, and which looks askance at any form of sport that can, by any stretch of extremest imagination, be regarded as dangerous: yet since we cannot all, for most obvious reasons, take our delight " wallowing in slimy spawn of lucre," something may surely be urged in favour of a sport that teaches, as no other teaches, endurance and mutual trust, and forces men occasionally to look death in its grimmest aspect frankly and squarely in the face. For though mountaineering is not, perhaps, more dangerous than other sports, it undoubtedly brings home to the mind a more stimulating sense of peril; a sense, indeed, that is out of all proportion to the actual risk. It is, for instance, quite impossible to look down the tremendous precipices of the Little Dru without feeling in each individual nerve the utter disintegration of everything human which a fall must involve; and the contingency of such a fall is frequently brought before the mind —indeed, throughout the ascent, constant and strenuous efforts are needed to avoid it. The love of wager, our religious teachers notwithstanding, is still inherent in the race, and one cannot find a higher stake—at all events in these materialistic days, when Old Nick will no longer lay sterling coin against the gamester's soul—than the continuity of the cervical vertebræ; and this is the stake that the mountaineer habitually and constantly wagers. It is true the odds are all on his side, but the off-chance excites to honesty of thought and tests how far decay has penetrated the inner fibre. That mountaineering has a high educational value, few, who have the requisite knowledge to form a fair judgment, would deny. That it has its evil side I frankly admit. None can look down its gloomy death-roll without feeling that our sport demands a fearful price.

Mountaineering being a sport not wholly free from danger, it behoves us to consider the directions from which this danger may come, and the methods by which it may usually be met and conquered. Amongst the mountains, as elsewhere, "the unexpected always happens." It is the momentary carelessness in easy places, the lapsed attention, or the wandering look that is the usual parent of disaster. It may appear that to this extent dangers are avoidable, and the high authorities referred to above justified in their optimism. But which of us can boast that his attention to the slope and his companions never flags, that his eyes are always on the watch for falling stones, for loose rocks, for undercut ice, and all the traps and pitfalls that Madame Nature scatters with such profusion among the "lonely hills"? The chief source of danger is this need for incessant care, the unvarying readiness of ice, snow, and rock to punish relentlessly an instant's forgetfulness, or the most trifling neglect. The first lesson the novice has to learn is to be ever on his guard, and it is one that the oldest climber rarely fully masters. Unfortunately it is one which the beginner must find out for himself, it is a habit that must be acquired, and to which no road, other than constant practice, will ever lead him. It wants long experience to impress upon the mind that the chief danger of extremely difficult climbing is to be found on the easy places by which it is followed; that it lies less in the stress of desperate wrestling with the crags than in the relaxed attention which such work is apt to induce on the return to comparatively easy ground. Nothing is more usual than to hear a man say after some very formidable ascent—it may even be read in the Alpine Journal—that on the way up, certain preliminary rocks appeared distinctly difficult, but on the way down, after the terrible grapple with the cliffs above, these same rocks appeared "ridiculously easy." It is the delusive appearance of safety presented by these "ridiculously easy rocks" that swells the list of Alpine victims. There are few, even of the oldest and most cunning climbers, who do not have to struggle against the feeling that the difficulties are over and care is no longer essential. Twice have I seen incipient accidents arise from this cause, and on each occasion none but the fair goddess of luck could have rescued a friend from disaster.

There is, again, the impossibility of learning, except by actual experience, the length of time during which the nervous system may be relied on. The protracted strain of a long ice slope tells on men in wholly different ways. To some it means merely the sharpening of their faculties, and with every hour they get steadier and safer in their steps; with others it means utter exhaustion and collapse. It is distinctly unpleasant when a companion, whom you think is enjoying himself, suddenly informs you that he is doubtful of his power to stand in the steps, that his knees are wobbling, and that he may be expected to slip at any moment. At such times nothing but the fact that one has been brought up surrounded by the best religious influences, prevents the ejaculation of the strongest and most soul-satisfying expletives known to the English tongue. It may be said that such a man should not go climbing; but how is he to know that he is affected in this way till he has so gone? A man can never know his capabilities till he has tried them, and this testing process involves risk. Going over ground where a slip would not be serious is of no use; so long as this is the case he may be as good or better than his companions. It is the knowledge that he holds the lives of the party in his hand that masters and conquers him, not the mere technical difficulties of the slope, which, to a man who has good steps cut for him, may be practically nil.

It will be evident that all these dangers press on the novice far more than on the old and seasoned mountaineer. Those who have learnt the craft, and spent fifteen or twenty summers amongst the mountains, are scarcely likely to be unaware of their own failings and weaknesses, and may be trusted to be generally on the alert. The dangers to which such "old hands" are subject come in the main from other directions, and are chiefly connected with "new expeditions." In the Alps, such ascents can only be found on previously unclimbed sides of peaks, and the mountaineer usually has the knowledge that if he reaches the top he can descend by an easy and well-known route. The temptation to persevere in an ascent, especially if anything very formidable has already been passed, is extremely great, and a party may even be urged forward by the fear of retreat. This fear should, however, never be yielded to; it may easily result in forcing the party into difficulties from which they have neither the time nor the ability to extricate themselves. If a place cannot be descended it should never be climbed.

A somewhat similar and still more deceitful peril is involved by the ascent in the early morning of gullies, which, though fairly safe at that hour, are known to be the channel of avalanches and falling stones in the afternoon. Should any unforeseen cause stop the party high up on the mountain, no safe line of retreat is open. In this way, when Herren Lammer and Lorria, foiled by the ice-glazed rocks of the western face of the Matterhorn, were forced to return, they found the great couloir ceaselessly swept by stones and snow. Persisting, none the less, in the descent, they were carried down by an avalanche, and though, by extraordinary luck, they both escaped with their lives, they suffered very serious injuries. Unless, therefore, the climber is absolutely certain that the ascent can be completed, it is in the highest degree perilous to enter such gullies, and those who do so should clearly recognise that they are running very serious risks. If, however, the risk has been run and the party is checked high up on the mountain, it is usually the better course to spend the night on the rocks, and wait till frost has sealed up the loose stones, snow and ice. This expedient has been adopted more than once by my old guide, Alexander Burgener. On the memorable descent of the Col du Lion, it undoubtedly saved both Dr. Güssfeldt's life and his own.* I am aware that this procedure involves

* "In den Hochalpen," pp. 269, 270.

some slight risk from adverse changes in the weather, and extreme discomfort from cold, and possibly hunger, but these latter are mere trifles to strong men, properly clad; and as for the former, such places as the great couloir of the western Matterhorn are far safer in a snowstorm than when the setting sun is blazing on the great slopes above. Indeed, when snow falls at a low temperature it instantly dries up the trickles of water, stops the melting of the great pendent icicles, and generally checks the fall of missiles, thus rendering slopes and couloirs, which one dare not climb in fine weather, fairly safe. On the other hand, a summer snow squall followed by a wind above freezing point (a not infrequent phenomenon), will convert rock slopes, usually innocent, into cascades of water, armed and rendered terrible by stones and dislodged crags. It will thus be seen that most accurate judgment is necessary, and the requisite knowledge for this judgment is hardly to be obtained till the climber has learnt, by dangerous experience, to grasp the exact nature of the storm, and the effect it is likely to have on the slope he is dealing with.

Climbers sometimes write as though it were possible to avoid all slopes down which stones or ice can ever fall. In actual fact, though such slopes may, to some extent, be avoided on the days and at the hours when such falls may be most expected, it is impossible to keep wholly clear of them.

Mountaineers of the widest experience and most approved prudence, even presidents and ex-presidents of the Alpine Club, have been known to descend, for hours on end, shelterless slopes of rock and ice, liable at any moment to be raked from top to bottom by falling stones and ice. The orthodox critic may protest, but none the less those who seek to effect new passes will occasionally find themselves in positions which leave them no endurable alternative. The pseudo mountaineer can, it is true, almost wholly avoid these dangers. Accompanied by guides who know every step of the way, he is led by a fairly sheltered route, or, if none such exists, he is told this fact before he starts, and can alter his plans accordingly. But the repetition of an accurately timed and adjusted performance, under the rigid rule of a guide as stage manager, does not commend itself to the real mountaineer. His delight and pleasure in the sport are chiefly derived from the very uncertainty and difficulties which it is the main function of such a guide to eliminate. Even if the pass is not exactly new, he likes to encounter it without the exact knowledge of the route which reduces it to a mere tramp of so many hours duration, and as a consequence he cannot invariably avoid all risk.

As a matter of fact, very few of the usual and customary ascents are quite free from ice and rock falls. Even the Chamonix route up Mont Blanc passes one place where the track is sometimes swept by stones from the Aiguille du Midi, and a second, where ice avalanches from the Dôme du Goûter threaten, and sometimes slay, the traveller. There is, in fact, no absolute immunity from this danger, and it is desirable, therefore, that the young mountaineer should learn the various methods by which it may most suitably be grappled. To acquire the art of watching a falling stone, and, at the critical moment, to remove oneself from the line of fire, is essential to the cragsman. To attain the knowledge requisite to judge where and when ice and snow avalanches may be expected to fall, is equally necessary for the safe guidance of a party. It requires, however, the best teaching that the oldest and steadiest guides can give, combined with a long experience of the upper snows. Those who aspire to lead a party cannot devote too great attention to this subject, and should be able to judge, with tolerable certainty, the effects which new snow on the one hand, or persistently fine weather on the other, has caused in the séracs towering above the lower glacier. Beginners are apt to forget that at no time is falling ice more greatly to be feared than when protracted sunshine has wrought havoc amongst the leering monsters poised above their track. To adapt the expedition to the weather is frequently of critical importance, and may make not merely the difference between success and failure, but even between health and jollity, and irremediable disaster.

In this connection it is desirable to notice that an unroped party is safer than a roped one, and that its chances of escape from the missiles at the mountain's disposal vary, at the very least, inversely with its size. With three on the rope the middle man is more or less of a fixture, and has very little chance of saving himself from falling stones unless cover is close at hand. If no cover is available, the fact that the party is spread over a considerable extent of rock renders it highly probable that the true line of escape for its first and last members will lie in opposite directions. Should this be the case no movement is immediately possible, and the middle man occupies a most unenviable position. Personally I much prefer discarding the rope in all such places, and if this is not desirable, consider two quite the maximum permissible. I may add that this opinion is shared by such men as Alex. Burgener and Emile Rey. I have known each of them object to add a third to the party, on the ground that it would prevent rapidity of movement in places where such rapidity might be desirable. There is also the very serious risk of stones upset by the leader, and which may acquire very dangerous velocity before they pass the lowest man when several climbers are on the slope. During the first ascent of the Rothhorn from

Zermatt, disaster was narrowly escaped from this very cause.*

There are many gullies in which it is absolutely impossible to avoid dislodging stones, and as a consequence large parties are forced to "close up." Whilst this, to some extent, obviates the risk from falling stones, it negatives any advantage from the rope, and frequently compels all but the first man to be simultaneously on bad ground. Even then I have, more than once, seen a man badly hurt by such stones, and it is difficult to avoid the conclusion that some unexplained accidents may have resulted from a dislodged stone knocking a companion out of his steps, and his fall dragging the members of a "closed up" party, one after another, from their hold. On very steep ice, again, the leader is sometimes seriously hampered by the existence of a large party below him, and the consequent necessity of only cutting small pieces of ice with each stroke of the axe, and absolutely to avoid, on reaching rocks, any endeavour to clear the ice from them; the chance of detaching a fragment sufficiently large to knock a companion seventy or eighty feet below from his steps, being greater than the advantage of getting reliable footing.

These considerations of roping and numbers apply with even greater force to any danger arising from ice avalanches. Every additional

* "Above the Snow Line," pp. 49, 50.

man on the rope means a serious decrease of the extreme speed at which the party can move, and it is in speed, and in speed alone, that a party so surprised can hope for safety. In 1871 Mr. Tuckett's party were nearly swept away by a great avalanche falling from the Eiger, and he attributes his escape, in no small measure, to the fact that the party was not roped, and had, in consequence, much greater power of rapid movement than would otherwise have been the case.*

Of course if an incompetent man is included, the rope must be worn constantly, and at least two sound and reliable mountaineers must be watching over his idiosyncrasies; but parties so hampered should avoid such gullies as that ascended on the way up the Schreckhorn, or the pitiless slopes of the Italian side of the Col des Hirondelles.

There is one other condition in which the rope seriously increases the risks of competent mountaineers. In the event of an avalanche being started, a roped party is almost helpless. It may be frequently possible for any one of the party to escape from the seething snow, but he is, if roped, of necessity dragged back by his companions. In such a case escape from the avalanche is only possible if all can jump from the sliding snow on the same side and at the same moment, and even then only if they can free the rope from the wet masses of snow in which it is certain to have

* Alpine Journal, vol. ii. p. 341 et seq.

become somewhat involved. It is obvious, that under circumstances which may afford each single member of the party a dozen chances of escape, it will be highly improbable that all of them will get a simultaneous chance, and the rope in such a case is a veritable death-trap. In larger avalanches, where the utmost the climber can do is to keep his head above the crest of the wave, the roped climber is hampered, as a swimmer in a furious surf would be hampered, by the entanglement of his companions. One has only to read the account of the death of Bennen to realise how disastrous a rope may be.*

I have no wish to advocate the disuse of the rope, but merely to point out certain well-known facts that have been lost sight of in recent contributions to the literature of mountaineering. As a general rule it is of the utmost value, and where climbers are of unequal skill and experience, its constant use is demanded by the primary feelings of comradeship and good faith. There is, however, some danger of its being regarded as a sort of Providence, always ready to save the reckless and incompetent, no matter how slight their experience, no matter how little they may be fitted for the expeditions they undertake. Though I have dwelt at some length on the occasional disadvantages the rope entails, and said but little about the safety it so constantly assures, this is

* "Hours of Exercise in the Alps," pp. 204, 205.

merely because there seems no danger of the latter being overlooked, and much that the former will be wholly forgotten. It is, moreover, to be remembered that the conduct of guideless parties has been chiefly in view. Since each member of such a party should be absolutely certain never to slip, the monotony of this precaution may in many places be relaxed with safety, and sometimes even with advantage.

I am, of course, aware that high authorities assert that a party should always be roped, and that it should never consist of less than three—does not the All England series tell that " whatever number may be right, two is wrong " ? I must, however, confess that I fail to apprehend the reasons which have led to this unqualified dictum. It would rather appear that the best number depends on a variety of conditions, which vary with the expedition in view. For instance, on the Col du Lion, two is undoubtedly the best and safest number. Not merely is it desirable to reduce to the smallest dimensions the target offered to the mountain musketry and big guns, but it is also essential to move with the utmost speed attainable. Wherever this is the case each additional man is a source of danger.

Much recent writing on this question assumes that on steep slopes or cliffs three men are safer than two. It would, however, appear obvious that this is an error. If the leader slips, it almost of necessity involves the destruction of the party. In any case the whole impact of his fall must come on the man next him in the line, and if this man is dragged from his hold it is absurd to suppose that the third will be able to support the shock of the two men falling. Exactly the same may be said of a traverse; if the leader slips he must be held, if he is held at all, by the man next him in the line. No matter how many may be behind, they will, of necessity, be dragged, one after another, from their hold. It is obvious that if the leader is held by the man next him in the line, two are sufficient for safety; if he is not so held, then three, or any greater number, are equally doomed to destruction. Writers on this subject seem to assume that a party of three or more have no ends to the rope—that each member of the party is between two others—in which case, doubtless, fairly efficient help could be given. It is needless to point out, however, that this is impossible. In every party there are two men, the slip of either of whom, on a steep traverse, is extremely dangerous, if not fatal. The insertion of a third climber, between these two, in no way reduces or diminishes this danger, though, in circumstances which can readily be imagined, it may gravely add to it.

The truth would appear to be, that if from a party of three you remove the worst climber, the two remaining men will, on steep slopes, be distinctly safer than the whole party. If, on the other hand, from the party of three you remove either of the more competent men, then the remaining two will be very much less safe. It must be remembered that I am not arguing in favour of a party consisting of one mountaineer and a duffer, but of two men, equally competent and skilled in all that pertains to the climber's craft.

A careful consideration of the various possibilities that can assail the mountaineer on the steeper slopes would appear to lead to the conclusion that a party of three or four is as often too many, as a party of two is too few. The loss of time and the danger of upset stones, and even of ice and snow hewn out in the process of step cutting, appear to fairly balance the advantages of a greater number.

These advantages are chiefly, that in places where the second man is giving the leader a shoulder, a third man may be able to anchor the party with a hitched rope; or where the upper lip of a Schrund is almost out of reach, a third man can materially aid in the work of lifting and holding the leader on the shoulders of his companion whilst the necessary steps are being cut. It is also desirable, in all expeditions where much backing up is required, that the second man should be free from the encumbrance of the knapsack, spare rope, etc., and this, necessarily, involves a third to act as porter. It would appear then, that so far as the steeper slopes are concerned, the number of the party should be adapted to the nature of the expedition, and no attempt should be made to lay down any hard and fast rule.

The main strength of the objection to two men climbing alone is, perhaps, to be found in the common belief that if one man falls into a crevasse, his companion will be unable to pull him out. With regard to this extremely unpleasant supposition, it may be pointed out that there is no particular reason for him to fall in. Why any one should wish to dangle on the rope, in a dark and chilly chasm, is one of those profound and inscrutable mysteries which may be regarded as past all finding out. It is, of course, a quite unnecessary incident, and one which is not, perhaps, nearly so frequently indulged in as some people imagine. Once only have I been near falling into a crevasse, but on that occasion, being unroped, I felt it desirable to abandon such pleasure as this proceeding may afford.

A crevasse, except immediately after fresh snow, is always visible to any one who takes the trouble to look for it; and even if the leader is careless and does break through, the rope, if used with any readiness and skill, ought to check his going in beyond his waist.

It is a curious fact, that, from the very earliest

days of mountaineering, two guides, dismissed after crossing a pass, have been in the habit of returning home by themselves. So far as I have been able to learn, no single crevasse accident has ever happened to them. When it is remembered that such extensive and fissured fields of névé, as those traversed by the routes over the Col du Géant, the Mönch Joch, the Weiss Thor, the Col d'Hérens and the Brèche de la Meije, are amongst those which have been habitually crossed by two guides alone, it would appear that the danger to such parties is almost or quite non-existent. It is, indeed, obvious that if such parties *were* exposed to the danger alleged, it would be little short of criminal to take two men across an ice pass and dismiss them under conditions which practically involve their climbing two on a rope. To permit guides to run risks, which their employer is warned on no account to face, would be, to say the least of it, contrary to the traditions of Englishmen at large and the Alpine Club in particular.

The difficulty of reconciling practice and teaching on this point leads me to suppose that, possibly, these denunciations are levelled, not against parties of two mountaineers, but against parties of one mountaineer and one duffer. Politeness, that arch-corrupter of truth, has, perchance, led our teachers to say "a party should never consist of less than three, of whom two should be guides," in preference to saying that "a party should always consist of two mountaineers, with or without one or more pieces of animate luggage." It would, indeed, be passing strange, if my old friends Alex. Burgener and Emile Rey, being seized with a desire to cross the Col du Géant, were compelled to obtain the help of some weakly school girl, or decrepit tourist, before being able to face the perils of the pass! Yet this is the conclusion to which the doctrines of our prophets necessarily lead! Truly those who aspire to walk with the "quiet gods" on more than Olympian heights should shun the formal politeness which conceals truth and say their whole meaning, regardless of the feelings of the incompetent and the duffer. Two friends of mine once wished to cross an extensive Norwegian snow field; being learned in the written wisdom of the mountains, they felt that a third man was essential to their safety. They found him, and during the succeeding two days were able to rejoice in the security so afforded! Not only did he cause them to go so slowly that they were benighted in the most inconvenient quarters, not only did he do his best to drag them off the rocks whenever there was any possibility of his efforts being rewarded with success, but I am assured, on authority which is absolutely indisputable, that he indulged, at times, in the most profane and unbecoming language! From that time forth my friends have been firm converts to the doctrine, that if from a party of three you abstract the weakest member, the party is very materially strengthened and improved, and that two competent climbers constitute a far safer and better party than the two guides and a traveller, so dear to the orthodox authorities on mountaineering.

Since, however, it is conceivable that an extensive snow bridge might give way, and let the leader fall some distance before the rope could come into play, it may be of advantage to describe a method of using the rope by which, even in this case, a party of two should still be able to work out their own salvation. It is a fairly well known fact, attested by a considerable number of involuntary experiments, that one man can hold a companion who has fallen some distance into a crevasse. The friction of the rope on the edge of the crevasse, and the splendid holding ground which the soft, level snow affords, enables the fall to be checked without very grave difficulty. The crucial point is, however, to get your companion out again. This, with the rope used in the customary manner, is impossible. Ferdinand Imseng* and other of the experimenters referred to above have tried it and

---

* Happily on each of these occasions another party was within hail, and by its assistance the entombed climber's rescue was effected.

failed, and their experience may, I think, be taken as conclusive. If, however, instead of the usual rope, a rope of half its weight and strength be used *doubled*, the problem is easily solved. One of these ropes is provided with two loops, one close to each climber. In the event of a bridge breaking, and as soon as the fall has been checked, the remaining climber drives his axe into the snow, cuts himself free from the looped rope and slips this loop over the axe head. The position of affairs is now as follows. The man in the crevasse has hold of a rope fast to the ice-axe; round his waist is a second rope, also round his companion's waist and held by him. The man in the crevasse pulls on the rope fast to the axe, and the man outside pulls on the rope round his companion's waist: in other words two men are engaged in lifting one. Every advance is made secure and permanent by the man outside, who holds no slack in his hands but pushes his way back from the crevasse, step by step, as his companion nears the lip. Arrived at this point, where the ropes will have cut deep into the snow, the engulfed man has only to rest his whole weight on the rope round his waist, and he can then jerk the other rope free from the snow, and get fresh hold higher up, and, little by little, extricate himself.

Whilst the rope so used is a fairly effective safeguard against this danger—as efficient perhaps as the rope used in the ordinary way by a party of three—it may be admitted that those who have a constant and irresistible impulse to plunge into the blue depths of crevasses would be wise to travel with two or more companions. A light and portable windlass would, perhaps, be a judicious investment for any spare carrying power such a party might possess. Those, however, who have the fortitude to resist the blandishments of the crevasse, whose ears are stuffed with wax and do not hear the sirens singing in their depths, may adopt the precaution of the doubled rope and feel fairly assured of its efficacy. It ought, however, to be remembered that at least fifty feet should be put between two men, when they are on a glacier by themselves.

The habit of climbing alone is open to far other and more serious objections. It is true that under very exceptional circumstances, when, for instance, settled fine weather has rendered every crevasse visible, snow fields may be crossed in the early morning without much risk. At such times I have strolled over the Trift Joch, the Weiss Thor, the Col du Géant and other passes without experiencing any symptom of danger; but the sense of loneliness, a sense which, when fog and mists curl round the ridges, becomes almost painful, is apt to affect a man's steadiness and resource. It is certainly undesirable to push such solitary wanderings beyond very narrow limits.

On the other hand, nothing develops a man's faculties so rapidly and completely. No one detects a crevasse so readily as the man who is accustomed to traverse snow fields by himself. No one takes such careful note of the line of ascent as the cragsman who has got to find his way back alone. The concentration of all responsibility and all the work on a single individual forces him to acquire an all-round skill which is hardly to be gained in any other way. Climbing in parties is apt to develop one-sidedness. One man cuts the steps, another climbs the rocks, and a third always knows the way. Division of labour is doubtless excellent, and perchance deserves all that Adam Smith has said in its favour, but it does not develop the ideal mountaineer. In this department of human duty Mr. William Morris gives sounder advice. Of course this is merely another way of saying that the chamois hunter—*i.e.*, the solitary mountaineer—is the best raw material for a guide. The fact that a man has been in the habit of climbing alone, means that the law of the survival of the fittest has had full and ample opportunity of eliminating him should he be, in any way, a careless or incapable mountaineer.

From the individual's point of view this elimination may not, perhaps, appear wholly desirable. Yet, judging from his habits, the faithful climber, carried away by altruistic feelings and thinking merely of the welfare of future companions, prefers that the law of the survival of the fittest should have full scope and should pass him through its searching fires. Possibly critics may suggest other and less pleasing motives, perhaps I could even do so myself, but wherefore filch from the lurking foe the joy of a trenchant onslaught? Any way, no matter what his motive may have been, the man so proved is quite independent of the rope, and moves as freely, or more freely, without it than with. He suggests at every step that he adds to the pool of safety that may be regarded as embodied in it. Those, on the other hand, who are imbued with the text-books, and fear to move hand or foot when free from the trammels of loops and knots, insensibly suggest that they subtract from this same pool of safety.

It must not be supposed that I am an advocate of solitary climbing. It requires but a trifling knowledge of the average amateur to feel assured that at least nine out of every ten will break their necks if they seriously attempt it. All that it is desirable to do, is to point out to those who wish to go without guides, the direction in which they may seek for reliable companions. The more orthodox method of ascending peaks, between two good guides, has much to recommend it, but its votaries had best be avoided by those who aspire to face the great ridges, trusting exclusively in their own right arms and slowly won experience.

The rope should, indeed, be regarded by each member of the party, exclusively as an aid and protection to his companions. Those who feel its constant use essential to their own comfort, should regard this as indisputable evidence that they are engaging in expeditions too difficult for them; a practice which will never make good and self-reliant climbers. To be able to move safely and freely on a mountain slope should be the one object which the young mountaineer sets before himself. At occasional "mauvais pas" he may legitimately ask his companions to look after him and either give actual help, or rescue him from disaster should he slip, but this help should be quite exceptional. If he finds on any expedition that this protection is constantly required, he should frankly recognise that he is attempting work for which he is unfit.

The Matterhorn gives a curious illustration of the way in which the modern amateur is deteriorating. The early climbers roped at the "shoulder." In 1873 they roped at the old hut. In 1886 they roped some distance below the old hut. Now they rope at the new hut, and the exploits of a gentleman in 1893 render it not impossible that future climbers will rope at the Hörnli. Yet these unfortunates fail to recognise that they are attempting work altogether beyond their powers, and are being nursed and coddled by their guides in a way that is destructive of all proper self-respect and of every feeling of self-reliant manliness. Whilst the true mountaineer is undoubtedly

". . . the noblest work of God,"

a thing that is pushed and hustled up peaks by Swiss peasants, and which is so wholly unable to take care of itself that it cannot be trusted to sit on a crag unroped, is as contemptible an object as may easily be imagined. A man should never knowingly and deliberately thrust himself into places where he is hopelessly mastered and dominated by his environment. He who does this is regarded by his guides as a sort of " vache au lait," a convenient source of tariffs and Trinkgeld ; a butt for small jokes and witticisms ; an object to smear with grease, to decorate with masks and veils, and to button up in strange, chain-clad gaiters ; a thing to be wound up with wine and brandy, and which must never be lost sight of till safely handed over to the landlord of an inn. It is difficult to apprehend how men, who in other departments of life are not wanting in a sufficient sense of their own personal dignity, should consent to be treated in this way. It is not, even, as if it were the only form of mountain expedition open to them. Work within the powers of the least competent is abundant in every Alpine valley, much of it surrounded by the noblest scenery both of ice and snow. The art of mountaineering consists in being able to climb easily and securely, in being able to relate one's skill to the difficulties of the slopes above and around, and it may, to some extent, be practised and enjoyed, consistently with reasonable safety and self-respect, by every man, no matter how slight his natural aptitude and training may be. It is merely necessary that he should recognise the limits so imposed.

High proficiency in the sport is only attainable when a natural aptitude is combined with long years of practice, and not without some, perhaps much, danger to life and limb. Happily, the faithful climber usually acquires this skill at an age when the responsibilities of life have not yet laid firm hold upon him, and when he may fairly claim some latitude in matters of this sort. On the other hand he gains a knowledge of himself, a love of all that is most beautiful in nature, and an outlet such as no other sport affords for the stirring energies of youth; gains for which no price is, perhaps, too high. It is true the great ridges sometimes demand their sacrifice, but the mountaineer would hardly forego his worship though he knew himself to be the destined victim. But happily to most of us the great brown slabs bending over into immeasurable space, the lines and curves of the wind-moulded cornice, the delicate undulations of the fissured snow, are old and trusted friends, ever luring us to health and fun and laughter, and enabling us to bid a sturdy defiance to all the ills that time and life oppose.

www.ingramcontent.com/pod-product-compliance
Lightning Source LLC
Chambersburg PA
CBHW031416230426
43668CB00007B/326